구문 분석과 해설

중급영문독해

구문 분석과 해설

중급 영문독해

Intermediate English Reading

석종환 지음

경상대학교출판부

저자의 말

4차 산업혁명의 시대에 우리는 정보의 홍수 속에 살고 있다. 인터넷을 통해 시시각각으로 접할 수 있는 수많은 정보에 접근하는 데 필요한 언어가 바로 영어라 할 수 있다. 영어로 접하는 수많은 정보를 이해하고 활용하기 위해서는 영어독해력이 바탕이 되어야 할 것이다.

독해(reading)란 문장을 읽고 그 문장에 내포된 정보를 독자의 지식과 정보 및 경험을 토대로 그것을 이해하고 해석하기까지의 일련의 행위를 가리키는 개념이다. 독해력(reading comprehension)은 필자가 표현하고자 하는 문장의 구조에 대한 이해를 통해 문장의 주제 및 구성을 파악하고, 문장의 의미를 추론할 수 있는 능력이라 할 수 있다.

영어독해력에 직접적으로 영향을 미치는 요소는 문법력과 어휘력이라 할 수 있다. 문법력은 문장에 쓰인 문법적인 구조를 이해하는 능력이고, 어휘력은 단어의 의미를 알고 있는 능력이다. 영어독해력을 높이기 위해서는 문법력과 어휘력뿐만 아니라 영어사용자의 사회적, 문화적 배경을 아는 것도 중요하다. 여기에 덧붙여 영어의 관용적인 표현이나 은어 등에 대한 이해가 있다면 더욱 수준 높은 독해를 할 수 있을 것이다.

이러한 목적을 위해 본 저서는 영어로 쓰인 다양한 주제의 글들을 가져와 구문분석과 해석을 시도한다. 과학과 종교, 정의와 공정, 법과 도덕, 삶과 문학, 인공지능과 윤리, 언어와 사고 사이의 관계를 다루는 글과 함께 4차 산업혁명, 안락사, 사형제, 낙태, 페미니즘과 같이 현재 많은 논란이 있는 주제와 관련되는 글 읽기를 통해 영어의 독해력을 높일 수 있도록 하였다.

각 단원의 처음에는 WARMING UP을 두어 단원에 나오게 될 중요구문을 미리 학습해 볼 수 있도록 하였으며 본문 각 페이지의 좌측과 우측에는 중요 어휘의 뜻을 제시해 더욱 쉽게 문장의 의미를 파악할 수 있도록 하였다. 또한 본문의 끝에는 독해를 위해 필요한 아주 기본적인 문법을 정리해 둠으로써 문법력을 높일 수 있도록 하였으며, 마지막으로 PHRASES and STRUCTURES에서는 독해를 돕기 위해 중요한 관용적인 표현이나 어려운 구문에 대한 분석과 문장의 해석을 제시하고 있다.

인공지능을 통한 번역이 가능한 시대에 이와 같은 독해학습서가 필요한지에 대해 의문을 제기할 수 있겠으나 영어구문에 대한 보다 정확하고 확실한 이해를 위해서는 영어문장의 구조에 대한 분석과 어휘와 숙어의 이해가 없이는 높은 수준의 영어능력에 이를 수 없을 것은 분명해 보인다.

아무쪼록 이와 같은 구문분석 훈련을 통해 영어학습자의 영어능력이 보다 향상될 수 있기를 기대하면서 출판을 허락해 준 출판부 관계자에게 깊은 감사를 드린다.

2020년 8월

저자 석종환

Contents

Unit 1

My father's Hands[1)]

WARMING UP

- He could draw and saw a square **with quick accuracy**
- He **had been known to peel** his knuckles upside a tough jaw
- They were good hands **that** served him well and failed him in only one thing
- He would **take me by the shoulder**
- **If there were only one I would be saddened, remembering** my father and the pain he endured
- His mind **was keen**, his will **to** work unsurpassed
- Once he **had heard "a radio preacher" relate** that the Bible said ~
- Doc Green gave him medications, including nitroglycerin tablets to put under his tongue **should he feel an attack coming on**

1) This article was written by Calvin R. Worthington and published by Reader's Digest in the May of 1976. The source is http://www.mark.hagerman.name/website/MFH.html

His hands were *rough[1] and exceedingly strong. He could gently *prune[2] a fruit tree or firmly *wrestle an *ornery[3] mule into *harness[4]. He could *draw[5] and *saw[6] a square *with quick accuracy. *He had been known to *peel[7] his *knuckles[8] upside a tough jaw. But what I remember most is *the special warmth from those hands soaking through my shirt as he would *take me by the shoulder and, *hunkering down[9] beside my ear, point out the *glittering[10] *swoop[11] of a blue hawk, or a rabbit asleep in its *lair[12]. They were *good hands that served him well and *failed[13] him in only one thing: they never learned to write.

My father was *illiterate[14]. The number of illiterates in our country has steadily declined, but *if there were only one I would be saddened, remembering my father and the pain he endured because his hands never learned to write. He started first grade, *where the *remedy[15] for a wrong answer was ten ruler strokes across a stretched palm. For some reason, shapes, figures, and *recitations[16] just didn't fall into the right pattern inside his six-year-old *towhead[17]. Maybe he *suffered from some type of learning handicap such as *dyslexia[18]. His father *took him out of school after several months and *set him to a man's job on the farm.

Years later, his wife, with her fourth-grade education, would try to teach him to read. And *still later I would grasp his big fist between my small hands and *awkwardly[19] help him trace the letters of his name. He *submitted to the *ordeal[20], but soon *grew restless. *Flexing[21] his fingers and *kneading[22] his palms, he would declare

1. rough
거친
2. prune
(가지를) 잘라내다
3. ornery
고집이 센
4. harness
마구(馬具)
5. draw
(부드럽게) 끌어당기다
6. saw
톱으로 켜서
~으로 만들다
7. peel
껍질을 벗기다
8. knuckle
손가락 관절
9. hunker down
쪼그리고 앉다
10. glittering
눈부신, 성공적인
11. swoop
급강하
12. lair
(야생 동물의) 집(굴)
13. fail
도움이 못되다
14. illiterate
글을 (읽거나 쓸 줄)
모르는
15. remedy
해결책
16. recitation
암송
17. towhead
삼빛 머리카락을
가진 사람
18. dyslexia
난독증
19. awkwardly
어슬프게
20. ordeal
시련
21. flex
구부리다, 풀다
22. knead
주무르다

that he *had had enough and depart for a long, *solitary[23] walk.

Finally, one night when he thought no one saw, he *slipped away[24] with his son's second-grade *reader[25] and *labored[26] over the words, until they became too difficult. He pressed his forehead into the pages and wept. "Jesus – Jesus - not even a child's book?" Thereafter, *no amount of persuading could bring him to sit with pen and paper.

From the farm to road building and later factory work, his hands served him well. *His mind was keen, his *will[27] to work *unsurpassed[28]. During World War II, he was a *pipefitter[29] in a *shipyard[30] and installed the complicated *guts[31] of *mighty[32] fighting ships. *His enthusiasm and efficiency brought an offer to become line boss - *until he was handed the qualification test. His fingers could trace a path across the *blueprints[33] while his mind imagined *the pipes lacing through the heart of the ship. He could recall every *twist and turn[34] of the pipes. But he couldn't read or write.

After the shipyard closed, he went to the *cotton mill[35], where he labored at night, and *stole from his sleeping hours the time required to run the farm. When the mill shut down, he went out each morning looking for work - *only to return night after night and say to Mother as she *fixed[36] his dinner, "*They just don't want anybody who can't take their tests."

It had always been hard for him to stand before a man and make an "X" mark for his name, but *the hardest moment of all was he placed "his mark" by the name someone else had written for him,

23. solitary 혼자의
24. slip away 빠져나가다
25. reader 읽기교재
26. labor 애를 쓰다
27. will 의지
28. unsurpassed 그 누구에게도 뒤지지 않는
29. pipefitter 배관공
30. shipyard 조선소
31. nuts 소화관, (여기서는) 배관
32. mighty 강력한
33. blueprint 설계도
34. twist and turn 구불구불함
35. cotton mill 방적공장
36. fix 준비하다

and *saw another man walk away with the *deed[37] to his beloved farm. When it was over, he stood before the window and *slowly turned the pen he still held in his hands - gazing, unseeing, down the mountainside. I went to the *spring house[38] that afternoon and wept for a long while.

Eventually, he found another cotton-mill job, and we moved into a millhouse village with a hundred look-alike houses. He never quite *adjusted to[39] town life. The blue of his eyes faded; the skin across his cheekbones became a little *slack[40]. But his hands kept their strength, and their warmth still soaked through when he would sit me on his lap and ask me to read to him from the Bible. He took great pride in my reading and would listen for hours as I struggled through the *awkward[41] phrases.

*Once he had heard "a radio preacher" relate that the Bible said, "The man that doesn't *provide for his family is worse than a thief and an *infidel[42] and will never enter the kingdom of Heaven." Often he would ask me to read that part to him, but I was never able to find it. Other times, he would sit at the kitchen table *leafing through the pages *as though by a miracle he might be able to turn to the right page. Then he would sit staring at the Book, and I knew *he was wondering if God was going to refuse him entry into heaven because his hands couldn't write.

When Mother left once for a weekend to visit her sister, Dad went to the store and returned with food for dinner while I was busy building my latest homemade *wagon[43]. After the meal he said he

37. deed
(소유권을 증명하는) 증서

38. spring house
샘 위에 세운 냉장 오두막

39. adjust to
~에 적응하다

40. slack
쳐진

41. awkward
어려운

42. infidel
신앙심이 없는 사람

43. wagon
마차

had a surprise for dessert, and went out to the kitchen, where I could hear him opening a can. Then everything was quiet. I went to the doorway and saw him standing before the sink with an open can in his hands. "The picture looked just like pears," he *mumbled[44]. He walked out and sat on the back steps, and I knew he had been embarrassed before his son. *The can read "Whole White Potatoes," but the picture on the label did look a great deal like pears.

I went and sat beside him, and asked if he would point out the stars. He knew where the *Big Dipper[45] and all the other stars were located, and we talked about how they got there in the first place. He kept that can on a shelf in the *woodshed[46] for a long while, and a few times I saw him turning it in his hands as if the touch of the words would teach his hands to write.

Years later, when Mom died, I tried to *get him to come live with my family, but he insisted on staying in his small *frame house[47] on the edge of town with a few farm animals and a *garden plot[48]. His health was *failing[49], and he was in and out of the hospital with several mild *heart attacks[50]. Old Doc Green saw him weekly and gave him medications, *including nitroglycerin tablets to put under his tongue should he feel an attack coming on.

My last fond memory of Dad was watching as he walked across the *brow[51] of a *hillside meadow[52], *with those big, warm hands - now gnarled with age - *resting[53] on the shoulders of my two children. He stopped to point out, *confidentially[54], a pond where he and I had swum and fished years before. That night, my family and I

44. mumble
중얼거리듯 말하다

45. Big Dipper
북두칠성

46. woodshed
장작헛간

47. frame house
목조 가옥

48. garden plot
정원부지(남새밭)

49. fail
나빠지다

50. heart attack
심장마비

51. brow
등성이(꼭대기)

52. hillside meadow
산비탈 목초지

53. rest
기대다

54. confidentially
은밀하게

55. bothered
신경이 쓰이는

56. prescription
처방전

57. fill
(처방전대로) 조제하다

58. summon
요청하다

59. come to rest
멈춰서다

60. lose
패하다, 지다

61. leather-bound
가죽제본의

flew to a new job and new home, overseas. Three weeks later, he was dead of a heart attack.

I returned alone for the funeral. Doc Green told me how sorry he was. In fact, he was *bothered[55] a bit, because he had written Dad a new nitroglycerin *prescription[56], and the druggist had *filled[57] it. Yet the bottle of pills had not been found *on Dad's person. Doc Green felt that a pill might have kept him alive long enough to *summon[58] help.

An hour before the chapel service, I found myself standing near the edge of Dad's garden, where a neighbor had found him. In grief, I stopped to trace my fingers in the earth where a great man had reached the end of his life. My hand *came to rest[59] on a half-buried brick, which I aimlessly lifted and tossed aside, before noticing underneath it *the twisted and battered, yet unbroken, soft plastic bottle that had been beaten into the soft earth.

As I held the bottle of nitroglycerin pills, *the scene of Dad struggling to remove the cap and in desperation trying to break the bottle with the brick flashed painfully before my eyes. With deep anguish I knew why those big warm hands had *lost[60] in their struggle with death. *For there, imprinted on the bottle cap, were the words, "*Child-Proof Cap - Push Down and Twist to Unlock." The druggist later confirmed that he had just started using the new safety bottle.

I knew it was not a purely rational act, but I went right downtown and bought a *leather-bound[61] pocket dictionary and a gold pen set. I *bade[62] Dad good-by by placing them in *those big old hands, once so warm, which had lived so well, but had never learned to write.

62. bid
고하다, 말하다

GRAMMAR

문장의 구성단위

1. 문장의 구성요소는 무엇인가?

문장을 구성하고 있는 형식적인 단위: **단어(word), 구(phrase), 절(clause)**

1) **품사**(parts of speech)**란?**: 문장의 기본 단위인 단어를 부류별로 나눈 용어이다.

기본요소	명사, 대명사, 동사	연결요소	전치사, 접속사
보조요소	형용사, 부사	기타	감탄사

2) 구(phrase)란?

(1) 형태적 구분

단어가 하나의 중심어를 중심으로 이루어진 통사적 단위를 구라 한다.
I want the book **on the table**: 형태적 전치사구(전치사+명사)

(2) 기능적 구분

단어가 모여 이루어진 것으로 **주어와 술어를 포함하지 않으면서 문장 속에서 한 개의 단어와 같이 어떤 품사의 역할을 하는 단위**를 구라 한다.
I want the book **on the table**: 기능적 형용사구
(cf. I found it **on the table**: 기능적으로 부사구)

3) **절**(clause)**이란?**: 단어가 모여 **주어와 술어를 포함하되 독립적인 문장이 되지 못하고 어떤 품사와 같은 역할을 하는 단위**이다.

(1) 기능상의 분류

명사절	The weather announcer said **that there will be thunderstorms**. (목적어)
	When the meeting will be held has not been decided. (주어)
	This is **what you need**. (보어)
형용사절	This is the man about **whom I spoke**.
부사절	You may begin **when you are ready**.

(2) 의존성에 따른 분류

주절	**The weather announcer said** that there will be thunderstorms.
종속절	The weather announcer said **that there will be thunderstorms**.

2. 영어 문장 접근 방법

1) 주부와 술부의 구분(본동사를 찾는다)

The children who live in town **walk** home.
The stores along the street on the hill **began** to open.

(1) **주부**(subject): 문장의 머리에 해당되며 일반적으로 **행위를 수행하거나 기술되는 사람이나 사물**이다. **주부의 중심어를 주어**라하는데 주어는 **명사(명사구, 명사절), 대명사**로 구성되어 있다.

The **quarterback** passed the ball to his wide receiver. (주어는 행위를 수행한다)

He is talented. (주어는 기술된다)

(2) **술부**(predicate): 주부에 의해 시작된 **행위를 표현하거나 주부에 관한 서술을 하는 것**으로 그 중심어는 동사이다.

The goalkeeper has **blocked** the shot. (술어는 행위를 표현한다)

She **is** quick. (술어는 주어에 관한 서술을 한다)

2) 주성분과 부성분을 찾는다

주성분	
주어	문장의 주체가 되는 것으로 명사(구/절), 대명사가 주어가 된다. 한국어: **주격조사** '은', '는', '이', '가' 영어: 어순이 중요한 역할을 하는데 **보통 본동사 앞부분**이 된다.
술어	주어의 상태나 행위를 서술하는 것으로 동사가 술어의 핵심이 된다.
목적어	행위의 대상이 되는 것으로 명사(구/절), 대명사가 목적어가 된다. 한국어: **목적격조사** '을', '를' 영어: 보통 **본동사 뒷부분**이 된다.
보어	주어나 목적어의 상태를 나타내 주는 것으로 명사(구/절), 형용사(구/절)가 보어로 사용된다.

부성분	
수식어	**주성분을 수식하는** 것으로 **형용사(구/절), 부사(구/절)**이 수식어로 사용된다.
연결어	이들 **성분들을 연결해 문장을 확대하는 역할**을 하는 것으로 **전치사, 접속사**가 연결어로 사용된다.

3. 영어와 한국어의 주요 차이

1) 영어는 어순이 아주 중요

영어	Tom likes Mary ≠ Mary likes Tom
한국어	톰은 메리를 좋아 한다 = 메리를 톰은 좋아한다 S+V+O(주어+동사+목적어)와 S+O+V(주어+목적어+동사)

2) 영어는 전치사(preposition) 한국어는 후치사(postposition)

영어는 명사 앞에 전치사가 온다. 반면에 한국어는 명사 뒤에 후치사(조사)가 온다.

영어	I go **to** school	* 영어의 모든 전치사 뒤에는 반드시 **전치사의 목적어로 명사(구/절)**를 취해야 한다.
한국어	나는 학교**에** 간다	

3) 수식어의 위치

일반적으로 영어나 한국어에서 **형용사는 명사 앞에서 그 명사를 수식**한다. **영어는 형용사가 명사의 앞뒤에서 수식**을 할 수 있으나, **형용사구나 형용사절은 항상 뒤**에서 수식을 한다. 반면에 **한국어는 단어, 구, 절 모두가 항상 앞에서 수식**을 한다.

영어	한국어
a **beautiful** girl	**아름다운** 소녀
China **proper**(중국본토)	**고유의** 중국
the **present** members(현 회원)	**현재의** 회원
the members **present**(참석한 회원)	**참석한** 회원
the book **on the table**	**탁자 위의** 그 책 (구)
The book **I am reading now** is my brother's.	**내가 지금 읽고 있는** 그 책은 (절)

PHRASES and STRUCTURES

* **wrestle (타동사)** ~ ~와 맞붙어 싸우다

He wrestled an alligator. 그는 악어와 맞붙어 싸웠다.

wrestle (자동사) with ~ ~와 맞붙어 싸우다, 씨름하다

He began to wrestle with his opponent. 그는 상대와 맞붙어 싸우기 시작했다.

He wrestled with the problems. 그는 그 문제들과 씨름 했다.

* **with quick accuracy** 빠르고 정확하게

with + 추상명사 = 부사

with accuracy 정확하게

* He had been **known to peel** his knuckles upside a tough jaw.

그는 강한 턱의 위쪽 면으로 그의 관절의 껍질을 벗긴 것으로 알려졌다.

= They had known him to peel his knuckles upside a tough jaw.(능동형)

know + 목적어 + to + do 목적어가 ~한 것을 알다

⇒ **목적어 + be + known + to + do(수동태)** 목적어가 ~한 것으로 알려져 있다

I know him to be honest. 나는 그가 정직하다는 것을 알고 있다.

⇒ He is known to be honest.(수동형)

* the special warmth from those hands **soaking** through my shirt

여기서 **soaking은 현재분사로 앞의 warmth를 수식하는 형용사 역할**을 함

The warmth soaks through my shirt. 따뜻함이 나의 셔츠 속으로 스며들다.

* **take me by the shoulder** 나의 어깨를 잡다

take + 대명사(사람) + by + 신체의 일부 = 사람의 신체 일부를 잡다

She took me by the wrist. 그 여자가 나의 손목을 잡았다.

He took me by the hand tightly. 그는 나의 손을 꼭 잡았다.

* good hands **that** served him well

그에게 큰 도움이 되었던 좋은 손

= good hands, **and + they(good hands)** served him well

that(= which)은 관계대명사 = and + they(good hands)

* If there were only one I would be saddened, remembering my father and the pain (**which**) he endured.
만일 오로지 한 사람만 있다면 나의 아버지와 그가 겪은 고통을 기억하고 나는 슬플 것이다.
= If there were only one I would be saddened, and I remember my father and the pain, **and** he endured **it(the pain)**.
If + 주어 + 과거동사, 주어 + would + 동사원형 가정법 과거(현재사실과 반대)
목적격 관계대명사 which = and + it(the pain)

* **where** = and there

* **suffer from** ~ ~로 고통 받다

* **took him out of school** 그를 학교에서 데리고 나왔다

* **set him a man's job on the farm** 그에게 농장의 남자 일을 맡게 하였다
set+목적어+전치사+명사 (목적어를) 배치하다, 보내다
He **set** the detective **on** the case. 그는 그 형사에게 그 사건을 맡게 하였다.

* **still later** 그 후에도 여전히

* **submitted to** ~ ~에 굴복하다

* **grew restless** 안절부절 못하게 되었다
grow + 형용사 = 형용사 되다

* **had had enough** 진절머리가 난다, 신물이 난다

* No amount of persuading could **bring him to sit** with pen and paper.
아무리 설득해도 그가 펜과 종이를 가지고 앉고 싶은 마음이 생기게 할 수 없었다.
Once she had made up her mind, no amount of persuading could change it.
그녀는 일단 결심을 하면 아무리 설득해도 마음을 바꿀 수 없었다.
bring + 목적어(사람) + to + do 목적어가 ~할 마음이 생기게 하다

What brought you to buy the book? 어째서 너는 그 책을 살 마음이 생겼는가?

* His mind **was keen**, his will **to** work unsurpassed.

= His mind was keen (to work unsurpassed), and his will was keen to work unsurpassed.

그의 마음은 그 누구에게도 뒤지지 않고 싶어 했고 그의 의지도 그 누구에게도 뒤지지 않고 싶어 했다.

be keen to + 동사원형 간절히 ~하고 싶어 하다

Most managements are keen to avoid strikes.

대부분의 경영진들은 파업을 간절히 피하고 싶어 한다.

* His enthusiasm and efficiency brought an offer **to become** line boss.

그의 열정과 효율성이 작업라인의 장이 되는 제의를 가져왔다.

to become은 an offer를 수식하는 형용사 역할

* until he **was handed** the qualification test

→ until they **handed** him the qualification test (능동태)

그들이 그에게 자격시험을 치게 했을 때까지

* the pipes **lacing** through the heart of the ship

배의 중심부를 관통해서 끈으로 묶고 있는 파이프

lacing은 pipes를 수식하는 형용사역할을 하는 현재분사

* stole from his sleeping hours the time **required** to run the farm

잠자는 시간에서 농장을 운영하기 위해 필요한 시간을 빼앗았다(아꼈다)

= stole (from his sleeping hours) **the time (which is) required** to run the farm

required는 time을 수식하는 형용사역할을 하는 과거분사로 앞에 관계대명사+be동사**가 생략되어 있음**

* **only to return** night after night 매일 밤 결국 돌아왔다

night after night 매일 밤

only to + 동사원형 어떤 것이 놀랍거나 예기치 않거나, 헛된 것을 보이기 위한 표현

He had tasted freedom **only to lose** it again.

그는 자유를 잠깐 맛보았지만 결국 다시 잃게 되었다.

* They just don't want anybody **who** can't take their tests.
시험을 칠 수 없는 사람은 누구도 원치 않는다.
They just don't want anybody, **and he(anybody)** can't take their tests.
who = and + he(anybody)

* The hardest moment of all was he placed "his mark" by the name someone else had written for him.
모든 것 중에서 가장 힘든 것은 그가 누군가가 그를 대신해 썼던 이름 옆에 '그의 표시'를 했던 것이었다.
= The hardest moment of all was **(that)** he placed "his mark" by the name **(which)** someone else had written for him.
= The hardest moment of all was **(that)** he placed "his mark" by the name, **and** someone else had written **it(the name)** for him.
that = **접속사**
목적격 관계대명사 which 생략 = and + it(the name)

* **saw** another man **walk** away with the deed to his beloved farm
다른 사람이 그의 사랑하는 토지증서를 가지고 떠나버리는 것을 보는 것
지각동사(see) + 사람 (man)+ 동사원형(walk)

* slowly turned the pen he still held in his hands
그의 손에 여전히 잡고 있었던 그 펜을 천천히 돌렸다
= slowly turned the pen **(which)** he still held in his hands
= slowly turned the pen, **and** he still held **it(the pen)** in his hands
목적격 관계대명사 which 생략 = and + it(the pen)

* Once he had **heard** "a radio preacher" **relate** that the Bible said.
한번은 그가 라디오 설교자가 성경이 말하고 있는 것을 연관시키는 것을 들었다.
지각동사(hear) + 사람 (preacher)+ 동사원형(relate)

* **provide for** ~ ~을 부양하다

* **as though** by a miracle he might be able to turn to the right page
마치 그가 기적적으로 바로 그 페이지로 돌아갈 수 있을지도 모르는 것처럼
as though = 마치 ~인 것처럼

* **leaf through** 대충 넘겨보다

* He was wondering if God was going to refuse him entry into heaven.
신이 그가 천국으로 들어오는 것을 거부하려고 할까 궁금해하고 있었다.
The Immigration Department refused him entry.
출입국 관리소는 그의 입국을 거부했다.

* The can **read** "Whole White Potatoes"
그 캔에는 "통 흰 감자"라고 적혀있었다.

* get him to come live with my family
그를 나의 가족과 함께 살게 하다
get + 목적어 + to + do ~시키다(하게하다)
I **got him to prepare** for our journey.
나는 그에게 우리의 여행 준비를 시켰다.

* **including** nitroglycerin tablets to put under his tongue **should he feel an attack coming on**
그런데 그 약들은 니트로글리세린 알약을 포함하고 있었는데 니트로글리세린 알약은 만일 그가 마비가 온다고 느끼게 되면 그의 혀 아래에 두기 위한 것이었다
= **and they(medications) included** nitroglycerin tablets to put under his tongue **if he should feel an attack coming on**
including(분사구문) = ~~and they(medications)~~ included
should he feel an attack coming on = if he should feel an attack coming on

* **with** those big, warm **hands - now gnarled** with age - **resting** on the shoulders of my two children
그 크고 따뜻한 손을 - 그런데 그 손은 이제 나이 때문에 울퉁불퉁해졌는데 - 나의 두 아이들의 어깨에 얹은 채
now gnarled(분사구문) = ~~and~~ now ~~the hands are~~(being) gnarled
그런데 그 손은 지금은 나이 때문에 울퉁불퉁해진
with + 목적어 + 동사원형+ing 목적어를 ~한 채

* **on Dad's person** 아버지가 몸에 지니고
on one's person 몸에 지니고, 휴대하고

* the twisted and battered, yet unbroken, soft plastic bottle **that** had been beaten into the soft earth

꼬여지고, 두드려졌지만 깨어지지 않은 부드러운 플라스틱 병, 그런데 그 병은 부드러운 흙에 대고 두드려졌었다

= the twisted and battered, yet unbroken, soft plastic bottle, **and it(the bottle)** had been beaten into the soft earth

주격 관계대명사 that = and + it(the bottle)

and it(the bottle) had **been beaten** into the soft earth

→ and he had **beaten** it(the bottle) into the soft earth (능동태)

* **The scene** of Dad **struggling** to remove the cap and in desperation **trying** to break the bottle with the brick **flashed** painfully before my eyes.

아버지가 그 병뚜껑을 열려고 안간힘을 쓰고 절망에 빠져 벽돌로 그 병을 깨려고 하는 장면이 나의 눈앞에 고통스럽게 번쩍거렸다.

scene이 주어이고 본동사는 flash

struggling과 trying이 scene를 수식하고 있음

* For there, **imprinted** on the bottle cap, were the words.

왜냐하면 다음과 같은 글이 병뚜껑 위에 새겨진 채로 있었기 때문이다.

= For there were the words, **(and they(the words) were) imprinted** on the bottle cap.

imprinted(분사구문) = ~~and they(the words) were~~(being) imprinted

* Child-Proof Cap - Push Down and Twist to Unlock.

어린이 보호용 뚜껑 – 열기위해 눌러서 돌리시오.

* those big old hands, once so warm, **which** had lived so well, but had never learned to write

그 큰 늙은 손, 한 때는 너무나 따뜻했던 손이었는데, 그 손은 너무나 잘 살아왔었지만 결코 글 쓰는 법을 배우지 못했었다

= those big old hands, **once so warm, and they(those hands)** had lived so well, but had never learned to write

, once so warm, = , ~~and those big old hands were~~(being) once so warm,

which = and + they(those hands)

Unit 2

Yes, there is a war between science and religion[1)]

WARMING UP

- **The claims that** science and religion are compatible **grow louder**
- I'll **construe** "science" **as** the set of tools we use to find truth about the universe
- trying your hardest to prove **that** your hypothesis is wrong to test your confidence **that** it's right
- I'll define religion as **does** philosopher Daniel Dennett
- Social systems **whose** participants avow belief in a supernatural agent or agents **whose** approval is to **be sought**
- If there be no resurrection of **the dead**, then is Christ not risen
- rests on the methods **(which)** they use to decide **what** is true, and **what** truths result
- for how can you reject the divine in your laboratory but accept that the wine **(which)** you sip on Sunday is the blood of Jesus?

1) The author is Jerry Coyne, Professor Emeritus of Ecology and Evolution, University of Chicago and this article was published by The Conversation in the December of 21, 2018. The source is http://theconversation.com/yes-there-is-a-war-between-science-and-religion-108002

As the West becomes more and more *secular[1], and the discoveries of *evolutionary biology[2] and *cosmology[3] *shrink[4] the boundaries of *faith[5], *the claims that science and religion are *compatible[6] grow louder. If you're a believer who doesn't want to seem *anti-science[7], what can you do? You must argue that your faith – or any faith – is perfectly compatible with science.

*And so one sees *claim after claim from believers, religious scientists, *prestigious[8] science organizations and even *atheists[9] *asserting not only that science and religion are compatible, but also that they can actually help each other. This claim is called "*accommodationism[10]."

But I argue that this is *misguided[11]: that science and religion *are not only in conflict – even at "war" – but also represent incompatible ways of viewing the world.

Opposing methods for *discerning[12] truth

My argument runs like this. *I'll construe "science" as the set of tools we use to find truth about the universe, *with the understanding that these truths are *provisional[13] rather than absolute. These tools include observing nature, *framing[14] and testing hypotheses, *trying your hardest to prove that your hypothesis is wrong to test your confidence that it's right, doing experiments and above all *replicating[15] your and others' results to increase confidence in your *inference[16].

And *I'll define religion as does philosopher Daniel Dennett:

1. secular
세속적인
2. evolutionary biology
진화생물학
3. cosmology
우주론
4. shrink
줄어들게 하다
5. faith
신앙, 종교
6. compatible
양립할 수 있는,
사이좋게 지낼 수 있는
7. anti-science
반 과학(의)
8. prestigious
권위 있는
9. atheist
무신론자
10. accommodationism
수용론
11. misguided
잘못된, 틀린
12. discern
발견하다
13. provisional
일시적인, 잠정적인
14. frame
틀을 잡다, 만들어내다
15. replicate
복제하다, 되풀이하다
16. inference
추론

17. fit
맞다

18. tout
장점을 내세우다

19. edifice
조직, 체계

20. Resurrection of Christ
그리스도의 부활

21. authoritative teaching
권위 있는 가르침

22. resurrection
부활

23. risen
부활한

24. vain
헛된, 소용없는

25. theologian
신학자

"*Social systems whose participants avow belief in a supernatural agent or agents whose approval is to be sought." Of course many religions don't *fit[17] that definition, but *the ones whose compatibility with science is *touted[18] most often – the Abrahamic faiths of Judaism, Christianity and Islam – fill the bill.

Next, realize that both religion and science rest on "truth statements" about the universe – claims about reality. The *edifice[19] of religion differs from science by additionally dealing with morality, purpose and meaning, but even those areas rest on a foundation of empirical claims. You can hardly call yourself a Christian if you don't believe in the *Resurrection of Christ[20], a Muslim *if you don't believe the angel Gabriel dictated the Qur'an to Muhammad, or a Mormon if you don't believe that *the angel Moroni showed Joseph Smith the golden plates that became the *Book of Mormon[2)]. After all, why accept a faith's *authoritative teachings[21] if you reject its truth claims?

Indeed, even the Bible notes this: "But if there be no *resurrection[22] of *the dead, then is Christ not *risen[23]: And if Christ be not risen, then is our preaching *vain[24], and your faith is also vain."

Many *theologians[25] emphasize religion's empirical foundations, *agreeing with the physicist and Anglican priest John Polkinghorne:

"The question of truth is as central to [religion's] concern as it is in science. Religious belief can guide *one in life or strengthen one at

2) Book of Mormon 모르몬 경전.

the approach of death, but *unless it is actually true it can do neither of these things and so would amount to no more than an *illusory[26] exercise in comforting fantasy."

The conflict between science and faith, then, *rests on the methods they use to decide what is true, and what truths result: These are conflicts of both methodology and outcome.

In contrast to the methods of science, religion *adjudicates[27] truth not empirically, but via *dogma[28], *scripture[29] and authority – *in other words, through faith, defined in Hebrews 11 as "the substance of things hoped for, the evidence of things not seen." In science, faith without evidence is a *vice[30], while in religion it's a *virtue[31]. Recall what Jesus said to "*doubting Thomas[3)]," who insisted in *poking[32] his fingers into the *resurrected Savior[4)]'s wounds: "*Thomas, because thou hast seen me, thou hast believed: blessed are they that have not seen, and yet have believed."

*And yet, without supporting evidence, Americans believe a number of religious claims: 74 percent of us believe in God, 68 percent in the *divinity[33] of Jesus, 68 percent in Heaven, 57 percent in the *virgin birth[34], and 58 percent in the Devil and Hell. Why do they think these are true? Faith.

26. illusory 환상에 불과한
27. adjudicate 판결(정)을 내리다
28. dogma 교리, (독단적인) 신조
29. scripture 성서, 경전
30. vice 악, 악덕
31. virtue 선, 미덕
32. poke 찌르다
33. divinity 신성
34. virgin birth (마리아의) 처녀 잉태설

3) doubting Thomas 의심이 많은 사람을 가리키는데 직접적인 개인 경험 없이는 믿기를 거부하는 사람을 가리킴. 사도 토마스에 대해 말하는 것에서 유래했는데 사도 토마스는 십자가에서 예수에 의해 입은 상처를 보고 느낄 수 있을 때까지는 부활한 예수가 10명의 다른 사도에게 나타났다는 것을 믿기를 거부했음.

4) resurrected Savior 부활한 구세주, 즉 예수그리스도를 말함.

35. conflicting 상반(충)되는
36. sect 종파
37. creed 신념, 신조
38. compartmentalize 영역을 구분하다
39. reconcile 화해시키다
40. point to ~을 들먹이다

But different religions make different – and often *conflicting[35] – claims, and there's no way to judge which claims are right. There are over 4,000 religions on this planet, and their "truths" are quite different. (Muslims and Jews, for instance, absolutely reject the Christian belief that Jesus was the son of God.) Indeed, new *sects[36] often arise *when some believers reject what others see as true. *Lutherans[5)] split over the truth of evolution, while *Unitarians[6)] rejected other *Protestants[7)]' belief that Jesus was part of God.

And while science has had *success after success in understanding the universe, the "method" of using faith has led to no proof of the divine. How many gods are there? What are their natures and moral *creeds[37]? Is there an afterlife? Why is there moral and physical evil? There is no one answer to any of these questions. All is mystery, for all rests on faith.

The "war" between science and religion, then, is a conflict about whether you have good reasons for believing what you do: whether you see faith as a vice or a virtue.

*Compartmentalizing[38] realms is irrational

So how do *the faithful *reconcile[39] science and religion? Often they *point to[40] the existence of religious scientists, like *NIH[8)]

5) Lutheran 루터 교도(16세기 독일 종교 지도자 마틴 루터의 가르침을 따르는 교회의 일원).

6) Unitarian 유니테리언 교도(삼위일체론을 부정하고 신격의 단일성을 주장하는 기독교의 한 파).
* 삼위일체론: 그리스도교도들은 하나의 신이 성부, 성자, 성령의 세 가지 '위격'을 취한다고 믿는데 이것이 삼위일체의 교리다. 유대인과 무슬림은 삼위일체를 별도의 세 개의 신으로 보기 때문에 삼위일체의 개념을 받아들이지 않으며, 유일신이 '아들'을 두었다는 생각도 인정하지 않음.

7) protestant 개신교도.

8) NIH National Institutes of Health (미국) 국립 보건원.

Director Francis Collins, or to the many religious people who accept science. But I'd argue that this is *compartmentalization[41], not *compatibility[42], *for how can you reject the divine in your laboratory but accept that the wine you *sip[43] on Sunday is the blood of Jesus?

Others argue that in the past religion *promoted[44] science and *inspired[45] questions about the universe. But in the past every Westerner was religious, and it's *debatable[46] whether, in the long run, the progress of science has been promoted by religion. *Certainly evolutionary biology, my own field, has been *held back[47] strongly by *creationism[9], which arises solely from religion.

What is not *disputable[48] is that today science is practiced as an *atheistic discipline[49] – and largely by atheists. There's a huge *disparity[50] in *religiosity[51] between American scientists and Americans as a whole: *64 percent of our elite scientists are atheists or *agnostics[10], compared to only 6 percent of the general population – more than a tenfold difference. Whether this reflects differential attraction of nonbelievers to science or science *eroding[52] belief – I suspect both factors operate – the figures are *prima facie evidence[53] for a science-religion conflict.

The most common *accommodationist[54] argument is Stephen Jay Gould's thesis of "*non-overlapping magisteria[11]." Religion and

41. compartmentalization
구획화

42. compatibility
양립성

43. sip
홀짝이다,
조금씩 마시다

44. promote
장려하다

45. inspire
영감을 주다

46. debatable
논란의 여지가 있는

47. held back
(진전, 발전) 방해하다

48. disputable
반론의 여지가 있는

49. atheistic discipline
무신론적 규율

50. disparity
차이

51. religiosity
종교성

52. erode
침식하다

53. prima facie evidence
일단 진실로 보는 증거

54. accommodationist
타협파의 사람

9) creationism 천지창조설(성서에 묘사된 대로 하느님이 우주를 창조했다는 믿음).

10) agnostic 불가지론자(인간은 신을 인식할 수 없다는 종교적 인식론자로 유신론과 무신론을 모두 배격함).

11) Non-overlapping magisteria(NOMA) 미국의 생물학자인 스티븐 제이 굴드가 주장하는 견해로 과학과 종교는 각각 서로 다른 탐구영역, 사실 대 가치관을 나타내기 때문에, 그들이 '정당한 교학권, 즉 교권 영역'을 가지고 있는 '망(nets)' 사이에는 차이가 있으며, 두 영역은 겹치지 않음.

55. document
뒷받침하다

56. factual
사실에 입각한

57. coordinate
조정하다

58. realm
영역

59. illuminate
밝히다, 분명히 하다

60. Abrahamic religion
아브라함 종교

61. bailiwick bailiff
(집달관)의 관할구, 전문분야

62. distinguished
유명한

63. fount
샘, 원천

64. wishful-thinking
희망사항

65. superstition
미신

66. undergird
~의 밑을 단단하게 묶다, 뒷받침하다

67. mind
사람

68. renowned
유명한, 명성 있는

69. dissonance
불협화음, (의견)충돌

70. prompt
사람에게 어떤 결정을 내리도록 하다(촉발하다)

science, he argued, don't conflict because: "Science tries to *document[55] the *factual[56] character of the natural world, and to develop theories that *coordinate[57] and explain these facts. Religion, on the other hand, operates in the equally important, but utterly different, *realm[58] of human purposes, meanings and values – *subjects that the factual domain of science might *illuminate[59], but can never resolve."

This fails *on both ends. First, religion certainly makes claims about "the factual character of the universe." In fact, the biggest opponents of non-overlapping magisteria are believers and theologians, *many of whom reject the idea that*Abrahamic religions[60] are "empty of any claims to historical or scientific facts."

*Nor is religion the sole *bailiwick[61] of "purposes, meanings and values," which of course differ among faiths. There's a long and *distinguished[62] history of philosophy and ethics – extending from Plato, Hume and Kant up to Peter Singer, Derek Parfit and John Rawls in our day – *that relies on reason rather than faith as a *fount[63] of morality. All serious ethical philosophy is secular ethical philosophy.

*In the end, *it's irrational to decide what's true in your daily life using empirical evidence, but then rely on *wishful-thinking[64] and ancient *superstitions[65] to judge the "truths" *undergirding[66] your faith. This leads to a *mind[67] (no matter how scientifically *renowned[68]) *at war with itself, *producing the cognitive *dissonance[69] that *prompts[70] accommodationism. If you decide to have good reasons for holding any beliefs, then you must choose between faith and reason. And as facts become increasingly important for the welfare of our species and our planet, *people should see faith for what it is: not a virtue but a *defect[71].

71. defect
결함

GRAMMAR

구두점(Punctuation)의 역할

1. 콤마(comma)(,)

1) 구어체에서 쉼(pause) 역할을 문어체에서 콤마가 한다.

When the recruiter called, Kenneth Martin answered. (두 사람)
When the recruiter called Kenneth, Martin answered. (세 사람)

2) 등위접속사 앞에서 독립절을 연결한다

주어+ 술어, **and(but, for, nor, or, so, yet)** + 주어 + 술어

3) 독립절을 앞서는 종속절 다음에서 사용된다.

When you write, you make a sound in the reader's head

4) 분사가 이끄는 구나 절을 연결하기 위해 사용된다.

She was staring at the stranger, **her heart pounding** louder and louder.
For there, **imprinted** on the bottle cap, were the words

5) 수식어로 사용된 비필수적인 요소를 분리하기 위해 사용된다.

My sister, **who** lives in Denver, is visiting me.
= I have only one sister, and she happens to live in Denver.
My sister **who** lives in Denver, is visiting me.
= I have several sisters, and the one who is visiting is the one who live in Denver.

6) 도입어 다음에 사용된다.

Well, come on in and join the party.

Yes, I have a valid inspection sticker.

7) 대등한 요소들이 연속적으로 나타날 때 분리하는데 사용된다.

The sky was **cloudless, bright, and blue**.

8) 보충적인 동격어를 분리하는데 사용된다.

Even Milo Kim, **my friend**, let me down.

9) 삽입적인 요소들은 비필수적인 단어나 구이다.

An airline ticket, **for example**, can be delivered electronically.

10) 대조적인 요소들을 분리하기 위해 사용된다.

A planet, **unlike a star**, reflects rather than genertates light.

2. 세미콜론(semicolon)(;)

세미콜론은 등위접속사로 연결되지 않은 독립절을 연결한다.

독립절(주부+ 술부), **등위접속사** + 주부 + 술부

My web sites are interesting, but some are not accurate.

My web sites are interesting, however, some are not accurate.

독립절(주부+ 술부); 주부 + 술부

My web sites are interesting; some are not accurate.

3. 콜론(colon)(:)

1) 첫 번째 독립절을 확장하거나 설명하는 두 번째 독립절을 도입할 때 사용된다.

They were concerned mainly about speed: Not only they want a very fast computer, but they also had to have a very fast Internet connection.

2) 어떤 것들을 나열할 때 사용된다.

There were three winners: Asa, Vanna, and Jack
or The winners were as follows: Asa, Vanna, and Jack
But The winners included Asa, Vanna, and Jack

4. 대시(dash)(—)

1) 강조나 명확성을 위한 삽입요소를 분리하기 위해 사용된다.

In many smaller cities of this nation, cable television operators - with the connivance of local government - have a virtual monopoly.

2) 앞의 내용을 다시 설명하거나 보충하는 역할을 한다

Eager, determined to succeed, and scared to death - all of these describe my emotions the first day on the job.

5. 피어리드(.)

어떤 내용이 끝났음을 나타낸다.

Global warming is a serious problem.

PHRASES and STRUCTURES

* **The claims that** science and religion are compatible **grow** louder.
과학과 종교가 양립할 수 있다는 주장들이 더 커지게 되었다.
주어는 The claims, 본동사는 grow
The claims와 that절은 동격

* **And so = Accordingly** 따라서

* **claim after claim** 거듭된 주장

* **asserting** not only that science and religion are compatible, but also that **they** can actually help each other
그런데 그들은 과학과 종교가 양립할 수 있을 뿐만 아니라 과학과 종교는 실제로 서로 도울 수 있다고 주장한다
= **and they assert** not only that science and religion are compatible, but also that they can actually help each other
asserting(분사구문) = ~~and they~~ assert
they = science and religion

* **are in conflict** 대립하고 있다

* I'll **construe** "science" **as** the set of tools we use to find truth about the universe.
나는 과학을 도구들의 세트로 해석할 것인데, 우리는 우주에 관한 진리를 발견하기 위해 그 도구들의 세트를 사용한다.
= I'll construe "science" as the set of tools **(which)** we use to find truth about the universe.
= I'll construe "science" as the set of tools, **and** we use **it(the set of tools)** to find truth about the universe.
목적격 관계대명사 which 생략 = and + it(the set of tools)
construe A as B A를 B로 해석하다

* with **the understanding that** these truths are provisional rather than absolute
이러한 진리가 절대적인 것이 아니라 잠정적이라는 이해와 함께
the understanding과 that절은 동격

* **trying your hardest** to prove **that** your hypothesis is wrong to test **your confidence that it**'s right
가설이 옳다는 당신의 확신을 검증하기 위해 당신의 가설이 틀렸다는 것을 증명하기 위해 최선을 다하려고 하는 것
trying your hardest 최선을 다해서
첫 **that**은 **prove**의 목적절
뒤의 **that**은 **confidence**와 동격절
it = hypothesis

* I'll define religion as **does** philosopher Daniel Dennett.
철학자 대니얼 데니트가 정의하는 것처럼 종교를 정의할 것이다.
does는 define을 받고 있는 대동사

* Social systems **whose** participants avow belief in a supernatural agent or agents **whose** approval is to be sought
(종교는) 사회제도인데, 그 사회제도의 참가자(구성원)들이 초자연적인 대리인이나 대리인들을 믿겠다고 공언하는데, 사람들은 그들(대리인이나 대리인들)의 승인을 구하려고 한다
= (Religion is) social systems, **and their(social systems)** participants avow belief in a supernatural agent or agents, **and their(agent or agents)** approval is to be sought
= (Religion is) social systems, **and their(social systems)** participants avow belief in a supernatural agent or agents, **and people are to seek their(agent or agents)** approval (능동형)
whose = and + their(social systems')
whose = and + their(agent or agent's)

* The **ones whose** compatibility with science is touted most often - the Abrahamic faiths of Judaism, Christianity and Islam - fill the bill.
그 종교들, 그런데 그 종교들의 과학과의 양립성이 매우 자주 장점으로 내새워지는데, 가령

유대교, 기독교, 이슬람교의 아브라함 신앙은 꼭 들어맞는다.

= The ones, **and their(religions')** compatibility with science is touted most often – the Abrahamic faiths of Judaism, Christianity and Islam – fill the bill.

whose = and + their(religion's)

ones는 religions을 가리킴

fill the bill 꼭 들어맞다

* if you don't believe **(that)** the angel Gabriel dictated the Qur'an to Muhammad
만일 천사장 가브리엘이 모하메드에게 코란을 받아쓰게 했다는 것을 믿지 않는다면

* The angel Moroni showed Joseph Smith the golden plates **that** became the Book of Mormon.

천사 모로니가 조지프 스미스에게 그 황금 접시를 보여주었는데, 그 황금 접시는 모르몬교의 경전이 되었다.

= The angel Moroni showed Joseph Smith the golden plates, **and they(golden plates)** became the Book of Mormon

관계대명사 that = and + they(golden plates)

* **the dead** 망자

* **agreeing** with the physicist and Anglican priest John Polkinghorne:

= **and they agree** with the physicist and Anglican priest John Polkinghorne:

그런데 그들은 물리학자이면서 성공회교 신부인 존 포킹혼의 의견에 다음의 면에서 동의한다:

agreeing(분사구문) = ~~and they~~ agree

* **one in life** 생전의 사람

* **unless** it is actually true it can do neither of these things and so would **amount to no more than** an illusory exercise in comforting fantasy

= **if** it is **not** actually true, it can do ~

만일 그것(종교적인 믿음)이 실제로 사실이 아니라면 그것은 이러한 것들 중의 어느 것도 할 수 없고 그래서 종교적인 믿음은 위안을 주는 상상에서 단지 환상에 불과한 일에 지나지 않을 것이다

amount to ~ ~와 마찬가지다, ~에 이르다

no more than 단지 ~일 뿐

* rests on the methods they use to decide **what** is true, and **what** truths result
무엇이 진실이고 어떤 진실이 발생할지를 결정하기 위해 그들이 사용하는 방법에 달려있다
= rests on the methods **(which)** they use to decide what is true, and what truths result
= rests on the methods, **and** they use **them(methods)** to decide what is true, and what truths result
목적격 관계대명사 which 생략 = and + them(methods)
what = 의문대명사(무엇)
what = 의문형용사(어떤)

* in other words, through faith, **defined** in Hebrews 11 as "the substance of things **hoped for**, the evidence of things not **seen**"
다시 말해, 믿음을 통해, 그런데 그 믿음은 히브리 성서 11장에 "기대되어지는 사물의 본질, 보여 지지 않는 사물의 증거"로 정의된다
= in other words, through faith, **and it(faith) is defined** in Hebrews 11 as "the substance of things **(which is) hoped** for, the evidence of things **(which is)** not seen"
과거분사(defined, hoped) 앞에서 관계대명사의 주격(which)과 be동사 생략

* Thomas, because thou hast seen me, thou hast believed: blessed are they that have not seen, and yet have believed.
토마스, 그대는 나를 보았기 때문에 그대는 믿었다: 보지 못하였으나 믿었던 그대들은 복이 있도다.

* **And yet** 그럼에도 불구하고

* when some believers reject **what** others see as true
몇몇 신자들이 다른 신자들이 사실로 보는 것을 거부할 때
= when some believers reject **the thing which** others see as true
= when some believers reject the thing, **and** others see **it(the thing)** as true
what은 선행사를 포함하는 관계대명사

* **success after success** 연이은 성공

* **the faithful** 신자
  the + 형용사

* for how can you reject the divine in your laboratory but accept that the wine you sip on Sunday is the blood of Jesus?
  그렇지 않다면 어떻게 실험실에서 신을 거부하지만 일요일에 당신이 마시는 와인이 예수의 피라는 것을 받아들일 수 있겠는가?
  = for how **(else)** can you reject the divine in your laboratory but accept that the wine **(which)** you sip on Sunday is the blood of Jesus?
  = for how **(else)** can you reject the divine in your laboratory but accept that the wine, **and** you sip **it(the wine)** on Sunday is the blood of Jesus?
  목적격 관계대명사 which 생략 = and + it(the wine)

* Certainly evolutionary biology, my own field, has been held back strongly by creationism, **which** arises solely from religion.
  확실히 나의 분야인 진화생물학은 천지창조설 때문에 심하게 방해를 받아왔는데, 천지창조설은 오로지 종교로부터 생겨난다.
  = Certainly evolutionary biology, my own field, has been held back strongly by creationism, **and it(creationism)** arises solely from religion.
  which = and + it(creationism)

* 64 percent of our elite scientists are atheists or agnostics, **compare**d to only 6 percent of the general population - more than a tenfold difference.
  엘리트 과학자들 중의 64%가 무신론자이거나 불가지론자인데, 그 비율은 일반대중의 6% 밖에 안 되는 것과 비교된다 - 즉 그것은 열배 이상의 차이다.
  = 64 percent of our elite scientists are atheists or agnostics, **and it is compared** to only 6 percent of the general population - more than a tenfold difference.
  = 64 percent of our elite scientists are atheists or agnostics, **~~and it is~~(being) compare**d to only 6 percent of the general population - more than a tenfold difference.
  compared(분사구문) = and it is compared = ~~and it is~~(being) compared

* subjects **that** the factual domain of science might illuminate, but can never resolve
과학의 사실에 기반을 둔 영역이 밝힐지도 모르나 결코 해결할 수 없는 주제들
= **(and they(purposes, meanings and values) are)** subjects, **and** the factual domain of science might illuminate **them(subjects)**, but can never resolve
= and they(purposes, meanings and values) are
목적격 관계대명사 that = and + them(subjects)

* **on both ends** 두 방면에서

* **Many of whom** reject the idea **that** Abrahamic religions are "empty of any claims to historical or scientific facts.
그들(신자와 신학자) 중의 많은 사람들은 아브라함 종교는 역사적 혹은 과학적 사실들에 대한 어떠한 주장도 없다는 생각을 거부한다.
= **And** many of **them(believers and theologians)** reject the idea **that** Abrahamic religions are "empty of any claims to historical or scientific facts.
whom = and + them(believers and theologians)
the idea와 that은 동격절

* Nor is religion the sole bailiwick of "purposes, meanings and values," **which** of course differ among faiths.
또한 종교는 '목적, 의미, 가치'의 유일한 전문분야가 아닌데, 물론 그것들은 종교들 사이에서도 다르다.
= Religion is not the sole bailiwick of "purposes, meanings and values," **and they(purposes, meanings and values)** differ among faiths.
which = and + they(purposes, meanings and values)

* **that** relies on reason rather than faith as a fount of morality
그런데 그 역사는 도덕성의 원천으로 신앙보다는 이성에 의존한다
= **and it(history of philosophy and ethics)** relies on reason rather than faith as a fount of morality
that은 주격 관계대명사 = and + it(history of philosophy and ethics)

* **In the end** 결국

* **It**'s irrational **to decide what**'s true in your daily life using empirical evidence, but then **rely on** wishful-thinking and ancient superstitions **to judge** the "truths" undergirding your faith.
경험적인 증거를 사용해서 여러분의 일상생활에서 무엇이 사실인지 결정을 내리지만 그 후에 여러분의 신앙을 뒷받침하고 있는 '진리'를 판단하기 위해 희망사항과 고대의 미신에 의지하는 것은 이성적이지 않다.
가주어 It, 진주어 to decide 이하
what은 decide의 목적절을 이끄는 의문대명사(무엇)
to judge는 목적을 나타내는 부사구(판단하기 위하여)

* **at war with** 전쟁 중의

* **producing** the cognitive dissonance **that** prompts accommodationism
그것은 인지적인 충돌을 야기하는데 그 인지적인 충돌은 수용론을 결정내리도록 한다
= **and it produces** the cognitive dissonance, **and it(cognitive dissonance)** prompts accommodationism
producing(분사구문) = ~~and it~~ produces
주격 관계대명사 that = and + it(cognitive dissonance)

* People should **see faith for what it is**: not a virtue but a defect.
사람들은 신앙의 본색, 즉 미덕이 아니라 결함을 알아야 한다.
see something for what it is ~이 무엇인지를 알아보다, ~의 본색을 알아보다.

Unit 3

Justice and Fairness[1)]

WARMING UP

- Justice means giving each person **what** he or she deserves
- When people differ over **what (they believe)** should be given
- There would be **no point of talking** about justice or fairness
- **unless** they differ in ways **that** are relevant to the situation **in which** they are involved
- when a person is punished for something **over which** he or she had no control
- when the government gives benefits to the needy **that** it does not provide to more affluent citizens
- Justice is an acknowledgement **that** if we are to live together in an interdependent community we must treat each other as equals

1) This article was written by Manuel Velasquez, Claire Andre, Thomas Shanks, S.J., and Michael J. Meyer, and appeared originally in Issues in Ethics V3 N2 (Spring 1990). It was updated in August 2018. The source is https://www.scu.edu/ethics/ethics-resources/ethical-decision-making/justice-and-fairness/

Many *public policy[1] arguments focus on *fairness[2]. Is *affirmative action[3] fair? Are *congressional districts[4] drawn to be fair? Is our *tax policy[5] fair? Is our method for funding schools fair?

Arguments about justice or fairness have a long tradition in Western civilization. In fact, no idea in Western civilization has been more *consistently[6] linked to ethics and morality than the idea of justice. From the Republic, written by the ancient Greek philosopher Plato, to A Theory of Justice, written by the *late[7] Harvard philosopher *John Rawls[2)], every major work on ethics has *held[8] that justice is part of the central core of morality.

*Justice means giving each person what he or she *deserves[9] or, in more traditional terms, giving each person his or her *due[10]. *Justice and fairness are closely related terms that are often today used *interchangeably[11]. There have, however, also been more *distinct[12] understandings of the two terms. While justice usually has been used *with reference to a standard of *rightness[13], fairness often has been used *with regard to an ability to judge *without reference to one's feelings or interests; fairness has also been used to *refer to[14] the ability to make judgments that are not *overly[15] general but that are concrete and specific to a particular case. In any case, a notion of being treated as one deserves is *crucial[16] to both justice and fairness.

*When people differ over what they believe should be given, or when decisions have to be made about how benefits and burdens

1. public policy
공공정책
2. fairness
공정성
3. affirmative action
차별철폐조처
(소수 민족과 여성의 교육 기회와 고용에 있어서)
4. congressional district
(미)하원 의원 선거구
5. tax policy
조세정책
6. consistently
일관되게
7. late
고인이 된
8. hold
간주(생각)하다
9. deserve
~을 받을만하다
10. due
~에게 마땅히 주어져야 하는 것
11. interchangeably
교체해서, 구별 없이
12. distinct
뚜렷이 다른 (구별되는)
13. rightness
올바름
14. refer to
언급하다, 나타내다
15. overly
너무, 몹시
16. crucial
중대한

2) John Rawls 미국의 철학자(1921~2002).

17. distribute
나누어주다, 배분하다

18. inevitably
불가피하게,
필연적으로

19. ethicist
윤리학자

20. hold
(신념, 의견)가지다

21. goods
상품

22. scarce
부족한

23. fundamental
근본적인

24. equal
동등한 사람(것)

25. contemporary
동시대의, 현대의

should be *distributed[17] among a group of people, questions of justice or fairness *inevitably[18] arise. In fact, most *ethicists[19] today *hold[20] *the view that there would be no point of talking about justice or fairness if it were not for the conflicts of interest that are created when *goods[21] and services are *scarce[22] and people differ over who should get what. When such conflicts arise in our society, *we need principles of justice that we can all accept as reasonable and fair standards for determining what people deserve.

But saying that justice is giving each person what he or she deserves does not *take us very far. How do we determine what people deserve? What criteria and what principles should we use to determine what is due to this or that person?

Principles of Justice

The most *fundamental[23] principle of justice - one that has been widely accepted since it was first defined by Aristotle more than two thousand years ago - is the principle that "*equals[24] should be treated equally and unequals unequally." In its *contemporary[25] form, this principle is sometimes expressed as follows: "Individuals should be treated the same, *unless they differ in ways that are relevant to the situation in which they are involved." For example, if Jack and Jill both do the same work, and there are no relevant differences between them or *the work they are doing, then *in justice they should be paid the same wages. And if Jack is paid more than Jill simply because he is a man, or because he is white, then we have an injustice - a form of *discrimination[26] - because race and sex are not relevant to normal work situations.

*There are, however, many differences that we deem as *justifiable[27] criteria for treating people differently. For example, we think it is fair and just when a parent gives his own children more attention and care in his private affairs than he gives the children of others; *we think it is fair when the person who is first in a line at a theater is given first choice of theater tickets; we think it is just *when the government gives benefits to *the needy that it does not provide to more *affluent[28] citizens; we think it is just *when some who have done wrong are given punishments that are not meted out to others who have done nothing wrong; and we think it is fair when those who *exert[29] more efforts or who make a greater contribution to a project receive more benefits from the project than others. *These criteria - need, *desert[30], *contribution[31], and effort - we *acknowledge[32] as justifying *differential[33] treatment, then, are numerous.

*On the other hand, there are also criteria that we believe are not justifiable grounds for giving people different treatment. In the world of work, for example, we generally *hold[34] that it is unjust to give individuals special treatment on the basis of age, sex, race, or their religious *preferences[35]. If the judge's nephew receives a *suspended sentence[36] for armed robbery *when another *offender[37] unrelated to the judge goes to jail for the same crime, or the brother of the *Director of Public Works[38] gets the million dollar contract to install

26. discrimination 차별
27. ustifiable 정당한
28. affluent 부유한
29. exert 있는 힘껏 노력하다
30. desert 상[벌]을 받을 만한 가치
31. contribution 기여
32. acknowledge 인정하다
33. differential 차별을 하는
34. hold (무엇이 사실이라고) 간주[생각]하다
35. preference 선호(도)
36. suspended sentence 집행유예
37. offender 범죄자
38. Director of Public Works 공공사업 관리이사

sprinklers on the *municipal[39] golf course despite lower *bids[40] from other *contractors[41], we say that it's unfair. We also believe it isn't fair *when a person is punished for something over which he or she had no control, *or isn't compensated for a harm he or she suffered.

Different Kinds of Justice

There are different kinds of justice. *Distributive justice[42] refers to the extent to which *society's institutions[43] ensure that benefits and burdens are distributed among society's members in ways that are fair and just. When the institutions of a society distribute benefits or burdens in unjust ways, *there is a strong *presumption[44] that those institutions should be changed. For example, the American institution of slavery in the *pre-civil war[3] South was *condemned[45] as unjust because it was a *glaring[46] case of treating people differently on the basis of *race[47].

A second important kind of justice is *retributive[48] or *corrective[49] justice. *Retributive justice refers to the extent to which punishments are fair and just. In general, *punishments are held to be just to the extent that they *take into account relevant criteria such as the *seriousness[50] of the crime and the *intent[51] of the criminal, and *discount[52] irrelevant criteria such as race. It would be *barbarously[53] unjust, for example, to *chop off[54] a person's hand for stealing a *dime[55], or to impose the *death penalty[56] on a person who *by accident and without *negligence[57] injured *another party[58]. Studies

39. municipal 시의
40. bid 입찰가, 호가
41. contractor 계약자, 도급업자
42. distributive justice 분배의 공정
43. society's institution 사회제도
44. presumption 추정
45. condemn 비난하다
46. glaring 확연한, 두드러진
47. race 인종
48. retributive 인과응보의
49. corrective (이전의 잘못된 것을) 바로잡는
50. seriousness 심각함
51. intent 의도, 목적
52. discount 무시하다
53. barbarously 야만적으로
54. chop off ~을 잘라내다
55. dime 미국·캐나다의 10센트짜리 동전
56. death penalty 사형
57. negligence 부주의, 과실
58. another party 다른 사람

3) pre-civil war 미국 남북 전쟁(1861~1865년) 이전.

have frequently shown that when blacks murder whites, they are much more likely to receive death sentences than when whites murder whites or blacks murder blacks. These studies suggest that injustice still exists in the *criminal justice system[59] in the United States.

Yet a third important kind of justice is *compensatory[60] justice. Compensatory justice refers to the extent to which people are fairly compensated for their injuries by those who have injured them; *just compensation is *proportional[61] to the loss *inflicted[62] on a person. This is precisely the kind of justice that *is at stake in debates over damage to workers' health in *coal mines[63]. *Some argue that mine owners should compensate the workers whose health has been ruined. Others argue that workers *voluntarily[64] *took on this risk when they chose employment in the mines.

The foundations of justice can be traced to the notions of social *stability[65], *interdependence[66], and equal *dignity[67]. As the ethicist John Rawls has pointed out, the stability of a society - or any group, for that matter - depends upon the extent to which the members of that society feel that they are being treated justly. When some of society's members come to feel that they *are subject to unequal treatment, the foundations have been laid for social *unrest[68], *disturbances[69], and *strife[70]. The members of a community, Rawls holds, depend on each other, and they will retain their social unity only to the extent that their institutions are just. Moreover, as the philosopher Immanuel Kant and others have pointed out, human

59. criminal justice system
형법제도

60. compensatory
보상의

61. proportional
비례하는

62. inflict
가하다

63. coal mine
탄광

64. voluntarily
자발적으로, 자진해서

65. stability
안정성

66. interdependence
상호의존

67. dignity
존엄성

68. unrest
불안정

69. disturbance
소란

70. strife
갈등

71. arbitrary
임의적인

72. due
마땅한, 당연한

73. override
무시하다

74. mutual
상호간의, 서로의

75. acknowledgement
인정

beings are all equal in this respect: they all have the same dignity, and *in virtue of this dignity they deserve to be treated as equals. *Whenever individuals are treated unequally on the basis of characteristics that are *arbitrary[71] and irrelevant, their fundamental human dignity is violated.

Justice, then, is a central part of ethics and should be given *due[72] consideration in our moral lives. In evaluating any moral decision, we must ask whether our actions treat all persons equally. *If not, we must determine whether the difference in treatment is justified: *are the criteria we are using relevant to the situation at hand? But justice is not the only principle to consider in making ethical decisions. Sometimes principles of justice may need to be *overridden[73] *in favor of other kinds of moral claims such as rights or society's welfare. Nevertheless, justice is an expression of our *mutual[74] recognition of each other's basic dignity, and *an *acknowledgement[75] that if we are to live together in an interdependent community we must treat each other as equals.

GRAMMAR

관계대명사(Relative Pronoun)

1. 관계대명사란?

앞서는 명사(선행사)를 대신하면서 동시에 그 이후의 절을 선행사에 연결하는 역할을 하는 대명사를 말한다. 즉 **접속사와 대명사의 두 역할**을 한다.
다음 두 문장을 관계대명사를 사용해서 하나의 문장으로 만들어 보자.

> The boy is my brother. He is standing in the corner.

여기서 He는 The boy를 받는 대명사이기 때문에 없앨 수 있고, 그 대명사가 그 문장의 주어로 사용되고 있기 때문에 주격이 주어진다. 따라서 선행사가 사람이고, 주격인 관계대명사 who를 사용해서 다음과 같이 하나의 문장을 만들 수 있다.

> The boy who is standing in the corner is my brother.
> (모퉁이에 서 있는 그 소년은 나의 동생이다)

이때 관계대명사 who가 이끄는 절(who is standing)은 앞의 명사(선행사)를 꾸미는 형용사절이 된다.

관계대명사는 선행사가 무엇인지와, 원래의 대명사가 했던 역할(격)에 따라 여러 가지 형태로 나타난다.

2. 종류와 격변화

선행사 \ 격	주격	소유격	목적격
사람	who	whose	whom
사람	which	of which, whose	which
사람, 사물	that	×	that
선행사 포함	what	×	what

3. 관계대명사의 용법

1) 관계대명사는 **제한적(한정적) 용법과 비제한적(서술적 혹은 계속적) 용법**이 있다. 관계대명사가 앞의 선행사를 한정할 때는 제한적 용법이고, 선행사를 서술할 때는 비제한적 용법이다.

The boy who is standing in the corner is my brother.

이 문장에서 who가 이끄는 절은 앞의 선행사 the boy를 한정해 주고 있기 때문에 제한적 용법으로 사용된 것이다. 즉 많은 소년 중에서 모퉁이에 서있는 바로 그 소년을 나타낸다. 그러나 다음과 같은 문장에서는 '그 소년이 모퉁이에 서 있는데, 그는 나의 동생이다'를 의미하는 것으로 그 소년에 대해 서술해 주고 있는 비제한적 용법이다.

The boy, who is standing in the corner, is my brother.

2) who와 which, whose는 제한적 용법과 비제한적 용법으로 사용되지만 that은 비제한적 용법으로 사용될 수 없다.

This is the song which / that I like best.(제한적)

This is the song, which / *that I like best.(비제한적)

3) 관계대명사의 목적격은 생략될 수 있다.

The woman (whom/that) I wanted to see was away.

4. 관계대명사 what

what은 **선행사를 포함하는 관계대명사**로 that which(혹은 the thing which, all that)의 뜻을 갖는다. 이러한 관계대명사가 이끄는 절은 명사절이 된다.

I gave him just the money. He needed it(the money).

이 두 문장을 하나의 문장으로 연결하면

I gave him just the money that he needed.

이것을 다시 what으로 바꾸면 다음과 같이 된다.

I gave him what he needed.

5. 복합관계대명사

who, which, what이 -ever와 결합해서 복합관계대명사를 만드는데 whoever는 anyone who, whichever는 anything which, whatever는 anything that을 나타낸다. 이러한 복합관계대명사는 **선행사를 포함하는 명사절**이다.

Whoever(= Anybody who) comes will be welcome.
(오는 사람은 누구든지 환대 받을 것이다)
I will give it to whomever(= anyone whom) I meet first on the way.
(나는 길에서 처음 만난 누구에게든 그것을 줄 것이다)

6. 관계부사

선행사가 시간, 장소, 이유, 방법 등을 나타내는 경우에는 다음과 같은 과정에 의해 두 문장이 하나의 문장으로 되는데 이 때 사용되는 것이 관계부사이다.

> This is the place.
> He was born in the place(there).
>
> This is the place in which he was born. 혹은
> This is the place that he was born in.

여기서 in which와(that -in)을 한 단어로 바꾸면
This is the place where he was born이 된다.

PHRASES and STRUCTURES

* Justice means **giving** each person **what** he or she deserves.
정의는 모든 사람 각자에게 그 혹은 그녀가 마땅히 받을만한 것을 주는 것을 의미한다.
= Justice means giving each person **the thing which** he or she deserves.
= Justice means giving each person the thing, **and** he or she deserves **it(the thing)**.
what(관계대명사) = the thing which
give + 간접목적어 + 직접목적어 ~에게 ~을 주다
giving은 동명사로 mean의 목적어 역할을 함

* Justice and fairness are closely related terms **that** are often today used interchangeably.
정의와 공정함은 밀접하게 관련이 있는 용어들인데 그 용어들은 오늘날 종종 구별 없이 사용된다.
= Justice and fairness are closely related terms, **and they(terms)** are often today used interchangeably.
that은 주격 관계대명사 = and + they(terms)

* **with reference to** ~ ~와 관련하여

* **with regard to** ~ ~과 관련하여

* **without reference to** ~ ~와 상관없이

* When people differ over **what** (they believe) should be given
사람들이 그들이 믿기로 무엇이 주어져야하는지에 대해 서로 다를 때
they believe는 삽입절
what은 의문대명사(무엇)로 사용됨

* the view **that** there would be **no point of talking** about justice or fairness **if it were not for** the conflicts of interest **that** are created
만일 만들어지는 이익의 충돌이 없다면 정의나 공정성에 대해 말할 필요가 없을 것이라는 견해
= the view **that** there would be **no point of talking** about justice or fairness **if it**

were not for the conflicts of interest, **and they(conflicts of interest)** are created
the view와 that절은 동격
no point of ~ing ~할 필요가 없다
if it were not for ~ = but for ~ ~이 없다면
that은 주격 관계대명사 = and + they(conflicts of interest)

* We need principles of justice **that** we can all accept as reasonable and fair standards for determining what people deserve.
우리는 정의의 원칙들이 필요한데 우리 모두는 그 원칙들을 사람들이 마땅히 받을만한 것을 결정하기 위한 합리적이고 공정한 기준으로 받아들일 수 있다.
= we need principles of justice, **and** we can all **accept them(principles) as** reasonable and fair standards for determining **what** people deserve.
that은 목적격 관계대명사 = and them(principles)
accept A as B A를 B로 받아들이다
what은 선행사를 포함하는 관계대명사

* **take us very far** 우리를 매우 멀리 데려가다

* **unless** they differ in ways **that** are relevant to the situation **in which** they are involved
만일 그들(개인들)이 방식들에서 다르지 않다면, 그런데 그 방식들은 그들(개인들)이 관계되는 상황과 관련이 있다
= **if** they **do not** differ in ways, **and they(ways)** are relevant to the situation, **and** they are involved **in it(the situation)**
unless = if ~ not
주격 관계대명사 that = and + they(ways)
in which = and + in it(the situation)
be relevant to ~ ~와 관련이 있다
be involved in ~ ~에 개입되다, 관계되다

* the work they are doing 그들이 하고 있는 일
= the work **(which)** they are doing
= the work, **and** they are doing **it(the work)**
목적격 관계대명사 which 생략 = and + it(the work)

* **in justice** 공평하게 평하면

* There are, however, many differences **that** we **deem as** justifiable criteria for treating people differently.
그러나 많은 차이들이 있는데 우리는 그 차이들을 사람들을 다르게 대우하기 위한 정당한 기준으로 간주한다.
= There are, however, many differences, **and** we **deem them(differences) as** justifiable criteria for treating people differently.
that은 목적격 관계대명사 = and + them(differences)
deem A as B A를 B로 간주하다, 여기다

* We think it is fair when the person **who** is first in a line at a theater is given first choice of theater tickets.
우리는 극장에서 줄의 처음에 있는 사람에게 극장표의 첫 선택이 주어질 때 공정하다고 생각한다.
= We think **(that)** it is fair when the person, **and he** is first in a line at a theater is given first choice of theater tickets.
접속사 that이 생략되어 있음
who = and he(the person)

* when the government **gives** benefits to the needy **that** it does not provide to more affluent citizens
정부가 어려운 사람들에게 혜택들을 줄 때, 그런데 정부는 더 부유한 사람들에게는 그 혜택들을 제공하지 않는다
= when the government **gives** the needy benefits **that** it(government) does not provide to more affluent citizens
= when the government **gives** the needy benefits, **and** it(government) does not provide **them(benefits)** to more affluent citizens
that은 목적격 관계대명사 = and + them(benefits)
the needy 어려운 사람들
the + 형용사 = 복수보통명사
give + 간접목적어 + 직접목적어
= give + 직접목적어 + to + 간접목적어

* when some who have done wrong are given punishments **that** are not meted out to others **who** have done nothing wrong
나쁜 짓을 한 몇몇 사람들에게 벌이 주어질 때, 그런데 그 벌들은 어떠한 나쁜 짓도 하지 않은 다른 사람들에게는 할당되지(주어지지) 않는다
= when some, **and they** have done wrong are given punishments, **and they(punishments)** are not meted out to others, **and they** have done nothing wrong
주격 관계대명사 that = and + they(punishments)
who = and + they
do wrong 나쁜 짓을 하다
mete out 할당(배당)하다

* **These criteria** - need, desert, contribution, and effort - we acknowledge as justifying differential treatment, then, **are** numerous.
이러한 기준들은 - 필요성, 받을만한 자격, 기여, 노력 - 그런데 우리는 그러한 기준들을 차별을 하는 대우를 정당화하기 위해 인정하는 것들인데 아주 많다.
= These criteria - need, desert, contribution, and effort – **(which)** we acknowledge as justifying differential treatment, then, are numerous.
= These criteria - need, desert, contribution, and effort - **and** we acknowledge **them(criteria)** as justifying differential treatment, then, are numerous.
주어는 These criteria, 본동사는 are
목적격 관계대명사 which 생략 = and + them(criteria)
acknowledge A as B A를 B로 인정하다

* On the other hand, there are also criteria **that** we believe are not justifiable grounds for giving people different treatment.
다른 한편으로 또한 기준들도 있는데, 그 기준들은 (우리가 믿기에) 사람들에게 다른 대우를 주기위한 정당한 근거가 되지 않는다.
= On the other hand, there are also criteria, **and they(criteria)** (we believe) are not justifiable grounds for giving people different treatment
주격 관계대명사 that = and + they(criteria)
we believe는 삽입절

* when another offender **unrelated** to the judge goes to jail for the same crime

그 판사와 관련이 없는 다른 범죄자가 같은 죄목으로 교도소로 갈 때

= when another offender **(who is) unrelated** to the judge goes to jail for the same crime

= when another offender, **and he is** unrelated to the judge goes to jail for the same crime

과거분사(unrelated) 앞에서 관계대명사의 주격(who)과 be동사 생략

* when a person is punished for something **over which** he or she had no control

그나 그녀가 어떻게 할 수가 없는 어떤 것에 대해 벌 받게 될 때

= when a person is punished for something, **and** he or she had no control **over it(something)**

over which = and + over it(something)

have no control over 어떻게 할 수가 없다

* or isn't compensated for a harm **which** he or she suffered

혹은 그나 그녀가 입은 피해에 대해 보상받지 못할 때

= or isn't compensated for a harm, **and** he or she suffered **it(a harm)**

목적격 관계대명사 which = and + it(a harm)

suffer a harm 피해를 입다

* Distributive justice refers to the extent **to which** society's institutions ensure **that** benefits and burdens are distributed among society's members in ways **that** are fair and just.

분배의 정의는 사회제도가 혜택과 부담이 공정하고 정당한 방식으로 사회 구성원들 사이에 분배된다는 것을 보장하는 정도를 가리킨다.

= Distributive justice refers to the extent, **and to it(the extent)** society's institutions ensure that benefits and burdens are distributed among society's members in ways, **and they(ways)** are fair and just.

to which = and + to it(the extent)

첫 번째 that =접속사

두 번째 that은 주격 관계대명사 = **and + they(ways)**

refer to ~ ~을 나타내다

Accessibility **refers to the extent to which** a product or service can be used by as many people as possible.

접근성이란 가능한 한 많은 사람들이 제품 또는 서비스를 사용할 수 있는 정도를 말한다.

* There is **a strong presumption that** those institutions should be changed.
그러한 제도들이 바뀌어야 한다는 강한 추정이 있다.
that = presumption과 동격

* Retributive justice **refers to** the extent **to which** punishments are fair and just.
인과응보적 정의는 벌이 공정하고 정당하다는 정도를 가리킨다.
= Retributive justice refers to the extent, **and** punishments are fair and just **to it(the extent)**.
to which = and + to it(the extent)

* punishments **are held** to be just to the extent ~
벌은 ~정도에서 공정하다고 간주**된다**
→ People **hold** punishments to be just to the extent (능동형)
사람들은 ~정도에서 벌이 공정하다고 간주**한다**

* **take into account** ~ ~을 고려하다

* **by accident** 우연히

* Just compensation is proportional to the loss **inflicted** on a person.
공정한 보상은 어떤 사람에게 가해진 손해에 비례한다.
= Just compensation is proportional to the loss **(which is) inflicted** on a person.
과거분사(inflicted) 앞에서 관계대명사의 주격(which)과 be동사 생략

* **is at stake** ~의 성패가 달려있다, 위기에 처해있다

* Some argue that mine owners should compensate the workers **whose** health has been ruined.
몇몇 사람들은 탄광 소유자들이 노동자들에게 보상해야 한다고 주장하는데 노동자들의 건강이 손상을 입었다.
= Some argue that mine owners should compensate the workers, **and their** health has been ruined.

whose = and + their
ruin somebody's health ~의 건강을 해치다

* **took on this risk** 이러한 위험을 떠맡다

* **are subject to** ~ ~를 받다

* **in virtue of** ~ ~덕분에(때문에)

* Whenever individuals are treated unequally on the basis of characteristics **that** are arbitrary and irrelevant
개인이 임의적이고 관련 없는 특성들의 토대 위에서 불평등하게 대우받을 때는 언제든지
= Whenever individuals are treated unequally on the basis of characteristics, **and they(characteristics)** are arbitrary and irrelevant
주격 관계대명사 that = and + they(characteristics)

* **If not**
= **If** we do **not** treat all persons equally

* Are the criteria we are using relevant to the situation at hand?
우리가 사용하고 있는 기준들이 가까이에 있는 상황과 관련이 있는가?
= Are the criteria **(which)** we are using relevant to the situation at hand?
= Are the criteria, **and** we are using **them(criteria)** relevant to the situation at hand?
목적격 관계대명사 which 생략 = and + them(criteria)
at hand 가까이에 있는

* **in favor of** ~ ~을 위하여, ~의 이익이 되도록

* **an acknowledgement that** if we are to live together in an interdependent community we must treat each other as equals
만일 우리가 상호의존적인 공동체에서 함께 살아가려고 한다면 우리는 서로서로를 동등한 사람으로 대우해야 한다는 인정
that 이하는 acknowledgement와 동격

Unit 4

Plato's Concept Of Justice: An Analysis[1)]

WARMING UP

- We **are to inquire** in this study the nature of justice
- **It** remains therefore **to** inquire what were the reasons for which he rejected those views
- The Government of any kind shall do **what** is good for the people **for whom** it exercises its art
- **Faced** with this situation they came to an agreement and instituted law and government through a sort of social contract and preached the philosophy of just
- Justice is **doing good** to friends and **harm** to enemies
- **It is** in this way **that** Plato condemned the position taken by Glaucon **that** justice is something **which** is external
- Justice is a 'human virtue' that **makes a man self consistent and good**
- Justice **is to** the soul **as** health **is to** the body

1) This article was written by D.R. Bhandari, and appeared in the Twentieth World Congress of Philosophy, in Boston, Massachusetts from August 10-15, 1998. The source is https://www.bu.edu/wcp/Papers/Anci/AnciBhan.htm

*Plato[2)] in his philosophy gives very important place to the idea of justice. *He used the Greek word "Dikaisyne" for justice which comes very near to the word 'morality' or '*righteousness[1]', it properly includes within it the whole duty of man. It also covers the whole field of the individual's conduct *in so far as it affects others. Plato contended that justice is the quality of soul, *in virtue of which men *set aside[2] the *irrational[3] desire to taste every pleasure and to get a selfish satisfaction out of every object and *accommodated themselves to the *discharge[4] of a single function for the general benefit.

Plato was highly dissatisfied with the discharge *degenerating[5] conditions in Athens. The Athenian democracy was *on the verge of *ruin[6] and was ultimately responsible for *Socrates'[3)] death. Plato saw in justice the only remedy of saving Athens from decay and ruin, for nothing *agitated[7] him in *contemporary[8] affairs more than *amateurishness[9], *needlesomeness[10] and political selfishness which was *rampant[11] in Athens of his day in particular and in the entire Greek world in general. In addition, **Sophistic teaching[12] of the ethics of self-satisfaction resulted in the excessive individualism also *induced[13] the citizens to capture the office of the State for their own selfish purpose and eventually divided "Athens in to two *hostile[14] camps of rich and poor, *oppressor[15] and oppressed. "Evidently, these two factors *amateur[16] needlesomeness and excessive individualism

1. righteousness 올바름
2. set aside ~을 고려하지 않다(무시하다)
3. irrational 비이성적인
4. discharge 이행
5. degenerate (도덕적, 육체적, 정신적으로) 악화되다
6. ruin 붕괴, 몰락
7. agitate 뒤흔들다, 선동하다
8. contemporary 당대의
9. amateurishness 미숙함
10. needlesomeness 바늘같음, 미미함
11. rampant 만연하는
12. Sophistic teaching 궤변적인 교리
13. induce 유도하다
14. hostile 적대적인
15. oppressor 억압하는 사람
16. amateur 아마추어의(미숙한)

2) Plato 플라톤(B.C. 427~B.C. 347) (그리스의 철학자).

3) Socrates 소크라테스(B.C. 470~B.C. 399) 고대 아테네의 철학자.

became main targets of Plato's attack. *The attack came in the form of the construction of an ideal society in which "Justice" *reigned supreme[17], since Plato found in justice the remedy for curing these evils. Thus, *we are to inquire in this study the nature of justice as *propounded[18] by Plato as a fundamental principle of *well-ordered[19] society.

It is to be noted that before Plato many theories of justice were *prevalent[20]. The *inquiry[21] about justice goes from the *crudest[22] to the most *refined[23] interpretation of it. *It remains therefore to inquire what were the reasons for which he rejected those views. Thus before discussing Plato's own concept of justice, it is necessary to analyze those traditional theories of justice rejected by him.

**Cephalus[4] who was a representative of traditional morality of the ancient *trading class[24] established the traditional theory of justice. According to him justice *consists in speaking the truth and paying one's debt. Thus Cephalus *identifies justice with right conduct. *Polemarchus[5] also holds the same view of justice but *with a little alteration. According to him "justice seems to consist in giving what is *proper[25] to him". The simple *implication[26] of this conception of justice may be that "*justice is doing good to friends and harm to enemies." This is also a traditional *maxim[27] of Greek morality.

*The views *propounded[28] by Cephalus and Polemarchus were

17. reign supreme
최고를 차지하다
18. propound
(사상·설명 등을 사람들이 고려해 보도록) 제기하다
19. well-ordered
질서가 잡힌
20. prevalent
널리 퍼져있는
21. inquiry
연구, 조사
22. crude
대충의, 조잡한
23. refined
정제된, 세련된
24. trading class
무역계급
25. proper
(사회적, 도덕적으로) 올바른
26. implication
함축, 암시
27. maxim
격언
28. propound
제기하다, 제안하다

4) Cephalus 케파루스 플라톤의 『국가』에 등장하는 인물로 방패공장을 운영. 폴레마르쿠스이 아버지.
5) Polemarchus 폴레마르쿠스(5세기 ~ B.C 404) 고대 아테네 철학자.

criticized by Plato. The *view point[29] of Cephalus was criticized *on the ground that there may be cases in which this formula may involve the violation of the spirit of right and his formula does not admit of being taken as a sound universal principle of life. It is not right to *restore[30] *deadly[31] weapons to a man after he has gone mad. And the *contention[32] of Polemarchus was condemned by Plato on the ground that it was only easy to speak of giving good to friend and evil to enemies. But if the friends are only a friend *in seeming, and an enemy in reality, then what will happen? Then under such circumstances whether we should *rigidly[33] follow the definition and do him good or we may use *discretion[34] and do him evil? But to do evil to anybody, including one's enemy was *inconsistent[35] with the most elementary conception of morality. Thus, this conception of justice *regulated[36] the relations between individuals on *individualistic[37] principles and ignores the society as a whole.

*Thrasymachus[6)] who represented the new and critical view, propounded the *radical[38] theory of justice. He defines justice as "the interest of the stronger". In other words, *might[39] is right. For while every man acts for himself and tries to get what he can, the strongest *is sure to get what he wants and as in a state the Government is the strongest, it will try to get and it will get, whatever it wants for itself.

29. view point
관점

30. restore
돌려주다

31. deadly
치명적인

32. contention
주장, 견해

33. rigidly
엄격하게

34. discretion
재량(권)

35. inconsistent
부합하지 않는

36. regulate
규제하다, 통제하다

37. individualistic
개인주의적인

38. radical
급진적인

39. might
힘, 권력

6) Thrasymachus 트라시마쿠스(B.C. 459 ~ B.C. 400) 그리스의 소피스트로, 플라톤의 《국가》에 등장하는 인물. 플라톤은 《국가》 1권에서 '정의란 무엇인가?'라는 물음을 제기하였는데 1권에 등장하는 케팔루스, 폴레마르쿠스, 그리고 트라시마쿠스가 각각 이 질문에 대하여 대답하고 있음. 트라시마쿠스는 '정의'를 '더 강한 자의 이득', '통치자들에게 복종하는 것', 그리고 '남에게 좋은 것'이라는 세 가지 규정을 제시하였음. 소크라테스는 트라시마쿠스의 주장과는 반대로, '정의'란 궁극적으로 인간적 훌륭함이기 때문에 1차적으로 피통치자나 더 약한 자에게 이득이 되는 것이라는 입장을 택하여, 국가 1권 후반부에서부터 10권까지 트라시마쿠스의 주장이 잘못되었다는 논의를 전개하였음.

Thus, for Thrasymachus justice means personal interest of the *ruling group[40] in any state or we can further define it as "another's good". Laws are made by the *ruling party[41] *in its own interest. Those who violate such laws are punished because violation of such laws is treated as violation of justice. Socrates criticizes the definition of justice given by Thrasymachus and he says just as a *physician[42] studies and *exercises[43] his power not in his interest but in the interest of a patient, *the Government of any kind shall do what is good for the people for whom it exercises its art. But Thrasymachus advances some more arguments in support of his concept of justice and injustice.

An unjust *is superior to a just in character and intelligence.

Injustice is a source of strength.

Injustice brings happiness.

Socrates attacks these points of Thrasymachus and *throws light on the nature of justice.

Justice implies *superior[44] character and intelligence while injustice means *deficiency[45] in both respects. Therefore, just men are superior in character and intelligence and are more effective in action. As injustice implies *ignorance[46], *stupidity[47] and badness, it cannot be superior in character and intelligence. A just man is wiser because he acknowledges the principle of limit.

Unlimited *self-assertion[48] is not a source of strength for any group organized for common purpose. Unlimited desire and claims lead to

40. ruling group
통치 집단

41. ruling party
제 1당, 여당

42. physician
의사

43. exercises
(권력, 권리)
행사하다

44. superior
우수한, 우월한

45. deficiency
결점, 결함

46. ignorance
무지

47. stupidity
어리석음

48. self-assertion
자기권리 주장

*conflicts[49].

Life of just man is better and happier. *There is always some specific *virtue[50] in everything, which enables it to work well. If it *is deprived of that virtue, it works badly. The soul has specific functions to perform. When it performs its specific functions, it has specific excellence or virtue. If it is deprived of its peculiar virtue, it cannot possibly do its work well. It is agreed that the virtue of the soul is justice. The soul which is more virtuous or in other words more just is also the happier soul. Therefore, a just man lives happy. A just soul, in other words a just man, lives well; an unjust cannot.

*At this juncture the new point of view is stated by *Glaucon[7)] and he *put forward a form of what was later to be known as a *social contract theory[8)], *arguing we are only moral because, it pays us or we have to be. Glaucon describes the historical evolution of the society where justice as a *necessity[51] had become the *shield[52] of the weaker. In the *primitive[53] stage of society without law and government, man was free to do whatever he likes. So *the stronger few enjoyed the life *at the sufferance of *the weaker many. The weaker, however, realized that they suffered more injustice. *Faced with this situation they came to an agreement and *instituted[54] law and government through a sort of social contract and *preached[55] the philosophy of just. Therefore, justice is in this way something artificial and unnatural. It is the "product of *convention[56]". *It is

49. conflict 갈등, 충돌
50. virtue 미덕
51. necessity 불가피한 것
52. shield 방패
53. primitive 초기의, 원시적인
54. institute (제도정책 등을) 도입하다
55. preach (특정 종교·생활 방식·체제 등을 남이 받아들이도록) 전하다
56. convention 관습

7) Glaucon(B.C. 445 ~ B.C. 4세기)(글라우콘) 고대 아테네 철학자로 플라톤의 형님.

8) social contract theory(사회계약설) 국가 혹은 정치적 단위사회의 기원(起源)을 구성원들의 계약에 두는 학설로 성원들의 합의에 의해 정치사회가 구성되는 것으로 보고 성원들의 자발성이 합의의 기초가 된다고 하였음.

57. selfishness
이기적임

58. dictate
(따라야 하는) 명령(요구)

59. habitation
거주지

60. condition
상태

61. inward
안쪽으로 향한

62. grace
품위

63. analogy
비유

through this artificial rule of justice and law that the natural *selfishness[57] of man is chained. A *dictate[58] of the weaker many, for the interest of the weaker many, *as against the natural and superior power of the stronger few.

Plato realizes that all theories propounded by Cephalus, Thrasymachus and Glaucon, contained one common element. That one common element was that all of them treated justice as something external "an accomplishment, an importation, or a convention, while none of them carried it into the soul or considered it in the place of its *habitation[59]." Plato proves that justice does not depend upon a chance, convention or upon external force. It is the right *condition[60] of the human soul by the very nature of man when seen in the fullness of his environment. *It is in this way that Plato condemned the position taken by Glaucon that justice is something which is external. According to Plato, it is internal as it resides in the human soul. "It is now regarded as an *inward[61] *grace[62] and its understanding is shown to involve a study of the inner man." It is, therefore, natural and no artificial. It *is therefore, not born of fear of the weak but of the longing of the human soul to do a duty according to its nature.

Thus, *after criticizing the conventional ideas of justice presented differently by Cephalus, Polymarchus, Thrasymachus and Glaucon, Plato now gives us his own theory of justice. Plato strikes an *analogy[63] between the human organism on the one hand and social organism on the other. Human organism according to Plato contains three elements - Reason, Spirit and *Appetite[64]. An individual is just when each part of his or her soul performs its functions without interfering with those of other elements. For example, the reason should rule *on behalf of the entire soul with wisdom and *forethought[65]. The element of spirit will *subordinate[66] itself to the rule of reason. Those two elements are *brought into harmony by combination of mental and bodily training. *They are set in command over the appetites which form the greater part of man's soul. Therefore, *the reason and spirit have to control these appetites which are likely to grow on the bodily pleasures. These appetites should not be allowed, to *enslave[67] the other elements and **usurp[68] the *dominion[69] to which they have no right. When all the three agree that among them the reason alone should rule, there is justice within the individual.

*Corresponding to these three elements in human nature there are three classes in the social organism - Philosopher class or the ruling class which is the representative of reason; *auxiliaries[70], a class of warriors and *defenders[71] of the country is the representative of spirit; and the appetite instinct of the community which consists of farmers, *artisans[72] and are the lowest *rung[73] of the ladder. Thus, *weaving[74] a web between the human organism and the social organism, Plato asserts that functional *specialization[75] demands from every social class to specialize itself in the station of life allotted to it. *Justice, therefore to Plato is like a manuscript which exists in two copies, and one of these is larger than the other. It exists

64. appetite
욕구

65. forethought
사전숙고

66. subordinate
종속시키다

67. enslave
노예가 되게 하다

68. usurp
빼앗다

69. dominion
지배, 영토

70. auxiliary
보조원

71. defender
수비수, 옹호자

72. artisan
장인

73. rung
(사회, 조직 내 서열 상의)단계

74. weave
짜다

75. specialization
특수화

76. consistent
일관된, 변함없는

77. non-interference
불간섭

78. fulfill
이행하다

79. platonic
이상적인

80. co-ordination
조화

81. disintegrate
해체되다, 붕괴되다

82. dissolve
분해되다, 사라지다

both in the individual and the society. But it exists on a larger scale and in more visible form in the society. Individually "*justice is a 'human virtue' that makes a man self *consistent[76] and good: Socially, justice is a social consciousness that makes a society internally harmonious and good."

Justice is thus a sort of specialization. It is simply the will to fulfill the duties of one's station and not to *meddle with the duties of another station, and its habitation is, therefore, in the mind of every citizen who does his duties in his appointed place. *It is the original principle, laid down at the foundation of the State, "that one man should practice one thing only and the thing to which his nature was best adopted". True justice to Plato, therefore, consists in the principle of *non-interference[77]. *The State has been considered by Plato as a perfect whole in which each individual which is its element, functions not for itself but for the health of the whole. Every element *fulfills[78] its appropriate function. *Justice in the *platonic[79] state would, therefore, be like that harmony of relationship where the Planets are held together in the orderly movement. *Plato was convinced that a society which is so organized is fit for survival. Where man are out of their natural places, there the *co-ordination[80] of parts is destroyed, the society *disintegrates[81] and *dissolves[82]. Justice, therefore, is the citizen sense of duties.

Justice is, for Plato, *at once a part of human virtue and the bond, which joins man together in society. It is the identical quality that makes good and social. Justice is an order and duty of the parts of the soul, *it is to the soul as health is to the body. Plato says that justice is not mere strength, but it is a harmonious strength. Justice is not the right of the stronger but the effective harmony of the whole. *All moral conceptions revolve about the good of the whole - individual as well as social.

동사의 유형

동사는 목적어를 취하는지의 여부에 따라 **자동사**와 **타동사**로 나눌 수 있다. 자동사는 목적어를 필요로 하지 않는 동사이고, 타동사는 목적어를 필요로 하는 동사이다. 자동사는 다시 홀로 주어를 완전하게 기술해 주는 **완전자동사**와 그렇지 못하는 **불완전자동사**로 구분된다. 타동사는 완전한 목적어를 취하는 **완전타동사**와 그렇지 못하는 **불완전타동사**, 그리고 목적어를 두 개 취하는 **수여동사**로 구분된다.

He dances well.(완전자동사)
He is a dancer.(불완전자동사)
He dances ballet.(완전타동사)
We call him a dancer.(불완전타동사)
He showed us ballet.(수여동사)
* 같은 동사가 자동사로도, 타동사로도 사용될 수 있다.

1. **완전자동사:** 목적어나 보어 없이 홀로 쓰이는 동사
What happened?(동사 단독으로 사용됨)
The sun rises in the east.(부사구가 뒤따라 올 수 있다)
Look at him.(전치사가 따라와 목적어를 취하고 있다)

2. **불완전자동사:** 주어의 상태, 특성 등을 기술하는 보어를 필요로 하는 동사
a) be 동사: He is honest.
He is a student.
b) 상태의 변화: He grew old.
c) 상태의 지속: Please stay quiet.

d) 지각: The bread tastes good.

e) 기타: He seems (to be) angry.

3. 완전타동사: 목적어를 수반하는 동사

1) 자동사/타동사에 따라 뜻이 바뀌는 경우

He left a message for you (타동사)
He left at 10. (자동사)
He smelled the rose. (타동사)

It smelled good. (자동사)
We don't sell the book. (타동사)
The book sells well. (자동사)

2) 전치사를 취하는 것처럼 보이는 타동사.

We discussed the plan.
We discussed about the plan. (비문)

He will marry Jane.
He will marry with Jane. (비문)

4. 수여동사

The girl showed me the dress.

The girl showed the dress to me.

Mom made me the cake.

Mom made the cake for me.

5. 불완전타동사: 목적어와 목적격보어를 필요로 하는 동사

They called me president

Keep the milk cold.

I found the door open.

PHRASES and STRUCTURES

* He used the Greek word "Dikaisyne" for justice **which** comes very near to the word 'morality' or 'righteousness'.
그는 정의에 대해 그리스 단어 "디카이시네"를 사용했는데 정의는 '도덕성' 혹은 '올바름'이라는 단어에 아주 가깝다.
= He used the Greek word "Dikaisyne" for justice, **and it(the Greek word "Dikaisyne")** comes very near to the word 'morality' or 'righteousness'.
which = and + it(the Greek word "Dikaisyne")

* **in so far as ~** ~하는 한에 있어서는

* in virtue of **which** men set aside the irrational desire to taste every pleasure and to get a selfish satisfaction out of every object
그것(정신의 질)의 덕분으로 인간은 모든 쾌락을 맛보고 모든 대상에서 이기적인 만족을 얻으려는 비이성적인 욕구를 무시한다
= **and** in virtue of **it(the quality of soul)**, men set aside the irrational desire to taste every pleasure and to get a selfish satisfaction out of every object
목적격 관계대명사 which = and + it(the quality of soul)
in virtue of ~ ~ 때문에, ~의 덕분에

* **accommodate themselves to ~** ~에 적응하다

* **on the verge of ~** ~의 직전에, 막 ~하려는

* **Sophistic teaching** of the ethics of self-satisfaction **resulted** in the excessive individualism also **induced** the citizens to capture the office of the State for their own selfish purpose.
과도한 개인주의를 낳게 된 자기만족 윤리라는 궤변적 교리는 또한 시민들을 그들 자신의 목적을 위해 국가의 자리를 차지하도록 유도했다.
= Sophistic teaching of the ethics of self-satisfaction **(which was)** resulted in the excessive individualism also induced the citizens to capture the office of the State

for their own selfish purpose.

과거분사(resulted) 앞에서 관계대명사의 주격(which)과 be동사 생략

주어는 Sophistic teaching, 본동사는 induce

* The attack came in the form of the construction of an ideal society **in which** "Justice" reigned supreme.

공격은 이상사회의 건설 형태로 왔는데 이상사회에서 '정의'가 최고를 차지했다.

= The attack came in the form of the construction of an ideal society, **and** "Justice" reigned supreme **in it(ideal society)**.

in which = and + in it(ideal society)

* We **are to inquire** (in this study) the nature of justice as propounded by Plato as a fundamental principle of well-ordered society.

우리는 본 연구에서 질서가 잡힌 사회의 근본 원리로 플라톤에 의해 제기된 것과 같은 정의의 본질을 알아보려고 한다.

be to + 동사원형 예정: ~할 예정이다

의무: ~하여야 한다

You **are** not **to speak** in this room. 당신은 이 방에서 이야기를 해서는 안 된다.

가능(부정문에서): ~할 수 있다

Not a soul **was to be** seen on the street. 거리에는 사람 하나 볼 수 없었다.

* It **remains** therefore to inquire **what** were the reasons **for which** he rejected those views.

따라서 그가 그러한 견해들을 거부했던 이유들이 무엇이었는지는 여전히 의문이다.

= It **remains** therefore to inquire **what** were the reasons, **and** he rejected those views **for them(the reasons)**

for which = and + for them(the reasons)

remain 여전히 ~이다

It는 to 이하를 가리킴

what은 의문대명사(무엇)

* **Cephalus** **who** was a representative of traditional morality of the ancient trading class **established** the traditional theory of justice.

케파루스, 그런데 그는 고대 무역계급의 전통적인 도덕성의 대표자였는데, 정의의 전통적인 이론을 확립했다.

= Cephalus, **and he** was a representative of traditional morality of the ancient trading class established the traditional theory of justice.

who = and + he

주어는 Cephalus, 본동사는 established

* **consists in ~** ~에 있다

* **identifies** justice **with** right conduct 정의와 올바른 행동을 동일시하다

identify A with B A와 B를 동일시하다

* **with a little alteration** 약간 변형하여

* Justice is **doing good** to friends and **harm** to enemies.

정의는 친구에게 선을 베풀고 적에게 손해를 끼친다.

do good ~에게 선의를 베풀다

do harm ~에게 손해를 끼치다

* The views **propounded** by Cephalus and Polemarchus were criticized by Plato.

케파루스와 폴레마르쿠스에 의해 제기된 견해들은 플라톤에 의해 비판받았다.

= The views **(which were)** propounded by Cephalus and Polemarchus were criticized by Plato.

= The views, **and they(views)** were propounded by Cephalus and Polemarchus were criticized by Plato.

과거분사(propounded) 앞에서 관계대명사의 주격(which)과 be동사 생략

which = and + they(view)

* **on the ground that** there may be cases **in which** this formula may involve the violation of the spirit of right and his formula does not **admit of** being taken as a sound universal principle of life

경우들이 있을지도 모른다는 이유로, 그런데 그 경우들에서 이러한 공식은 옳음이라는 정신의 위반을 포함할 수도 있고, 그의 공식은 삶의 건전한 보편적인 원칙으로 받아들여지는 것을 허용하지 않는다

= on the ground that there may be cases, **and in them(cases)** this formula may involve the violation of the spirit of right

in which = and + in them(cases)

on the ground that ~ ~의 이유로

admit of ~ ~을 허용하다

* **in seeming** 겉보기에는

* **is sure to** 반드시 ~하다, 분명이 ~일(할) 것이다

* **in its own interest** 그 자신의 이익을 위하여

* The Government of any kind shall do **what** is good for the people **for whom it** exercises **its** art.
모든 종류의 정부는 그 국민들에게 좋은 것을 행해야하는데, 그 정부는 정부의 기술을 그 국민들을 위해 행사한다.
= The Government of any kind shall do what is good for the people, and it exercises its art **for them(the people)**.
for whom = and + for them(the people)
what은 선행사를 포함하는 관계대명사
it = The Government

* **is superior to ~** ~보다 더 뛰어나다

* **throws light on ~** ~을 설명하다, (문제)해결의 실마리를 던져 주다

* There is always some specific virtue in everything, **which** enables **it** to work well.
항상 모든 것에서 어떤 특정 미덕이 있는데, 그 미덕은 공정한 사람의 삶이 잘 작동될 수 있게 한다.
= There is always some specific virtue in everything, **and it(virtue)** enables **it(life of just man)** to work well.
which = and + it(virtue)
it = life of just man

* **is deprived of ~** ~을 빼앗기다

* **At this juncture** 이 시점(단계)에서

* **put forward** 제안하다

* **arguing** we are only moral because, it pays us or we have to be
그는 다음과 같이 주장했는데, 그것(사회계약설)이 우리에게 (대가를)지불하기 때문에, 다시 말해 우리에게 지불을 해야 하기 때문에 우리는 오로지 도덕적이다
= **and he argues (that)** we are only moral because, it pays us or we have to be (paid).
arguing(분사구문) **= ~~and he~~ argues**

* **the stronger few** 더 강한 소수

* **at the sufferance of ~** ~의 묵인 하에서

* **the weaker many** 더 약한 다수

* **Faced** with this situation they came to an agreement and instituted law and government through a sort of social contract and preached the philosophy of just.
이러한 상황에 직면하게 되자 그들은 합의에 이르게 되었고 일종의 사회적 계약을 통해서 법과 정부를 도입했고 정의의 철학을 설파했다.
= (**When they are**) **faced** with this situation, they came to an agreement and instituted law and government through a sort of social contract and preached the philosophy of just.
Faced(분사구문) **= ~~When they are~~(being) faced**

* **It is** through this artificial rule of justice and law **that** the natural selfishness of man is chained.
인간의 정상적인 이기적임이 구속을 받는 것은 바로 이러한 인위적인 정의와 법의 규칙을 통해서이다.
It is ~ that 강조구문

* **as against ~** ~과 대조적으로, ~에 비해

* **It is** in this way **that** Plato condemned **the position** taken by Glaucon **that** justice is something which is external.
  바로 이런 식으로 플라톤은 글라우콘에 의해 받아들여졌던 입장을 비난했는데 그의 입장은 정의는 외적인 어떤 것이라는 것이다.
  It is ~ that 강조구문
  뒤의 that은 the position과 동격

* **is born of** ~ ~에서 태어나다
  not A but B A가 아니라 B다

* After criticizing the conventional ideas of justice **presented** differently by Cephalus, Polymarchus, Thrasymachus and Glaucon, Plato now gives us his own theory of justice.
  케파루스, 폴리마르쿠스, 트라시마쿠스와 글라우콘에 의해 제시된 정의에 대한 관습적인 생각을 비판한 후에 플라톤은 이제 우리에게 그 자신의 정의론을 제시한다.
  = After criticizing the conventional ideas of justice **(which were) presented** differently by Cephalus, Polymarchus, Thrasymachus and Glaucon, Plato now gives us his own theory of justice.
  과거분사(presented) 앞에서 관계대명사의 주격(which)과 be동사 생략

* **on behalf of** ~ ~을 대신하여, ~을 위하여

* **brought into harmony** 조화를 이루다

* They are **set in command over** the appetites **which** form the greater part of man's soul.
  그들(이성과 정신)은 인간의 정신의 가장 큰 부분을 형성하는 욕구에 지배된다.
  = They are set in command over the appetites, **and they(the appetites)** form the greater part of man's soul.
  which = and + they(the appetites)
  set in command over ~ ~을 지배한다

* The reason and spirit have to control these appetites **which** are likely to grow on

the bodily pleasures.

이성과 정신은 이러한 욕구들을 통제해야 하는데 이러한 욕구들은 신체의 쾌락위에서 자랄 것 같다.

= The reason and spirit have to control these appetites, **and they(appetites) are likely to** grow on the bodily pleasures.

which = and + they(appetites)

be likely to ~ ~일(할) 것 같다

* usurp the dominion **to which** they have no right

그들이 그 영토에 대해 어떠한 권리도 없는 그 영토를 빼앗다

= usurp the dominion, **and** they have no right to **it(the dominion)**

to which = and + it(the dominion)

* **Corresponding to ~** ~와 상응해서

* Justice, therefore to Plato is like a manuscript **which** exists in two copies.

따라서 플라톤에게 정의란 두 개의 복사본으로 존재하는 하나의 원고와 같다.

= Justice, therefore to Plato is like a manuscript, **and it(the manuscript)** exists in two copies.

which = and + it(the manuscript)

* Justice is a 'human virtue' **that** makes a man self consistent and good.

정의는 '인간의 미덕'인데 그 미덕은 인간자신이 일관되고 선하게 하는 것이다.

= Justice is a 'human virtue', **and it(human virtue)** makes a man self consistent and good.

주격 관계대명사 that = and it(human virtue)

make + 목적어 + 보어(형용사) 목적어가 ~되게 하다

* **meddle with ~** ~에 관여(간섭)하다

* It is the original principle, **laid** down at the foundation of the State, "that one man should practice one thing only and the thing **to which** his nature was best adopted".

한 사람이 단지 하나의 일, 그리고 그의 본성이 가장 잘 채택되는 일을 실행해야 한다는 것이

바로 국가의 기초에 규정되어 있는 원래 원칙이다.

It is the original principle, **(and it(the original principle) is) laid** down at the foundation of the State, "**that** one man should practice one thing only **and** the thing, and his nature was best adopted **to it(the thing)**".

It is ~ that 강조구문

laid(분사구문) = ~~and it(the original principle) is~~(being) laid

to which = and + to it(the thing)

lay down 규정하다, 단언하다

* The State has been considered by Plato as a perfect whole **in which** each individual **which** is its element, functions not for itself but for the health of the whole.

국가는 플라톤에 의해 완벽한 전체로 간주되어져 왔는데 그 전체 속에서 전체의 요소인 각각의 개인은 전체 자체를 위해서가 아니라 전체의 건강을 위해 기능 한다.

= The State has been considered by Plato as a perfect whole, **and in it(the perfect whole)** each individual, **and it(each individual)** is its element, functions not for itself but for the health of the whole.

in which = and + in it(the perfect whole)

which = and + it(each individual)

consider A as B A를 B로 간주하다

not A but B A가 아니라 B다

* Justice in the platonic state would, therefore, be like that harmony of relationship **where** the Planets are held together in the orderly movement.

이상 국가에서 정의는 따라서 관계의 그러한 조화와 같은데 관계에서 행성들은 질서있는 움직임 속에서 함께 결합된다.

= Justice in the platonic state would, therefore, be like that harmony of relationship, **and there(relationship)** the Planets are held together in the orderly movement.

where = and + there(relationship)

* Plato was convinced that a society **which** is so organized is fit for survival.

플라톤은 그렇게 조직된 사회는 생존에 적합하다고 확신했다.

= Plato was convinced that a society, **and it(the society)** is so organized is fit for survival.

which = and + it(the society)

* **at once** a part of human virtue **and** the bond
인간 미덕의 일부이기도 하고 결속이기도 하다
at once A and B A이기도 하고, B이기도 하다

* **It(justice) is to** the soul **as health is to** the body.
정의의 정신에 대한 관계는 건강의 신체에 대한 관계와 같다.
A is to B as(what) C is to D A의 B에 대한 관계는 C의 D에 대한 관계와 같다
Reading is **to the** mind **what** food **is to** the body.
독서의 정신에 대한 관계는 음식의 몸에 대한 관계와 같다.

* All moral conceptions **revolve about** the good of the whole - individual as well as social.
모든 도덕적 개념들은 사회적 뿐만 아니라 개인적인 전체의 선 주위를 돈다.
revolve about 주위를 돌다

Unit 5

Law and Morality: the eternal debate[1)]

WARMING UP

- Any woman **who** slept with a man outside marriage was to be treated as **no better than** a common prostitute
- The suppression of vice is **as much** the law's business **as** the suppression of subversive activities
- The fundamental link between sex and procreation had been sundered, and so, Sir James seemed to be saying, had **that** between morality and law
- **what** a society **regards as** most worthwhile
- **The principle that** promises should be kept **lies** beneath the law of contract
- The law **which** they apply is still based on and reflects values
- The rights **set** out in the Human Rights Act 1998 were a good guide, **if not** an exhaustive one, to **what** our society regarded as fundamental values

1) This article is written by Paul Magrath, who is Head of Product Development and Online Content at ICLR, publishers of the official series of The Law Reports since 1865. He is a regular contributor to the ICLR blog and reviews books for a number of legal and literary journals. The source is https://www.counselmagazine.co.uk/articles/

1. senior judge 원로판사
2. reignite 재 점화하다
3. ember 불씨
4. flare up 확 타오르다
5. common ground 공통점
6. promote 고취하다
7. enforce 강요하다
8. legal process 법적 절차
9. prominent 두드러진, 눈에 잘 띄는
10. keynote address 기조연설
11. entitle 제목을 붙이다
12. directed to ~으로 향하다
13. sincere 진실한

Last autumn two *senior judges[1] gave speeches concerning the relationship between law and morality, *thus *reigniting[2] the *embers[3] of a debate which has *flared up[4)] repeatedly over the last two centuries.

Although they were not in any sense *putting forth rival views, they approached their *common ground[5] from different directions. While both felt it was not for judges to *promote[6] or *enforce[7] religious or sexual morals, as had been done in *Victorian times[2)], they differed slightly on the role of moral values in the modern *legal process[8].

The more *prominent[9] of the two judges was Sir James Munby, President of the *Family Division of the High Court[3)], giving the *keynote address[10] to the Law Society's Family Law Annual Conference on 29 October 2013. *Although his paper, *entitled[11] "Law, Morality and Religion in the Family Courts," was more widely reported on his remarks about the role of religion in our law courts ("Religion … is not the business of government or the secular courts"), much of what he said was really *directed to[12] the wider issue of morals, which can be derived from religion, but need not be. And he *was careful to *remind his listeners of the distinction between enforcing religious principles or the morality derived from them on the one hand, and respecting and protecting the right to hold *sincere[13] beliefs on the other.

2) Victorian times (영국) 빅토리아 (여왕) 시대(1837~1901).

3) Family Division of the High Court 고등법원 가족부.

Sir James began by citing a case from 1905 in which a judge in a *family case[14] had *confidently[15] asserted that the function of judges was "to promote virtue and morality and to *discourage[16] vice and immorality". *He gave various examples from the 19th and early 20th century in which courts had decided cases on moral grounds, applying the sexual morality of Victorian *righteousness[17] according to which any woman who slept with a man *outside marriage[18] was to be treated as no better than a common prostitute[19], and could be *stripped[20] of rights over *property[21] or children simply *by virtue of her, well, lack of virtue. Needless to say, the same *strictures[22] were not applied to men.

The Victorian *hang-up[23] about sex (or *stern[24] *Canutism[4)] in the face of progress) was most *startlingly[25] exemplified by in re Besant (1878) 11 Ch D 508, in which it was held that the *publication[26] by the activist Annie Besant of a book about *contraception[27], which was found to *constitute[28] an *obscene[29] *libel[30], was sufficient grounds for removing her seven-year-old daughter from her *custody[31].

Sir James then stepped back from the *arena[32] of family law, and considered the wider question of the relationship between law and morality, saying:

"Happily for us, the days are past when the business of the judges was the enforcement of morals or religious belief. That was a battle

14. family case 가사사건
15. confidently 자신 있게
16. discourage 단념시키다
17. righteousness 정의
18. outside marriage 혼인 외 (혼외)
19. prostitute 매춘부
20. strip 빼앗다, 박탈하다
21. property 재산
22. strictures 제한, 제약
23. hang-up 문제, 콤플렉스
24. stern 단호한, 가혹한
25. startlingly 놀랍도록
26. publication 출판
27. contraception 피임
28. constitute ~이 되다
29. obscene 외설적인, 음란한
30. libel 명예훼손
31. custody 보호, 관리
32. arena 무대

4) Canutism 카뉴트적 태도, 카뉴트주의(끝까지 변화에 저항하고자 하는 완고한 태도).

33. fight out
(갈등 등에 대해) 해결[결판]이 날 때까지 싸우다

34. libertarian
자유주의적인

35. warrant
보증서, 근거

36. interfere
간섭하다, 참견하다

37. prevent
막다, 방지하다

38. fraternity
형제애, 박애

39. restraint
규제, 제한

40. safeguard
보호(안전)장치

41. criminal
형사상의

42. civil
민사상의

43. reiterate
되풀이하다

44. established
확실히 자리를 잡은

45. suppression
억제

46. subversive
체제전복적인

*fought out[33] in the nineteenth century between *John Stuart Mill[5] and *Sir James Fitzjames Stephen(Stephen J)[6] and in the middle of the last century between Professor Herbert Hart and Sir Patrick Devlin (Devlin J). *The philosophers had the better of the argument, and rightly so."

*The debate in the 19th century began with Mill's *On Liberty*, published in 1859, in which the philosopher put forth the *libertarian[34] argument that the only *warrant[35] for *interfering[36] with anyone's actions was to *prevent[37] harm to others. Stephen J responded with his book Liberty, Equality, *Fraternity[38], published in 1873, *in which he asserted that "*restraints[39] on immorality are the main *safeguards[40] of society against influences which might be fatal to it". The purpose of the law, both *criminal[41] and *civil[42], was to promote virtue and prevent vice.

A century later, *in reaction to the liberalizing proposals contained in the Report of the Committee on Homosexual Offences and Prostitution (*The Wolfenden Committee*) (1957), Sir Patrick Devlin, in The Enforcement of Morals, *reiterated[43] Stephen J's view, asserting that "an *established[44] morality is as necessary as good government to the welfare of society", and that "*the *suppression[45] of vice is as much the law's business as the suppression of *subversive[46] activities".

Taking up the opposing, libertarian view, was another philosopher,

5) John Stuart Mill(1806~1873) 영국의 철학자, 경제학자.

6) Sir James Fitzjames Stephen(1829~1894)영국의 법률가, 판사, 작가.

Professor Herbert Hart, who in his book Law, Liberty, and Morality, *echoed[47] what J. S. Mill had said a century earlier, that essentially it was not the law's business to *regulate[48] morality.

*Having *set out[49] the opposing positions, Sir James Munby P went on to *demonstrate[50] how history had proved the philosophers to have had "the better of the argument". He cited the poet *Philip Larkin[7]'s famous lines about how "*Sexual intercourse[51] began/In nineteen sixty-three…" Modern sexual morality, said Sir James, was a product of the 1960s.

That decade had begun with what Sir James called the "*last hurrah[52] of the *ancient regime[53]", the decision of the *House of Lords[8] in Shaw v Director of Public Prosecutions [1962] AC 220, *upholding[54] the *appellant's[55] *conviction[56] for, *inter alia[57], *conspiracy[58] to corrupt public morals, after he had published an *illustrated[59] *directory[60] of prostitutes. In his *judgment[61] Viscount Simonds, at p 267, said the "*supreme[62] and fundamental purpose of the law [was] to *conserve[63] not only the safety and order but also the moral welfare of the State".

*He might just as well have said, like *Madame de Pompadour[9]: "*après nous, le Déluge". The following year, the *prosecution[64] of Penguin Books for *obscenity[65] in publishing an *unexpurgated[66] version of *D. H. Lawrence's[10] *frankly[67] *explicit[68] novel, Lady

47. echo
그대로 따라하다
48. regulate
규제하다, 통제하다
49. set out
제시하다
50. demonstrate
입증하다, 증거를 들어가며 보여주다
51. sexual intercourse
성교
52. last hurrah
마지막 노력(시도)
53. ancient regime
구제도(체제)
54. uphold
(이전의 판결을) 확인하다
55. appellant
상고자, 항소자
56. conviction
유죄선고(판결)
57. inter alia
(L.)그중에서도, 특히
58. conspiracy
모의
59. illustrated
삽화를 넣은
60. directory
안내책자
61. judgment
판결
62. supreme
최고의
63. conserve
보호하다
64. prosecution
기소, 고발
65. obscenity
외설
66. unexpurgated
삭제되지 않은
67. frankly
노골적으로, 솔직히
68. explicit
분명한, 적나라한

7) Philip Larkin(1922~1985) 영국의 시인·소설가.

8) House of Lords (영국) 상원 cf. House of Commons 하원.

9) Madame de Pompadour 퐁파두르 후작부인. 프랑스의 궁정인이며, 로코코 문화의 상징적 존재. 평민 출신이지만, 문화적 교양을 지녔고, 타고난 미모와 야심으로 국왕 루이 15세의 정부가 됨.

10) D. H. Lawrence(1885 ~ 1930) 영국 소설가, 시인 겸 비평가로 《채털리 부인의 사랑》은 그의 성철학(性哲學)을 펼

69. notoriously 악명 높게
70. dawning 여명기의
71. legalize 합법화하다
72. decriminalize 기소[처벌] 대상에서 제외시키다
73. homosexuality 동성애
74. procreation 출산
75. sunder 가르다, 분리하다
76. adapt 조정하다
77. high court judge 고등법원판사
78. strikingly 눈에 띄게, 두드러지게
79. quotation 인용
80. straightforward 간단한, 쉬운

Chatterley's Lover, was *notoriously[69] unsuccessful, *marking a turning point in the public acceptance of the *dawning[70] sexual revolution for which the decade is remembered. Within a few years Parliament had *legalized[71] contraception and abortion and *decriminalized[72] *homosexuality[73]. *The fundamental link between sex and *procreation[74] had been *sundered[75], and so, Sir James seemed to be saying, had that between morality and law. At any rate, *it was not for judges to arrogate to themselves the custodianship of public morality: the job of *adapting[76] the law for a multi-cultural multi-faith society was now for Parliament, not the courts.

Law as a system of values

Although Sir James gave his speech several days later, he *made no reference to that given on 24 October 2013 by Sir Rabinder Singh, a high court judge[77] (Singh J), giving the Jan Grodecki lecture at the University of Leicester, under the title "Law as a system of values". Yet the content of the two speeches covered *strikingly[78] similar ground, and many of the same *quotations[79] were employed *in illustrating the points made.

Sir Rabinder said the relationship between law and values was "not a *straightforward[80] one". *By "values" he meant to include: *"what a society regards as most worthwhile. Often values are moral values but they need not be; and moral values certainly need not be

친 작품이며 외설시비로 오랜 재판을 겪은 후 미국에서는 1959년에, 영국에서는 1960년에야 비로소 완본 출판이 허용되었음.

*founded[81] on the doctrines of religion in general or any religion in particular."

It was clear, he said, that many legal rules were intended to "*give effect to certain basic values of a society", and this provided "much of the moral force which is needed to support positive rules of law, in particular the rules of criminal law." A society could not function without rules prohibiting murder or theft. "One thinks immediately of the *Ten Commandments[11]." *Such rules reflected fundamental values which might have derived from religious traditions but were needed even in a wholly secular society.

In civil law, *"the principle that promises should be kept lies beneath the law of contract; and much of the law of *equity[82] was historically founded upon principles of *conscience[83]." As for the law of *negligence[84], one *had only to recall Lord Atkin's famously Biblical description of the "*duty of care" as one owed to one's fellow man as a "neighbour".

Likewise, *legislation[85] often sought to reflect and promote (even if it could not always enforce) certain values, such as that of *equality[86] between human beings regardless of race, sex, colour, ability etc, in the *anti-discrimination laws[87].

*The key point which Sir Rabinder wished to make was that even though the secular courts now *disavow[88] any duty or intention to enforce morals, the law which they apply is still based on and

81. found
~에 기반을 두다

82. equity
공정

83. conscience
양심

84. negligence
부주의, 과실

85. legislation
입법, 법률의 제성

86. equality
평등

87. anti-discrimination law
차별금지법

88. disavow
부인하다

11) Ten Commandments 십계명은 B.C. 13세기 고대 이스라엘 민족의 지도자였던 모세가 시나이 산에서 하느님으로부터 받은 10개조의 계율로서, '모세의 십계'라고도 불림.

reflects values. Although a judge *was not entitled to impose on society his or her own subjective views of what was morally right or wrong, there were many occasions when simply applying a system of *black letter rules was not enough. An obvious example was *sentencing[89], where section 125 of the *Coroners and Justice Act[12)] 2009 *provided[90] that the court should follow any relevant guideline *issued[91] by the *Sentencing Council[13)], unless it would be contrary to the "interests of justice". That phrase was not, however, defined in the Act.

Other examples could be found in the civil law, under which a contract might not be *enforceable[92] if it would be "contrary to public policy", where a *covenant[93] might be in "unreasonable" restraint of trade, or a duty of *confidentiality[94] *overridden[95] where it was "in the public interest" to do so (and where, one might add, there was an obligation of "*good faith[96]" in insurance contracts).

How was a judge to determine these questions without applying values? *Where were the values to be found if not in the subjective views of the individual judge?

The answer, Sir Rabinder said, was to be found in using the *conventional[97] techniques of *legal reasoning[98], by referring to relevant legal materials, such as *binding[99] *precedents[100] or legislation, and by reference to the "fundamental values which are well established in our system of justice". The principle of

89. sentence (형을) 선고하다
90. provide 규정하다
91. issue 공표하다
92. enforceable 강제할 수 있는
93. covenant 약속, 계약
94. confidentiality 비밀
95. overridden 기각된
96. good faith 선의
97. conventional 관습적인
98. legal reasoning 법률적 추론
99. binding 구속력 있는
100. precedent 선례, 판례

12) Coroners and Justice Act(검시관과 형사법) 영국 의회의 법령으로 잉글랜드와 웨일즈에서의 검시관과 형사법에 관한 법을 바꾸었음.

13) Sentencing Council 판결위원회.

*proportionality[101], for example, in relation to sentencing. *The rights *set out[102] in the *Human Rights Act[14)] 1998 were a good guide, if not an *exhaustive[103] one, to what our society regarded as fundamental values.

Most observers of the English legal system would acknowledge that its values included the concepts of fairness, equality, democracy and the rule of law. Sir Rabinder continued: "*Although the law does not any longer attempt (or even think that it should attempt) to *enforce[104] morals in the sense that Lord Devlin thought it should 50 years ago, that is not to say that the law is immoral or even *amoral[105]. *It is based on values, which lie at its *foundations[106], but one of those values is that we do not necessarily think it right to impose a subjective *code[107] of private or sexual morality on an individual."

He then cites what Lord Devlin had argued about the enforcement of morals, and Professor Hart *in reply, *much as Sir James also does in his lecture. But interestingly, there's another *passage[108] from Hart (which Sir James does not quote), in which he speaks in the language of values: "*The *unimpeded[109] *exercise[110] by individuals of free choice may be held to be a value in itself with which it is *prima facie[111] wrong to interfere; or it may be thought valuable because it enables individuals to experiment – even with living – and to discover things valuable both to themselves and others."

The fact that the law *is no longer concerned with the enforcement

101. proportionality 비례의 원칙(과잉조치 금지의 원칙)
102. set out 공표하다
103. exhaustive 철저한(완전한)
104. enforce 강요하다
105. amoral 도덕적 관념이 없는
106. foundation 토대
107. code 관례, 규칙
108. passage 구절
109. unimpeded 방해받지 않는
110. exercise 권리행사
111. prima facie (나중에 거짓으로 드러날지라도) 처음에 진실로 여겨지는, 일단 볼 때

14) Human Rights Act 인권법.

112. abundantly
풍부하게, 아주

113. triumphantly
의기양양하게

114. value-free
가치 판단적이 아닌

of morals (as Sir James makes *abundantly[112], and perhaps *triumphantly[113], clear) does not mean, says Sir Rabinder, that "the law has become a *value-free[114] zone. *Far from it. It means that the values of the law are now different from what they were 50 years ago." But it could still be said that the law was a system of values.

GRAMMAR

시제(Tense)와 상(Aspect)

1. 시제란?

동사의 어형변화를 통해 시간관계를 표현하는 양식을 말한다. 영어의 시제는 **현재**와 **과거 시제**가 있다. 현재시제는 주로 동사의 원형으로 나타내고, 주어가 3인칭 단수이면 동사 뒤에 -s를 붙여서 나타낸다.

현실세계에서의 시간과 혼동하지 않는 것이 중요한데 현실세계에서의 시간은, 현재, 과거, 미래로 구분되지만 영어의 시제에서 미래라는 시제는 없다고 할 수 있다.

현재	원형, 혹은 주어가 3인칭 단수일 때 동사 뒤에 -s, -es
과거	규칙형은 일반적으로 동사원형 뒤에 -ed를 붙여 만든다. 불규칙형은 동사별로 기억해야 할 것이다(was, did, had, ran, put, came, caught, brought 등)

2. 상이란?

진행(계속), 완료(미완료), 습관(반복적 동작) 등을 나타내는 동사의 의미와 형식을 말한다. 다음의 예를 보자.

a) He reads the Bible every day(습관). b) He is reading a newspaper(진행).
c) He has just read her letter(완료).

위의 문장은 시제란 관점에서 본다면 모두 현재시제형(현재, 현재진행, 현재완료)이다. 그러나 습관, 진행, 완료라는 상(aspect)이 다르다. 그러나 다음의 문장을 보자.

a) He is reading a book. b) He was reading a book.

위의 문장은 진행상은 동일하나 시제는 다르다(현재진행과 과거진행). 다음의 문장은

완료라는 상은 동일하나 시제는 현재(완료)와 과거(완료)로 다르다.

a) He has just read her letter.　　b) He had just read her letter.

진행상	be 동사 + 동사원형 + -ing
	be 동사로 시제를 표시한다(is, am, are, was, were)
완료상	have 동사 + 과거분사(past participle)
	have 동사로 시제를 표시한다 (have, has, had)

현재완료	Have(has) + been + 동사원형 + -ing
진행상	He has been studying English.

이처럼 영어는 시제와 상이 뒤섞여 동사에 여러 가지 형태의 변화를 줌으로써 시간과, 습관, 진행, 완료 등을 표현한다. 이러한 시제와 상을 정리해 보면 다음과 같다.

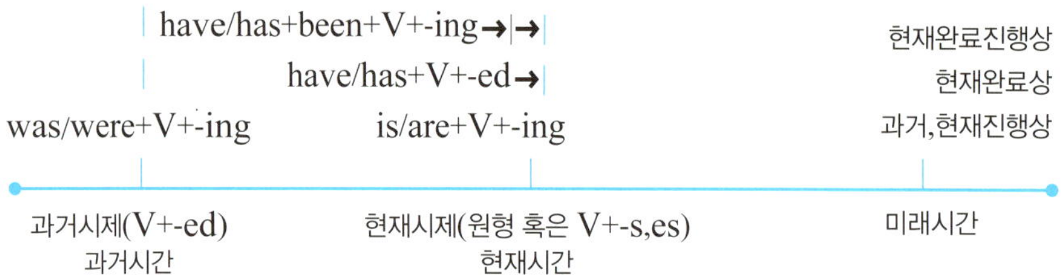

3. 미래를 표현하는 양식

1) 현재진행상(is/are + V+-ing): 이미 계획한 것

I am playing tennis on Monday afternoon.

2) 현재시제(동사원형+(s, es): 시간표나 일정표

I start my new job on Monday.

3) be going to do: 이미 하기로 결정한 것

I'm going to write some letters.

4) will: 말하는 순간에 하기로 결정한 것

"What would you like to drink?"
"I'll have some orange juice, please, please."

5) 미래진행상(will be+V+-ing): 미래시점에서의 행위의 지속

I'll be watching the game then.

6) 미래완료상(will+have+V+-ing): 미래의 어떤 시점 이전에 이미 끝나게 될 때

The movie will already have started by the time we get to the theater.

PHRASES and STRUCTURES

* thus **reigniting** the embers of a debate **which** has flared up repeatedly over the last two centuries
이렇게 하여 그들은 논란의 불씨들을 다시 불붙였는데, 그 논란은 지난 2세기에 걸쳐 반복적으로 타올랐던 것이다
= thus **they(two senior judges) reignited** the embers of a debate, **and it(the debate)** has flared up repeatedly over the last two centuries
reigniting(분사구문) = thus they(two senior judges) reignited
which = and + it(the debate)

* **put forth** 의견을 제시하다

* Although his paper, **entitled** "Law, Morality and Religion in the Family Courts," was more widely reported on his remarks about the role of religion in our law courts, much of **what** he said was really directed to the wider issue of morals, **which** can be derived from religion, but need not be.
비록 그의 논문은, '가족 법원에서의 법, 도덕성, 그리고 종교'로 제목이 붙여졌는데, 우리의 법정에서 종교의 역할에 관한 그의 언급에 관해 더 널리 보도되었다 하더라도 그가 말했던 많은 것들은 도덕이라는 더 넓은 문제로 향했는데 그 문제는 종교로부터 생겨날 수 있지만 생겨날 필요는 없다.
= Although his paper, **(and it was) entitled** "Law, Morality and Religion in the Family Courts" was more widely reported on his remarks about the role of religion in our law courts, much of **what** he said was really directed to the wider issue of morals, **and it(the issue)** can be derived from religion, but need not be
과거분사(entitled) 앞에서 관계대명사의 주격(which)과 be동사 생략
entitled = which was entitled = ~~and it was~~(being) entitled
what은 선행사를 포함하는 관계대명사(그가 말했던 것)
which = and + it(the issue)

* **was careful to ~** ~에 주의하다

* **remind A of B** A에게 B를 생각하게 하다 (상기시키다)

* He gave various examples from the 19th and early 20th century **in which** courts had decided cases on moral grounds, **applying** the sexual morality of Victorian righteousness according to **which** any woman **who** slept with a man outside marriage was to be treated as no better than a common prostitute.
그는 19세기와 20세기 초에서 다양한 예들을 들었는데, 그 예들에서 법원은 도덕적 토대위에서 사건들을 판결했고, 그렇게 해서 빅토리아시대의 정의라는 성적인 도덕성을 적용했는데, 그 성적인 도덕성에 따라 혼인 외에 어떤 남자와 잠을 잔 모든 여성은 일반적인 창녀와 다름없이 간주되어져야했다.
= He gave various examples from the 19th and early 20th century, **and in them(examples)** courts had decided cases on moral grounds, **and they(courts) applied** the sexual morality of Victorian righteousness, **and** according to **it(the sexual morality)** any woman, **and she(woman)** slept with a man outside marriage was to be treated as **no better than** a common prostitute.
in which = and in them(examples)
applying(분사구문) = ~~and they(courts)~~ applied
목적격 관계대명사 which = and + it(the sexual morality)
who = and + she(woman)
no better than ~ ~와 다름없는

* **by virtue of ~** ~ 때문에, ~의 이유로

* The philosophers **had the better of** the argument, and rightly so.
철학자들이 논쟁에서 유리한 입장에 있었고 마땅히 그럴만했다.

* The debate in the 19th century began with Mill's *On Liberty*, published in 1859, in which the philosopher put forth the libertarian argument that the only warrant for interfering with anyone's actions was to prevent harm to others.
19세기의 논란은 밀의 책 *On Liberty*와 함께 시작되었는데, 그 책은 1859년에 출판되었고, 그 책에서 그 철학자(밀)는 자유주의적 주장을 제시하였는데 그 주장은 어떤 사람의 행동에 간섭하는 유일한 근거는 다른 사람들에 대한 해를 막기 위한 것이었다.
= The debate in the 19th century began with Mill's *On Liberty*, **(and it was)**

published in 1859, **and in it(the book)** the philosopher put forth **the** libertarian **argument that** the only warrant for interfering with anyone's actions was to prevent harm to others.
in which = and in it(the book)
the argument와 that절은 동격

* **in which** he asserted that "restraints on immorality are the main safeguards of society against influences **which** might be fatal to it
그 책에서 그는 비도덕성에 대한 제약들은 사회에 치명적일 수도 있는 영향에 대비하는 사회의 주요한 보호 장치들이라고 주장했다
= **and in it(the book)**, he asserted that "restraints on immorality are the main safeguards of society against influences, **and they(influences)** might be fatal to it(=society)
in which = and in it(the book)
which = and + they(influences)

* **in reaction to ~** ~에 반응해서

* The suppression of vice is **as much** the law's business **as** the suppression of subversive activities.
악덕의 억제는 체제 전복적인 활동의 억제 못지않게 법이 할 일이다.

* **Having set out** the opposing positions, Sir James Munby P went on to demonstrate how history had proved the philosophers to have had "the better of the argument".
반대 입장을 제시한 후 제임스 먼비 경은 계속해서 철학자들이 논쟁에서 유리한 입장에 있었는지를 역사가 어떻게 입증했는지를 예증했다.
= **After Sir James Munby P had set out** the opposing positions, he went on to demonstrate how history had proved the philosophers to have had "the better of the argument".
Having set out(분사구문) = ~~After Sir James Munby P~~ had set out

* He might just as well have said. ~라고 말하는 것이 나았을지도 모른다
might as well ~ ~하는 편이 낫다

* après nous, le Déluge (우리가) 죽은 뒤에 무슨 일이 일어나든 아무 상관없다

* **marking** a turning point in the public acceptance of the dawning sexual revolution **for which** the decade is remembered
그런데 그것은(성공하지 못한 것) 여명기의 성적인 혁명에 대한 대중의 수용성에 있어서 전환점이 되었는데, 그 수용성으로 그 십년이 기억된다
= **and it marked a turning point** in the public acceptance of the dawning sexual revolution, and the decade is remembered **for it(the public acceptance)**
mark a turning point 전환점을 찍다
marking(분사구문) = ~~and it~~ marked
for which = and + for it(the public acceptance)

* The fundamental link between sex and procreation had been sundered, and so, Sir James seemed to be saying, had **that** between morality and law.
성과 출산 사이의 근본적인 관련성이 분리되게 되었고, 도덕성과 법 사이의 관련성도 또한 그렇게 되었다고 제임스 경이 말하고 있는 것처럼 보였다.
= The fundamental link between sex and procreation had been sundered, and **that (the link)** between morality and law, Sir James seemed to be saying, **had (been sundered)**.
that은 link를 받고 있음
so + 동사 + 주어

* **It** was not **for** judges **to** arrogate to themselves the custodianship of public morality.
공공의 도덕성이라는 보호임무를 가로채는 것은 판사가 아니다.
arrogate to yourself something 가로채다
It ~ for ~ to + 동사원형

* **made no reference to ~** ~을 전혀 언급하지 않았다

* in illustrating the points **made**
제시된 주장을 예증하는데
= in illustrating the points **(which were)** made

과거분사(made) 앞에서 관계대명사의 주격(which)과 be동사 생략

* By "values" he meant to include: 가치라는 말은 다음을 포함 한다:

* **What** a society regards as most worthwhile. Often values are moral values but they need not be.
사회가 가장 가치 있다고 간주하는 것. 종종 가치들은 도덕적 가치이지만 그 가치들이 도덕적 가치일 필요는 없다.
= **The thing which** a society regards as most worthwhile. Often values are moral values but they(values) need not be (moral values).
= The thing, **and** a society regards **it(the thing)** as most worthwhile. Often values are moral values but **they(values)** need not be **(moral values)**.
regard A as B A를 **B**로 간주하다
What은 선행사를 포함하는 관계대명사로 regard의 목적으로 사용됨
what = the thing which

* **give effect to** 실행(시)하다

* Such rules reflected fundamental values **which** might have derived from religious traditions but were needed even in a wholly secular society.
그러한 규칙들은 근본적인 가치들을 반영했는데, 그 가치들은 종교적인 전통에서 파생했을지도 모르지만 심지어 완전히 세속적인 사회에서도 필요 되었다.
= Such rules reflected fundamental values, **and they(values)** might have derived from religious traditions but were needed even in a wholly secular society.
which = and + they(values)
might have + p.p. ~였을지도 모른다

* **The principle** that promises should be kept **lies** beneath the law of contract.
약속은 지켜져야 한다는 원칙은 계약법 아래에 있다.
that은 the principle과 동격
주어는 the principle, 본동사는 lies

* **had only to ~** ~하기 만 하면 되었다

* **duty of care** 주의의무

* **The key point which** Sir Rabinder wished to make **was that** even though the secular courts now disavow any duty or intention to enforce morals, the law **which** they apply is still based on and reflects values.
라빈더 경이 주장하고 싶어 했던 요지는 비록 세속적인 법원이 지금 도덕을 강요하는 모든 의무나 의도를 부인한다 하더라도 법원이 적용하는 법은 여전히 가치에 기초하고 있고 가치를 반영한다는 것이었다.
= **The key point**, and Sir Rabinder wished to make **it(the point) was that** even though the secular courts now disavow any duty or intention to enforce morals, the law, **and** they(courts) apply **it(the law)** is still based on and reflects values.
목적격 관계대명사 which = and + it(the point)
make the point 주장하다, 강조하다
주어는 the key point, 본동사는 was
that은 was 의 보어절
that 절속에 even though는 부사절을 이끄는 종속적이고, 주절은 the law이하가 됨
목적격 관계대명사 which = and + it(the law)

* **be entitled to ~** ~할 자격이 있다

* **black letter rules** 검은색 글자로 된 규칙, 여기서는 활자화 된 규칙을 가리킴

* Where were the values to be found **if not** in the subjective views of the individual judge?
만일 개인적 판단이라는 주관적인 견해들 속에 그 가치들이 없다면 그 가치들은 어디서 발견될 수 있겠는가?
= Where were the values to be found **if (they(values) were) not** in the subjective views of the individual judge?
be to + 동사원형 = 가능
if not = if (they(values) were) not

* The rights **set** out in the Human Rights Act 1998 were a good guide, **if not** an exhaustive one, to what our society regarded as fundamental values.

1998년의 인권법에서 공표된 권리들은 비록 완전한 지침이 아니라 하더라도 우리 사회가 근본적인 가치들로 간주했던 것에 대한 좋은 지침이다.

= The rights **(which were) set** out in the Human Rights Act 1998 were a good guide, **(even)if (they(= rights) are) not** an exhaustive **one(= a guide)**, to **what** our society regarded as fundamental values.

과거분사**(set)** 앞에서 관계대명사의 주격**(which)**과 **be**동사 생략 = **which were set**

if not = (even)if (they(= rights) are) not

one = a guide

a good guide to ~ ~에 대한 좋은 지침

what은 관계대명사

regard A as B A를 **B**로 간주하다

* Although the law does not any longer attempt (or even think that it should attempt) to enforce morals in **the sense that** Lord Devlin thought it should 50 years ago

데블린 경이 50년 전 법이 도덕을 당연히 강요해야한다고 생각했던 의미에서 비록 법이 더 이상 도덕을 강요하려고 시도하지 않는다 하더라도(심지어 법이 시도해야 한다고 생각조차 않는다하더라도)

= Although the law does not any longer attempt (or even think that it should attempt) to enforce morals in **the sense that** (Lord Devlin thought) it(= the law) should (enforce morals) 50 years ago

not any longer ~ 더 이상 ~아니다

Lord Devlin thought는 삽입절

the sense와 that절은 동격

* It is based on values, **which** lie at its foundations, but one of those values is that we do not necessarily think it right to impose a subjective code of private or sexual morality on an individual.

그것(법)은 가치들에 기초하고 있는데, 그 가치들은 법의 토대를 이루고 있지만 그러한 가치들 중의 하나는 우리가 개인적인 혹은 성적인 도덕성이라는 주관적인 규칙을 개인에게 가하는 것이 반드시 옳다고는 생각하지 않는다는 것이다.

= It is based on values, **and they(values)** lie at its foundations, but one of those values is **that** we do not necessarily think **it** right **to** impose a subjective code of private or sexual morality on an individual.

which = and + they(values)
that은 is의 보어절
think + 목적어 + to + 동사원형 목적어가 ~라고 여기다
it은 가목적어 to impose이하는 진목적어

* **in reply** 답으로

* **much as ~** ~이긴 하지만

* The unimpeded exercise by individuals of free choice may be held to be a value in itself **with which** it is prima facie wrong to interfere.
개인들의 자유로운 선택이라는 방해받지 않은 권리행사가 본질적으로 가치라고 여겨질 수 있는데, 그 가치를 방해하는 것은 일단 보기에는 잘못이다.
= The unimpeded exercise by individuals of free choice may be held to be a value in itself, **and it** is prima facie wrong **to** interfere **with it(the value)**.
with which = and + with it(the value)
in itself 본질적으로
it은 가주어, to이하는 진주어

* **is concerned with ~** ~와 관계가 있다

* **be far from it** 전혀 (그렇지 않다)(오히려 그 반대이다)

Unit 6

The Ethics of Ending Life: Euthanasia and Assisted Suicide[1)]

WARMING UP

- We need to anticipate **what** ethical questions remain to be answered
- **It** may be reasonable **to** assume that a suicide **in which** a physician provides aid **that** a non-physician would not have been able to provide does constitute physician-assisted suicide
- Prescriptive assistance by a physician in a suicide requires that **the physician use** his or her unique privileges as a physician
- The core value supporting **that** motive must be altruism
- This concept is **so** engrained in our society **that** euthanasia often is referred to as "mercy killing"
- When he injected elderly patients with lethal doses of narcotics **so that** he could inherit money left to him in their wills
- **While commonly used**, these terms add nothing to a simpler definition of euthanasia

1) This article was written by Gail Van Norman, M.D., Professor of Anesthesiology and Pain Medicine and Adjunct Professor of Biomedical Ethics, University of Washington, Seattle. The source is https://csahq.org/docs/default-source/news-and-events-docs/csa-bulletin-docs/volume-61-number-1/end_of_life_61_1.pdf?sfvrsn=2

Last November, New Zealand *forensic[1] scientist Sean Davidson was *sentenced[2] to five months' *detention[3] for assisting a suicide. His crime? At the request of his 85-year-old *terminally ill[4] mother, he *crushed up[5] a bottle of morphine tablets, *dissolved[6] them in a glass of water, and *handed[7] it to her so that she could *voluntarily[8] drink it to end her life. The original *charge[9] of *attempted[10] murder eventually was reduced to counseling and *procuring[11] a suicide because of public *outcry[12] including the *testimonial[13] support of such *luminaries[14] as *Bishop Desmond Tutu[2)]. Such stories are becoming increasingly common.

The moral limits of relieving suffering at the end of life, and where our responsibilities as physicians should lie, are more frequently debated as *populations age[15] and the diseases and *disabilities[16] of old age present increasing challenges. *In the balance are crucial issues: personal autonomy, dignity, compassion, ending suffering, protection of the *vulnerable[17], promotion of good *palliative[18] care, and redefinition of the role of the physician in death and dying. In the last 15 years, the Netherlands, Belgium, and three states (Oregon, Washington and Montana) have passed laws permitting physician-assisted suicide and/or *euthanasia[19]. In Switzerland, the law even permits *assisted suicide[20] by non-physicians. *Debate about assisted suicide is currently in full swing in Great Britain, where *prosecution[21] of family members who have assisted desperate patients to travel abroad to commit suicide has *elicited[22] public

1. forensic 법의학의
2. sentence (형을) 선고하다
3. detention 구금, 구류
4. terminally ill 말기의
5. crush up 가루로 만들다
6. dissolve 녹이다
7. hand 건네주다
8. voluntarily 자발적으로, 자진해서
9. charge 기소
10. attempted 미수에 그친
11. procure 알선하다
12. outcry 격렬한 반응
13. testimonial 증명이 되는
14. luminary 전문가(권위자)
15. populations age 인구노령화
16. disability 장애
17. vulnerable 취약한, 연약한
18. palliative 일시적인, 임시방편의
19. euthanasia 안락사
20. assisted suicide 조력자살
21. prosecution 기소, 고발
22. elicit 끌어내다

2) Bishop Desmond Tutu 남아프리카공화국의 성직자(1931~) 1984년 노벨 평화상 수상자.

23. specialty 전문, 전공
24. legislator 입법자, 국회의원
25. anticipate 예상하다
26. detail 상세히 알리다(열거하다)
27. legislative 입법의
28. refer to ~을 나타내다, 지칭하다
29. intrinsic 고유한, 본질적인

outcry.

As moral dilemmas about ending life become increasingly common, physicians of all *specialties[23] will be confronted with questions from patients and their families, from our own friends and families, and from our *legislators[24] and the media. We need to know precisely what is meant by "assisted suicide" and "euthanasia," understand why some societies have legalized such actions, and **anticipate[25] what ethical questions remain to be answered. Part I of this discussion reviews common terminology and definitions relevant to assisted suicide and euthanasia, while Part II (to appear in the Spring 2012 CSA Bulletin) reviews ethical issues about ending life and *details[26] *legislative[27] differences regarding physician-assisted suicide and euthanasia in various countries.

The term "euthanasia" comes from Greek roots eu(good) and thanatos(death). In modern usage, *the term always *refers to[28] an act of killing that meets certain criteria described in this article. Not every killing is an act of euthanasia, but all euthanasia is killing. Furthermore, even though the Greek roots appear to imply moral "goodness," the term "euthanasia" itself has no *intrinsic[29] moral value: an act of euthanasia may be moral or immoral depending on the context and on society's values.

Suicide and Assisted Suicide

*Suicide is "self-killing," which may or may not require the aid of another person. *"Assisted suicide" is a suicide that does require the aid of another person. In the United States, legally permitted suicide is almost always discussed in the context of physician-assisted suicide (for example, by writing a *lethal[30] prescription of *barbiturates[31].

However, not every act by a physician is carried out as a physician. In Switzerland, for instance, any citizen can legally assist suicide, yet a Swiss physician cannot ethically assist a suicide as a physician but may do so as a private person. Indeed, *it may be reasonable to assume that a suicide in which a physician provides aid that a non-physician would not have been able to provide does constitute physician-assisted suicide. Purchasing a gun for another person for purposes of suicide is assisting them, but does not constitute physician-assisted suicide even if the *purchaser[32] is a physician. Almost any citizen can provide the service. However, *writing a prescription is a privilege *afforded[33] to physicians and only a few other *allied[34] health professionals, such as some *nurse practitioners[35] and some physician assistants. *Prescriptive assistance by a physician in a suicide requires that the physician use his or her *unique[36] privileges as a physician, and therefore this does constitute physician-assisted suicide.

Euthanasia

Euthanasia always requires the act of *another party. *When more than one person is involved in a sequence of actions that results in death, then that death is *termed[37] a suicide when the last person

30. lethal
치명적인

31. barbiturate
신경안정제

32. purchaser
구입한 사람

33. afford
제공하다

34. allied
관련된

35. nurse practitioner
임상간호사

36. unique
고유의

37. term
칭하다, 일컫다

38. homicide
살인

39. intention
의도, 목적

40. desired
바랐던, 희망했던

41. mercy
자비

42. altruism
이타심

43. engrained
뿌리 깊게 박혀있는

44. mercy killing
안락사

45. serial killer
연쇄살인자

46. commit
(범죄를) 저지르다

47. inject
주사하다, 주입하다

48. dose
복용량, 투여량

49. narcotic
마약, 마취제

50. will
유언장

51. invalidate
무효화하다

52. anguish
괴로움

53. inspire
불어넣다

54. revulsion
혐오감, 공포감

55. accompany
동반하다

56. beheading
참수

who acts in the sequence is the one who dies. If the last "actor" is someone other than the one who dies, the death is termed a *homicide[38] (one human being killing another), even if the person who dies agreed to it.

Euthanasia always involves a special motive. *Intentions[39] are the specific goals and *desired[40] outcomes of an act; *"motives" are the reasons for which we have those intentions. In the case of euthanasia, the motive always is required to be *mercy[41], and *the core value supporting that motive must be *altruism[42]. *This concept is so *engrained[43] in our society that euthanasia often is referred to as "*mercy killing[44]." Harold Shipman, a British physician and *serial killer[45], *committed[46] murder and not euthanasia *when he *injected[47] elderly patients with lethal *doses[48] of *narcotics[49] so that he could inherit money left to him in their *wills[50]. Even if his actions actually relieved suffering in some, his motive *invalidates[51] a claim of euthanasia.

When is a homicide considered euthanasia? The term "euthanasia" implies a "good" death, and therefore the act should meet commonly agreed criteria for "goodness." Such criteria may be that it is swift, relatively painless, and *causes minimal if any psychological suffering, such as fear, *anguish[52] or deep regret. The death should not intentionally *inspire[53] horror or *revulsion[54], nor be *accompanied[55] by signs of suffering from the dying person. The motive should not be to punish. *Beheading[56], for example, might be swift and even relatively painless, but because it is usually intended to inspire horror in *victims[57] and *witnesses[58] alike and to punish the *recipient[59], then it would generally not be considered an act of euthanasia.

"Passive" Euthanasia: A Problematic Term

Intention and foresight are critical aspects in both the moral and the legal considerations of whether an act *constitutes[60] euthanasia, represents another kind of homicide, or is even an act of killing at all. Euthanasia and suicide both require the primary intention of causing death. *Foresight involves conceiving of possible outcomes, some of which we may neither desire nor intend. Certain acts can be *reasonably[61] *foreseen[62] to result in death, but may nevertheless be committed primarily for reasons other than death.

One example is *discontinuing[63] medical treatments at the request of an *autonomous[64] patient. *Patients have the legal right in the U.S. to say what will be done to them, and in *withdrawing[65] such treatments we not only respect their autonomy, but obey the law. Because our intention is to respect autonomy and not to kill, withdrawal of medical treatments under those circumstances is neither suicide nor euthanasia, and it does not even constitute killing because death is not the primary intention even though it is a foreseen result. Some authors use the term "passive euthanasia" to describe withdrawal of *life-sustaining treatments[66] when death is a *virtually[67] certain outcome, but not the primary intention.

Karen Ann Quinlan survived nine and a half years after her parents

57. victim
희생자

58. witness
목격자

59. recipient
받는 사람

60. constitute
…이 되는 것으로 여겨지다, …이 되다

61. reasonably
합리적으로, 타당하게

62. foresee
예견하다

63. discontinue
중단하다

64. autonomous
자율적인

65. withdraw
중단하다, 철회하다

66. life-sustaining treatment
생명유지(연명)치료

67. virtually
사실상

68. ventilator therapy 산소호흡기 치료
69. comment 견해를 밝히다
70. indignity 수모, 모욕
71. premeditated 사전에 계획된, 계획적인
72. negligent 부주의한, 과실의
73. misleading 오해의 소지가 있는
74. enlighten 이해를 시키다
75. voluntarism 자발적인 행동
76. incompetent 결정권이 없는
77. medical condition 질환
78. competent 결정권이 있는
79. merciful death 안락사

won the legal right to end her *ventilator therapy[68]. Her parents *commented[69] that their intention had never been to kill Karen, but rather to allow her to live her life, *however shortened it might turn out to be, without the *indignity[70] of unwanted therapy. The law itself recognizes the crucial difference between intention and foresight: *premeditated[71] (intentional) murder is punished differently from *negligent[72] homicide (carelessness or negligence that results in a death that might be predictable, but isn't intended). The primary and necessary intention of euthanasia is always to cause death. Without that primary intention the act is not euthanasia.

The term "passive euthanasia" is therefore problematic. *In the first place, euthanasia is an act, and therefore it cannot be passive. *The term is further *misleading[73] in that it confuses foresight with intention. For these reasons "passive euthanasia" is a term that often confuses rather than *enlightens[74] and should not be used.

Competence, Autonomy and *Voluntarism[75] in Euthanasia

Patient voluntarism is not necessary for euthanasia. Patients who are *incompetent[76] and non-autonomous as a result of *medical conditions[77], or who never were *competent[78] or autonomous due to age or other medical issues, may nevertheless be suffering in ways in which a *merciful death[79] is desirable, even though they cannot ask for it or agree to it. *Yet if a patient is competent to make decisions, killing them against their will violates other necessary criteria for euthanasia (kindness, mercy, preservation of dignity, and avoidance of *distress[80]). *Furthermore, euthanizng a patient who is capable of making a decision and refuses euthanasia is prohibited by other primary ethical principles, such as respect for autonomy, *beneficence[81] and *nonmaleficence[82].

Some authors have coined *yet[83] other terms such as "voluntary euthanasia" for patients who are competent and agree to be euthanized; "non-voluntary euthanasia" for those who have never been competent; and "*involuntary[84] euthanasia" for which a competent or previously competent patient's wishes are unknown. *While commonly used, these terms add nothing to a simpler definition of euthanasia (as a morally *neutral[85] term) that requires, in the case of competent patients, that their permission be obtained and, in the case of incompetent patients, that *deliberation[86] is undertaken by the appropriate *surrogate[87] *decision-makers[88] and after review of the patient's *advance directive[89], if available.

"Physician Aid-in-Dying": A Term of Uncertain Meaning and Limited Value

In the theater of political debate, terminology is often used to *polarize[90] or to unite. When the debate involves such a fundamentally morally uncomfortable concept as whether certain forms of killing should be legalized, one might expect that vocabulary will develop to enable comfortable discussion, or to *ignite[91] debate. However, *it is important to understand that such political terms often have little moral, ethical, or medical meaning

80. distress
고통

81. beneficence
자선

82. nonmaleficence
해악금지

83. yet
거기에 또

84. involuntary
자기도 모르게 하는, 원치 않은

85. neutral
중립적인

86. deliberation
숙고, 신중함

87. surrogate
대리의

88. decision-maker
의사결정자

89. advance directive
사전지시

90. polarize
양극화하다

91. ignite
불을 붙이다

92. obfuscate
혼란스럽게 만들다

93. ambiguous
애매모호한,
중의적인

94. encompass
포함하다, 아우르다

95. simultaneously
동시에

96. administer
(약을)투여하다

97. symptom
증상

98. intervention
개입, 간섭

99. equivalent
동등한

100. procedurally
절차상으로

101. facilitate
용이하게 하다

and not only may not add to, but may even *obfuscate[92], our understanding of underlying issues. "Physician aid-in-dying" is one such term, because it is *ambiguous[93] and *encompasses[94] *a host of morally dissimilar actions while *simultaneously[95] implying that those actions are morally the same - and therefore should be treated similarly.

"Aid-in-dying," for example, could include such diverse actions as sitting at the bedside and holding the hand of a dying patient, *administering[96] medications to relieve *symptoms[97] such as pain, discontinuing life-sustaining medical *interventions[98], providing a lethal prescription for a patient to take voluntarily, or injecting a non-autonomous or incompetent patient with a lethal medication. These acts are morally dissimilar, and yet the term might imply that they can be discussed, understood, and managed as though they were morally the same. Discourse about legalized killing can be uncomfortable, but debating "aid-in-dying" as a morally *equivalent[99] group of actions is impossible. Whenever ethical debate is held regarding the ending of a life, vocabulary that is sufficiently *procedurally[100] and morally specific should be employed to *facilitate[101] meaningful discussion and avoid confusion. *The term "aid-in-dying" is far too vague and associates too many ethically diverse actions to be truly useful or enlightening in either political or medical discussion.

GRAMMAR

태(Voice)

1. 태(Voice)란?

주어와 술어동사의 능동과 수동 관계를 나타내는 형식을 태라 한다. 즉 행위자(agent)와 피행위자(patient) 사이의 관계를 나타내는 동사의 표현 양식을 말한다. 능동태(active voice)는 타동사+목적어의 형식으로 나타나며, 수동태(passive voice)는 능동태의 목적어를 주어로 삼고 동사는 be동사 + 과거분사의 형식을 취한다. 수동태는 행위에 의해 영향을 받는 사람이나 사물에 포커스를 둔다.

> Mr. Smith locks the gate at 6 o'clock every night. (능동태)
> The gate is locked at 6 o'clock every night. (수동태)

> The janitor always opens the door → The door is always opened by the janitor
> 행위자 피행위자 피행위자 행위자

1) 수동태가 주로 사용되는 구문은 다음과 같다.

(1) 특별히 피행위자를 드러내고자 할 때

My dog was hit by a car.

(2) 행위자가 중요하지 않거나 알려지지 않을 때

The United Jewerly store has been robbed several times.
(유나이티드 보석가게는 여러 번 강도 당했다)
The Yalta Agreement was signed during World War Two.
(얄타 협정은 2차 세계대전 중 조인되었다)

(3) 행위자를 드러내지 않으려 할 때

Your earliest reply will be appreciated. (빨리 답해 주시면 감사하겠습니다)

2) 수동태의 형태: be + 과거분사

am/is/are + 과거분사: 현재수동
was/were + 과거분사: 과거수동
has/have been + 과거분사: 현재완료수동
had been + 과거분사: 과거완료수동
am/is/are + being + 과거분사: 현재진행수동
was/were + being + 과거분사: 과거진행수동
has/have been + being + 과거분사: 현재완료진행수동
had been + being + 과거분사: 과거완료진행수동
will be + 과거분사: 미래수동
will be + being + 과거분사: 미래진행수동
will have been + 과거분사: 미래완료수동
will have been + being + 과거분사: 미래완료진행수동

2. 유사수동태

1) **be supposed to**는 다음 세 가지 의미로 사용된다.

(1) it is supposed to = it is said to

Let's go and see that movie. It's supposed to be very good.

(=it is said to be very good) (그 영화는 아주 좋다고 들었다)

(2) Something is supposed to happen = it is planned, arranged, or expected.
(~하기로 되어있다)
I'd better hurry. It's almost 8:00 and I'm supposed to meet Ann 8:15.
(=I have arranged to meet Ann; I said I would meet her)
(앤을 8:15에 만나기로 되어있다)

(3) You're not supposed to do something = it is not allowed or advisable for you to do it.(~하는 것이 허락되지 않는다)
You're not supposed to park your car here.(=you're not allowed to park here)
(너의 차를 여기에 주차해서는 안 된다)

PHRASES and STRUCTURES

* In the balance are crucial issues.
중요한 문제들이 불확실한 상태에 있다.
= Crucial issues are in the balance.
(be/hang) in the balance 앞날을 알 수 없는(불확실한) 상태에 (있다)

* Debate about assisted suicide is currently in full swing in Great Britain, **where** prosecution of family members **who** have assisted desperate patients to travel abroad to commit suicide has elicited public outcry.
영국에서는 현재 도움을 받는 자살에 관한 논란이 한창인데, 이곳에서 절망적인 환자가 자살을 하기 위해 해외로 여행하는데 도움을 주던 가족들에 대한 기소가 대중의 격렬한 항의를 이끌어 내었다.
= Debate about assisted suicide **is currently in full swing** in Great Britain, **and there(in Great Britain)** prosecution of family members, **and they** have assisted desperate patients to travel abroad to commit suicide has elicited public outcry.
is currently in full swing 현재 한창 진행 중이다
where = and there(in Great Britain)
who = and + they(family members)

* anticipate **what** ethical questions remain to be answered
답변되어야 할 어떠한 윤리적 문제들이 여전히 있는지 예상하다
what은 여기서 의문형용사로 사용됨(어떠한)

* The term always refers to an act of killing **that** meets certain criteria **described** in this article.
그 용어는 죽이는 행위를 지칭하는데, 그 행위는 이 기사에서 기술되는 몇 가지 기준들을 충족한다.
= The term always refers to an act of killing, **and it(the act of killing)** meets certain criteria **(which are) described** in this article
주격 관계대명사 that = and + it(the act of killing)
과거분사(described) 앞에서 관계대명사의 주격 + be 동사 생략

* Suicide is "self-killing," **which** may or may not require the aid of another person.
  자살은 스스로를 죽이는 것인데, 그것은 다른 사람의 도움을 필요로 할 수도 있고 하지 않을 수도 있다.
  = Suicide is "self-killing," **and it(self-killing)** may or may not require the aid of another person.
  which = and + it(self-killing)

* "Assisted suicide" is a suicide **that does** require the aid of another person.
  조력자살은 자살인데, 그것은 다른 사람의 도움이 반드시 필요하다.
  = "Assisted suicide" is a suicide, **and it(suicide)** does require the aid of another person.
  주격 관계대명사 that = and + it(suicide)
  does는 강조를 위해 사용되었음

* **It** may be reasonable **to** assume that **a suicide in which** a physician provides aid **that** a non-physician would not have been able to provide **does constitute** physician-assisted suicide.
  그런 자살이, 그런데 그 자살에서 의사는 도움을 제공하는데, 그 도움은 의사가 아닌 사람이 제공 할 수 없었을 도움으로, 바로 의사의 도움을 받는 자살이라고 가정하는 것이 합당할 것이다.
  = **It** may be reasonable **to** assume that **a suicide**, **and in it(the suicide)** a physician provides aid, **and** a non-physician would not have been able to provide **it(aid)** **does constitute** physician-assisted suicide.
  it은 **to** 이하를 가리킴
  that이하를 **to assume**하는 것은 합당할 것이다
  in which = and + in it(the suicide)
  목적격 관계대명사 that = and + it(aid)
  does는 강조의 do
  assume that절 속에서 주어는 a suicide 동사는 does constitute

* Writing a prescription is a privilege **afforded** to physicians.
  처방전을 쓰는 것은 의사에게 제공되는 특권이다.
  = Writing a prescription is a privilege **(which is) afforded** to physicians.

과거분사(afforded) 앞에서 관계대명사의 주격 + be 동사 생략

* Prescriptive assistance by a physician in a suicide **requires** that **the physician use** his or her unique privileges as a physician.
자살에서 의사에 의한 처방전의 도움은 그 의사가 그의 혹은 그녀의 의사로서의 고유의 특권을 사용할 것을 요구한다.
= Prescriptive assistance by a physician in a suicide requires that the physician **(should) use** his or her unique privileges as a physician.
require that절 속에서 주어가 3인칭 단수 현재라 하더라도 동사는 항상 원형을 사용함

* **another party** 다른 사람

* When more than one person is involved in a sequence of actions that results in death, then **that death** is termed a suicide when the last person who acts in the sequence is the one **who** dies.
한 명 이상의 사람들이 죽음을 가져오는 일련의 행동에 관여하게 되고, 그 후 그 연쇄에서 행동하는 마지막 사람이 죽는 사람일 때 그러한 죽음은 자살이라 일컬어진다.
= When more than one person is involved in a sequence of actions, **and it(a sequence of actions)** results in death, then that death is termed a suicide when the last person, **and he(the last person)** acts in the sequence is the one, **and he(the one)** dies.
a sequence of 일련의
주격 관계대명사 that = and + it(a sequence of actions)
that death에서 that은 지시형용사(그러한)
who = and + he(the last person)
who = and + he(the one)

* "motives" are the reasons **for which** we have those intentions.
동기들이 우리가 그러한 의도를 갖는 이유들이다.
= "motives" are the reasons, **and** we have those intentions **for them(reasons)**.
for which = and + for them(reasons)

* The core value **supporting that motive** must be altruism.
그러한 동기를 지지하는 핵심적인 가치는 이타심이어야 한다.

= The core value **which supports that motive** must be altruism.

supporting = which supports; supporting은 앞의 value를 수식하는 현재분사

that은 지시형용사(그러한)

* This concept is **so** engrained in our society **that** euthanasia often is referred to as "mercy killing."

이러한 개념은 우리 사회에 너무 뿌리 깊게 박혀 있어서 안락사가 종종 'mercy killing'이라고 일컬어질 정도이다.

so A that B 구문 '너무나 A해서 B할 정도이다'로 해석함

* when he injected elderly patients with lethal doses of narcotics **so that** he could inherit money **left** to him in their wills

그가 나이가 든 환자들에게 마취제의 치명적인 용량을 주사하고 그 결과 그가 그 환자들의 유언장에서 그에게 남겨진 돈을 상속할 수 있게 되었을 때

= when he injected elderly patients with lethal doses of narcotics **so that** he could inherit money (which is) **left** to him in their wills

so that ~ 구문 보통 so that ~ 앞에 ,가 없으면 '~할 목적으로'로 해석하지만 여기서는 편이하게 '그 결과 ~하게 되다'로 해석했음

과거분사(left) 앞에서 관계대명사의 주격(which) + be동사(is) 생략

* causes minimal if any psychological suffering

어떤 심리적인 고통이 있다하더라도 최소의 고통을 야기하다

= causes minimal (suffering) **(even) if (there is)** any psychological suffering

* Foresight involves conceiving of possible outcomes, **some of which** we may neither desire nor intend.

선견지명은 가능한 결과들에 관해 생각하는 것을 포함하는데, 우리는 약간의 결과들을 바라지도 의도하지도 않을 수 있다.

= Foresight involves conceiving of possible outcomes, **and** we may neither desire nor intend **some of them(outcomes).**

some of which = and + some of them(outcomes)

* Patients have the legal right in the U.S. to say **what** will be done to them.

미국에서 환자들은 그들에게 무엇이 행하여질 것인지를 말할 법적인 권리를 가진다.

= Patients have the legal right in the U.S. to say **they(people) will do what to them(patients).(능동형)**
what은 의문대명사로 '무엇'으로 해석함

* however shortened **it(her life)** might turn out to be
아무리 그것(그녀의 삶)이 짧은 것으로 판명난다 하더라도
turn out to be 판가름이 나다

* **In the first place** 우선, 먼저

* The term is further misleading in that it **confuses** foresight **with** intention.
그 용어는 선견지명이 의도와 혼동된다는 점에서 더 오해를 살 여지가 있다.
confuse A with B A와 B를 혼동하다

* Yet if a patient is competent to make decisions, **killing** them against their will **violates** other necessary criteria for euthanasia.
그렇지만 만일 환자가 결정을 내릴 수 있다면 그들의 의지에 반해서 그들을 죽이는 것은 안락사를 위한 다른 필요 기준들을 위반한다.
주어는 killing, 동사는 violates

* Furthermore, **euthanizng a patient who** is capable of making a decision and refuses euthanasia **is prohibited** by other primary ethical principles.
게다가 결정을 내릴 수 있고 안락사를 거부하는 환자를 안락사 시키는 것은 다른 일차적인 윤리적 원칙들에 의해 금지된다.
= Furthermore, euthanizng a patient, **and he(a patient)** is capable of making a decision and refuses euthanasia is prohibited by other primary ethical principles.
주어는 euthanizing a patient, 동사는 is prohibited
who = and + he(a patient)

* "involuntary euthanasia" for which a competent or previously competent patient's wishes are unknown
결정권이 있는 혹은 이전에 결정권이 있었던 환자의 바람이 그 원치 않는 안락사에 대해 알지 못한다.
= "involuntary euthanasia", **and** a competent or previously competent patient's

wishes are unknown **for it(involuntary euthanasia).**
for which = and + for it(involuntary euthanasia)

* **While commonly used**, these terms add nothing to a simpler definition of euthanasia.
이러한 용어들이 일반적으로 사용되지만, 이러한 용어들은 안락사라는 더 간단한 정의에 어떤 것도 덧붙이지 않는다.
While commonly used(분사구문) = While ~~these terms are~~(being) commonly used,

* It is important to understand that such political terms often **have little** moral, ethical, or medical meaning.
그런 정치적인 용어들은 종종 도덕적, 윤리적, 혹은 의학적 의미를 거의 가지고 있지 않다는 것을 이해하는 것이 중요하다.
It은 to이하를 받음
have little 거의 가지고 있지 않다(부정적으로 해석함)

* **a host of** 다수의

* The term "aid-in-dying" is far too vague and associates **too** many ethically diverse actions **to be** truly useful or enlightening in either political or medical discussion.
"죽음에서 도움"이라는 용어는 너무 지나치게 애매하고 너무나 많은 윤리적으로 다양한 행동들을 연상하게 해서 정치적 혹은 의학적인 논의에서 진정으로 유용할 수 없을 정도이거나 도움이 되지(밝혀주지) 못할 정도이다.
too A to B 너무나 A해서 B할 수 없다

Unit 7

The history of the death penalty[1)]

WARMING UP

- There were upwards of 25 crimes **that** resulted in the death penalty, the code stipulated, **including** the theft of temple or palace property, or **providing** refuge to an escapee slave
- at least in theory if not in practice, **with** 11 of those states **having** not carried out an execution in a decade or more
- fell even further **with** only 191 **killed** between 1960 and 1976
- Americans have the British to **blame** most **for** introducing the death penalty to their country
- the famous inventor **hailed as** the driving force
- The Eighth Amendment of the United States Constitution "**prohibits** the federal government **from imposing** excessive bail, excessive fines, or cruel and unusual punishment

1) This article was written by Oliver Pickup on August 31, 2018. The source is https://www.raconteur.net/current-affairs/the-history-of-the-death-penalty

Oliver Pickup investigates the history of the death penalty and asks: will *capital punishment[1] ever be completely *abolished[2] across the world?

Right now, 106 countries - just over half in the world - *have formally abolished the death penalty, according to the latest *figures[3], *produced[4] by *Amnesty International[2)] at the end of 2018. While those with a *progressive outlook[5] might determine that the number is *alarmingly[6] low in the 21st century there is good reason to be cheerful: consider that 40 years ago, in 1977, only 16 nations had formally abolished capital punishment.

For tens of thousands of years the death penalty has been a crucial feature of civilization, and its threat and application has been *justified[7] by ancient and modern leaders *across the globe to *keep societies in check. The first recorded death penalty laws can be *traced all the way back to the *reign[8] of *Hammurabi[3)], a Babylonian king who ruled from 1792 BC to 1750 BC. *There were upwards of 25 crimes that resulted in the death penalty, the *code[9] *stipulated[10], including the theft of temple or palace property, or providing refuge to an *escapee[11] slave. Murder was not on the list, *ironically enough.

1. capital punishment 사형제도
2. abolish 폐지하다
3. figure 수치
4. produce 보여주다
5. progressive outlook 혁신적인 전망
6. alarmingly 놀랄 만큼
7. justify 정당화시키다
8. reign 통치기간
9. code 법규
10. stipulate 규정하다, 명문화하다
11. escapee 도망자

History of capital punishment in America

America, where 31 of the 50 states still employ the death penalty -

2) Amnesty International 국제사면위원회.

3) Hammurabi(함무라비) 기원전 18세기경의 바빌로니아 왕으로 법령 제정으로 유명함.

12. executive director 전무(이사)
13. respectively 각각
14. prevailing 지배적인
15. country-wide = nationwide 전국에 걸쳐
16. quagmire 수렁
17. gallow 교수대
18. drown 익사시키다
19. pit 구덩이
20. baron 남작(귀족)
21. tenure 재임기간

*at least in theory if not in practice, with 11 of those states having not carried out an execution in a decade or more - is "in the midst of a climate change on capital punishment", in the words of Robert Dunham, *executive director[12] of the *Death Penalty Information Center (DPIC)[4].

Last year *there were 20 executions and 31 new death sentences handed out in the United States, marking a record low since 1991 and 1973 *respectively[13]. "We are witnessing a significant decline in the use of the death penalty, and it's a long-term decline," says Mr Dunham, suggesting that despite there being around 2,900 people *on death row the *prevailing[14] mood is that *country-wide[15] abolition is nearer than it has been for four decades. There is, however, *a fair way to go, and *Americans have the British to blame most for introducing the death penalty to their country.

When was the death penalty introduced in the UK?

There has been a long history of capital punishment in Britain. As early ago as 450 BC *the condemned were killed by being dropped into a *quagmire[16], though by the 10th century hanging from the *gallows[17] was the preferred method of execution. *Drowning[18] *pits[19] were dug and used by *barons[20] in the middle ages, and it is estimated that some 72,000 people *were put to death in *Henry VII's[5] bloody *tenure[21], from 1509 until 1547. By the 18th century

4) Death Penalty Information Center 사형정보센터.

5) Henry VII(1457~1509) 잉글랜드의 왕(재위 1485~1509). 보즈워스 전투에서 장미전쟁을 종식시킴과 동시에 튜더왕조를 개조함. 내란으로 혼란한 국내질서를 바로잡고 귀족세력을 약화시켰음. 재정을 튼튼히 하였으며, 왕권

more than 200 crimes were punishable by death in Britain, such as stealing 40 shillings from a house, or five shillings from a shop, or even cutting down a tree.

So, when was the death penalty abolished in Britain? Well, capital punishment for murder was abolished in 1965, a year after the last executions took place, and 1973 in Northern Ireland. And although the death penalty was unused henceforth it remained a legally *defined[22] punishment for *treason[23] until it was totally abolished in the UK in 1998. *America is some way behind, though gathering speed.

America's death penalty history begins in Britain

When British settlers *made landfall[24] in the Americas, in the age of discovery, they brought with them the practice of capital punishment. The first recorded execution in the colonies of the new world occurred in 1608, when Captain George Kendall was put to death in Virginia for *allegedly[25] spying for the Spanish.

Four years later Sir Thomas Dale, the governor of Virginia, *established[26] the Divine, Moral and Martial Laws. They *decreed[27] that even *petty[28] *offences[29], like *pinching[30] grapes, or *slaughtering[31] someone else's chickens, would be punished by death. Other colonies soon followed Virginia's *lead[32]. For example Duke's Laws, used from 1665 in New York, determined that the death penalty could be utilized if someone denied the existence of

22. defined 정의된
23. treason 반역죄
24. made landfall 상륙하다
25. allegedly 주장에 의하면, 이른바
26. establish 제정하다
27. decree 명하다, 선언하다
28. petty 사소한, 하찮은
29. offence 위법행위, 범죄
30. pinch 꼭 집다, (사소한 것을)훔치다
31. slaughter 도살하다
32. lead 본(보기), 선례

을 신장시켜 영국의 절대왕정의 기초를 굳혔음.

33. pivotal
중심이 되는

34. defeat
무산시키다

35. bill
청구서, 법안

36. solitary
단 하나의

37. electrocution
전기처형

38. viable
실행 가능한

39. bizarre
기이한, 특이한

40. incandescent
백열성의

41. embroiled
~에 휩쓸린

42. corporate battle
기업싸움

God, or hit their parents.

We are witnessing a significant decline in the use of the death penalty

*It wasn't until 1776's *Declaration of Independence* - the *pivotal[33] document announcing the 13 American colonies at war with Britain regarded themselves as independent sovereign states - that the first death penalty reforms were made in America. *Thomas Jefferson[6)], the principal author of the Declaration of Independence who would go on to become the third president of America, from 1801 to 1809, and four others were tasked with revising Virginia's laws. *The pioneering group recommended that the death penalty be used for treason and murder alone, and the proposed legislature *defeated[34] the *bill[35] by a *solitary[36] vote.

How the electric chair was invented

Before the late 1880s, hanging was the favoured death penalty method in America, though that all changed when *electrocution[37] entered the market as a *viable[38] alternative in rather *bizarre[39] circumstances. Edison Company, the organization of Thomas Edison - *the famous inventor hailed as the driving force behind the phonograph, the *incandescent[40] light bulb, and early motion picture cameras, among numerous other innovations - became *embroiled[41] in a *corporate battle[42] with Westinghouse Electric Company. The

6) Thomas Jefferson(1743~1826) 미국 제 3대 대통령.

former used *direct current[43] (DC) in its electrical systems, while the latter was pushing for nationwide electrification with *alternating current[44] (AC). To highlight the dangers of AC, a *determined[45] Edison decided to employ *shock tactics[46], and electrocuted animals with Westinghouse generators in various public *demonstrations[47].

Although Edison had proven his point, *albeit[48] in a *gruesome[49] fashion, he had also *inadvertently[50] invented the electric chair. In 1888 the state of New York, where most of the AC demonstrations had taken place, *dismantled[51] its gallows and built the first such seat of death in America. Two years later William Kemmler became the fatality-inducing furniture's earliest victim.

A third method of execution, *cyanide[52] gas, was introduced in 1924 by the state of Nevada, during a *tough[53] period when Americans were enduring *Prohibition[7)] and the *Great Depression[8)] and there was a *resurgence[54] in the use of the death penalty. Indeed, in the 1930s there were 167 executions per year, on average - the most in the country's history.

43. direct current 직류

44. alternating current 교류

45. determined 단호한

46. shock tactic 충격전술

47. demonstration 설명, 입증

48. albeit = though 비록 ~일지라도

49. gruesome 소름끼치는

50. inadvertently 우연히, 의도치 않게

51. dismantle 해체하다

52. cyanide 청산가리

53. tough 힘든, 어려운

54. resurgence 부활

Public opinion *turns against the death penalty

*In the 1950s, following World War II - during which over 60 million people died (equal to three per cent of the planet's population) - the Americans began to turn against the death penalty.

7) Prohibition (미국에서) 금주법 시행 시대(1920년~1933년).

8) Great Depression 1929년 뉴욕 증권시장의 주가대폭락을 계기로 1930년대 엄습한 세계적인 공황. '검은 목요일'로 불리는 1929년 10월 24일, 뉴욕 주식시장의 대폭락에 의하여 촉발되어 전 세계로 확대된 경제 공황을 의미함. 당시 세계는 극심한 경제적 혼란 상태로 접어들었고 이로 인하여 기업들의 도산, 대량 실업, 디플레이션 등이 초래되었음.

55. plummet
곤두박질치다, 급락하다

56. rule
판결하다

57. arbitrariness
독단, 임의성

58. capriciousness
변덕스러움

59. bail
보석(금)

60. fine
벌금

61. statute
법규

62. void
무효로 하다

63. commute
감형하다

64. hastily
급히, 서둘러서

65. lethal
치명적인

Many of America's allies started to abolish, or at least limit, capital punishment, and the number of executions in the US *plummeted[55] from 1,289 in the 1940s to 715 in the next decade, and *fell even further with only 191 killed between 1960 and 1976.

Public support for the death penalty in America reached a record low in 1966, and in the landmark **Furman v. Georgia* case[9)], which concluded on June 29, 1972, *the Supreme Court *ruled[56] that the *arbitrariness[57] and *capriciousness[58] of sentencing violated the Eighth Amendment of the United States Constitution, which "prohibits the federal government from imposing excessive *bail[59], excessive *fines[60], or cruel and unusual punishment". Therefore, 40 death penalty *statutes[61] were instantly *voided[62] and 629 death sentences *commuted[63].

Many states *hastily[64] re-wrote their statutes, though it was 1977 - the same year Oklahoma became the first state to adopt *lethal[65] injection as a means of execution - before the death penalty was used again, in Utah. And following an increase in the 1990s (with 98 executions in 1999 the highest amount in the last four decades) the numbers have steadily declined in the 21st century.

The death penalty in America *is on the way out

DPIC statistics show that in the so-called modern era of the death penalty in America, from 1976, there have been 1,458 executions (as of July 31), and since 2007 alone seven states - Connecticut,

9) Furman v. Georgia case 1972년 미국 대법원이 5대 4 판결로 미국에서 모든 사형제를 폐지했던 형사 사건.

Delaware, Illinois, Maryland, New Jersey, New Mexico, and New York - have abolished it.

It could take another decade, or even a century, before America as a whole can join the majority of the world's countries in formally abolishing capital punishment, *such is the complicated *state-to-state[66] legal structure. When that inevitable day finally arrives, other nations will surely *follow suit, such is America's influence. And *given that the indications are it will happen sooner rather than later, there is yet another reason for those who oppose the death penalty to be optimistic.

66. state-to-state 주마다의

GRAMMAR

가정법(Subjunctive Mood)

1. 법(Mood)이란?

말할 내용에 대한 화자의 태도를 나타내는 방식을 법이라 한다. 예를 들어 명령이나 요구를 표현하기 위해 사용하는 동사의 표현 양식은 명령법(Imperative Mood)이 되고, 비현실적인 것, 소망, 추측, 긴급성 등을 나타내기 위한 것은 가정법(Subjunctive Mood)이 되고, 명령법이나 가정법을 요하지 않는 모든 상황에서 사용되는 것은 직설법(Indicative Mood)이 된다. 가정법은 다음과 같은 상황을 나타낸다.

1) 비현실적인 조건

If I were you, I would go to bed early.(가정법 과거로 현재시간을 나타냄)

(내가 너라면 일찍 잠자리에 들텐데)

If I had been you, I would have gone to bed early.(가정법 과거완료로 과거시간)

(내가 너였더라면 일찍 잠자리에 들었을 텐데)

2) 소망

I wish that I were you.(가정법 과거로 현재의 소망을 나타냄)

I wish that I had been you yesterday.(가정법 과거완료로 과거의 소망)

* 만일 소망이 현재나 미래에 실현될 가능성이 조금이라도 있으면 that 절에 조동사의 과거형을 사용한다.

I wish that it would stop raining.(비가 멎었으면 하고 바란다)

I wish I might see him once more.(다시 한 번 더 그를 만날 수 있기를 바란다)

3) 추측

He acts as if he were a king.(가정법 과거로 현재시간을 나타냄)

He acts as if he had been a king once.(가정법 과거완료로 과거시간)

4) 어느 정도의 긴급성

He insisted that his wife be on time.(가정법 현재형)

It is necessary that he be on time.(가정법 현재형)

2. 가정법과 직설법

> a) If he has some money, he will lend you.(직설법)
> b) If he had some money, he would lend you.(가정법)

a)는 의미상으로는 '가정'을 나타내지만 직설법이라고 하는 것은 조건절(If절)에 사용된 동사(has)가 인칭과 시제의 일치를 따라 어형이 바뀌는 정형동사이기 때문이다. 반면에 b)를 가정법이라 하는 것은 조건절에 사용된 동사(had)가 인칭이나 시제의 일치를 따르지 않고 사용되는 어형이기 때문이다. 이와 같이 가정법에서는 인칭, 시제, 수 등과 상관없이 특정한 동사의 어형으로 사용된다.

3. 가정법의 시제

1) 가정법 과거

종속절	주절
If + 주어 + 동사의 과거형 ~	주어 + would/should/could/might + 동사원형

가정법 과거는 **현재 사실과 반대되는 가정**을 나타낸다. 위의 예에서 If he has some money(그가 돈을 좀 가지고 있다면)(직설법)은 그가 돈을 가지고 있을 가능성을 배제하지 않지만(돈을 가지고 있는지 확실하게 알 수는 없지만), If he had some money(그가 돈을 좀 가지고 있다면)(가정법)은 "그는 돈을 가지고 있지 않는데"라는 사실을 전제로 한다.

2) 가정법 과거완료

종속절	주절
If + 주어 + had + 동사의 과거분사 ...	주어 + would/should/could/might/would + have + 동사의 과거분사

가정법 과거완료는 **과거의 사실에 반대되는 가정**을 나타낸다.

If I had been you, I should have done so.

(만일 내가 너였더라면 당연히 그렇게 했었을 텐데)

3) 가정법 현재

가정법 현재는 인칭이나 시제에 관계없이 항상 동사의 원형을 술어동사로 사용하는 문장형식을 가리키는데 이 표현은 고어체나 격식체에 속하며 현대영어에서는 많이 사용되지 않는다.

종속절	주절
If + 주어 + 동사의 원형...	주어 + will/can/may/shall + 동사원형

If gold rust, what shall iron do?

(금이 녹슨다면 하물며 철이야 어떻겠는가)

If this be the case, then we must help him at once.

(만일 이것이 사실이라면, 우리는 당장 그를 도와야 할 것이다)

때때로 법조문 같은데서 사용된다.

If any person be found guilty, he shall have the right of appeal.

(유죄판결을 받을 경우 그 사람은 항소의 권리를 갖는다)

또한 주어의 요구, 주장, 권고, 간청 등을 나타내는 술어동사가 이끄는 절이나 주관적 판단을 나타내는 형용사(necessary, important, urgent, imperative 등)가 보어로 사용된 구문에서 사용된다. 주로 미국영어에서는 원형을 사용하지만 영국영어에서는 should + 동사원형이 사용된다.

I demanded that she leave the place immediately.

It was necessary that she leave the place immediately.

* 조건절에서 동사의 현재형이 사용되는 경우는 직설법 현재형을 주로 미래의 불확실한 사실을 나타낸다. 즉 조건절에서 현재시제형이 미래대신 사용된다.

4) 가정법 미래형

가정법 미래시제형은 앞으로 일어날 가능성이 아주 희박할 때 사용된다. 이때 주절의 동사 형식은 여러 가지로 나타난다.

종속절	주절
If + 주어 + should + 동사원형 ...	주어 + would/will/could/might/may/should + 동사원형

If you should change your mind, no one would blame you.
(설사 네가 너의 마음을 바꾼다하더라도 아무도 너를 욕하지 않을 거야)

4. 가정법 관련 구문

1) as if / as though

You talk as if you knew a great deal about this.
It looks as though it might rain.

2) If의 생략형

Were I as rich as he(=If I were as rich as he), I would go abroad.
Had I known(=If I had known) you didn't have a key, I wouldn't have locked the door.

3) If 절의 대용

Without air(=If there were no air), no living things could exist.

But for your assistance(=If it had not been for your assistance), I could not have succeeded.

I am very busy this week; otherwise(=If I were not busy) I would certainly come to your party.

To look at him(=If you looked at him), you could hardly help laughing.

A true friends would have acted differently.

(친한 친구라면 그렇게는 행동하지 않았을 텐데)

4) 조건절의 생략

He could easily do it.(그는 쉽게 할 수 있을 텐데)

5) 주절의 생략

Had I but known it!(그것을 알기만 했더라도!)

PHRASES and STRUCTURES

* have formally abolished the death penalty, according to the latest figures, **produced** by Amnesty International
가장 최근의 수치에 따르면, 그런데 그 수치는 국제사면위원회에 의해 보여 졌는데, 공식적으로 사형제를 폐지했다
= have formally abolished the death penalty, according to the latest figures, **(and they(figures) were) produced** by Amnesty International
produced(분사구문)= ~~and they(figures) were(being~~) produced

* **across the globe** 전 세계에서

* **keep societies in check** 사회를 억누르다

* **traced all the way back to** ~ ~까지 거슬러 추적하다

* There were upwards of 25 crimes **that** resulted in the death penalty, the code **stipulated, including** the theft of temple or palace property, or **providing** refuge to an escapee slave.
25개 이상의 범죄들이 있었는데, 그 범죄들은 사형을 야기했으며(사형에 처하도록 했으며), 사형은 명문화된 법규였고, 그 법규는 사원이나 궁전 재산을 훔치는 것 혹은 도망친 노예에게 피신처를 제공하는 것을 포함했다.
= There were upwards of 25 crimes, **and they(crimes)** resulted in the death penalty, the code **(which was) stipulated, and they(crimes) included** the theft of temple or palace property, or **providing** refuge to an escapee slave.
주격 관계대명사 that = and + they(crimes)
the death penalty, the code stipulated **,와 the code는 동격**
과거분사(stipulated) 앞에서 관계대명사의 주격(which)과 be동사 생략
including(분사구문) = ~~and they(crimes)~~ included
providing(동명사) = 제공하는 것
upwards of ~ ~의 이상

* **ironically enough** 아주 역설적이게도

* at least in theory if not in practice, **with** 11 of those states **having** not carried out an execution in a decade or more
  실제는 아닐지라도 적어도 이론적으로는, 사형제를 운영하는 31개 주 중에 11개 주는 십년 이상 동안에 사형을 집행하지 않고 있는데
  with + 명사 + 현재분사 명사가 ~한 채
  carry out execution 사형을 집행하다

* There were 20 executions and 31 new death sentences **handed out** in the United States, **marking** a record low since 1991 and 1973 respectively.
  미국에서 배포된 20건의 집행과 31건의 사형선고가 있었는데 그것들은 각각 1991년과 1973년 이래로 기록적인 낮은 수치를 나타낸다.
  = There were 20 executions and 31 new death sentences **(which were) handed** out in the United States, **and they mark** a record low since 1991 and 1973 respectively.
  과거분사**(handed) 앞에서 관계대명사의 주격(which)과 be동사 생략**
  hand out 배포하다
  marking(분사구문) = ~~and they~~ mark

* **on death row** 사형 선고를 받고 집행을 기다리는
  death row (교도소의) 사형수 수감 건물

* **a fair way to go** 마땅히 가야할 길

* Americans have the British to **blame** most **for** introducing the death penalty to their country.
  미국인들은 미국에 사형제를 도입 한 데 대해 영국인들을 가장 큰 책임으로 돌렸다.
  blame A for B A를 B의 책임으로 돌리다
  They **blamed** me **for** the accident. 그들의 그 사고에 대한 책임을 나에게 돌렸다.

* **the condemned** (to death) (사형)선고가 내려진 사람들(사형수)
  the + 형용사 = 복수보통명사

* **were put to death** 사형에 처해졌다
be put to death 사형에 처하다

* America is **some way** behind, though gathering speed.
미국은 비록 속도를 올리고 있다하더라도 다소 뒤쳐져 있다.
some way 얼마간, 어느 정도

* **It wasn't** until 1776's Declaration of Independence - the pivotal document announcing the 13 American colonies at war with Britain regarded themselves as independent sovereign states - **that** the first death penalty reforms were made in America.
미국에서 이루어진 첫 번째 사형제 개혁은 1776년의 독립선언서 까지 단행되지 않았다. 독립선언서는 영국과의 전쟁에서 미국의 13개 식민지들이 그들 자체가 독립적인 주권국가로 간주된다고 선언한 중심 문서이다.
it is ~ that 강조구문
- A - = (and it is) A

* The pioneering group **recommended** that the death penalty be used for treason and murder alone, and the proposed legislature defeated the bill by a solitary vote.
그 개척적인 집단은 사형제가 반역과 살인에 대해서만 사용되어져야 한다고 권고했는데 발의를 받은 입법부는 단 한 표 차이로 그 법안을 무산시켰다.
recommend(insist, require, suggest, order) + that + 주어 + (should) + 동사원형
The motion was **defeated** by 19 votes.
그 안건은 19표 차이로 무산되었다.

* the famous inventor **hailed as** the driving force
원동력으로 불리어졌던 유명한 발명가
= **(and he is)** the famous inventor **(who was) hailed** as the driving force
= **(and he is)** the famous inventor, people **hailed** him(the inventor) **as** the driving force (능동형)
과거분사(hailed) 앞에서 관계대명사의 주격(which)과 be동사 생략
hail A as B A를 B라고 부르다

* **turns against ~** ~에 대해 등을 돌리다

* In the 1950s, **following** World War II - **during which** over 60 million people died (equal to three per cent of the planet's population) -
1950년대에, 그런데 1950년대는 2차 세계대전을 뒤따르는데, 그 기간 중에 6000만 명 이상이 죽었다(그 수치는 전 세계 인구의 3%와 같다)
= In the 1950s, **and it(1950s)** followed World War II - **and during it(World War II)** over 60 million people died **((and it(over 60 million people) is) equal to** three per cent of the planet's population) -
following = ~~and it(1950s)~~ followed
during which = and + during it(World War II)
equal to = ~~and it(over 60 million people) is~~(being) equal to
equal to ~ ~와 같은

* fell even further **with** only 191 **killed** between 1960 and 1976
1960년과 1976년 사이에 단지 191명만 죽게 되면서 (미국에서의 사형집행의 수가) 훨씬 더 떨어졌다
with + 명사 + 과거분사 명사가 ~가 되면서

* The Supreme Court ruled that the arbitrariness and capriciousness of sentencing violated the Eighth Amendment of the United States Constitution, **which "prohibits** the federal government **from imposing** excessive bail, excessive fines, or cruel and unusual punishment."
대법원은 선고의 임의성과 변덕스러움이 미국 헌법 수정조항 8조를 위반했다고 판결했는데, 그 수정조항 8조는 연방 정부가 과도한 보석, 과도한 벌금, 혹은 잔인하고 특이한 처벌을 하지 못하게 한다.
= The Supreme Court ruled that the arbitrariness and capriciousness of sentencing violated the Eighth Amendment of the United States Constitution, **and it(the Eighth Amendment)** "prohibits the federal government from imposing excessive bail, excessive fines, or cruel and unusual punishment."
which = and + it(the Eighth Amendment)
prohibit(prevent) + 목적어 + from + doing 목적어가 ~하지 못하게 하다

* **is on the way out** 나가는 길이다

* Such is the complicated state-to-state legal structure.

그런데 그러한 것(사형제)은 복잡한 주마다의 법률 구조이다.
= **(and)** such is the complicated state-to-state legal structure.

* **follow suit** 방금 남이 한대로 따라 하다, 전례를 따르다

* **given that** the indications are **(that)** it will happen sooner rather than later, there is yet another reason **for** those who oppose the death penalty **to be** optimistic
그 표시들이 그것(사형제 폐지)이 조만간 일어날 것이라는 것을 고려하면 사형제도를 반대하는 사람들이 낙관적일 수 있는 또 다른 이유가 있다
given that ~ ~을 고려(감안)하면
sooner rather than later 조만간
for 이하는 to 부정사(to be)의 의미상의 주어

Unit 8

Ethicists Generally Agree: The *Pro-Life[1] Arguments Are Worthless[1)]

WARMING UP

- Opposition to abortion **is far from** unanimous
- Yet **few** seem to take notice
- **The view that** abortion is, with rare exceptions, seriously immoral has received **little support** in the recent philosophical literature
- **Lacking** good reasons or **armed** with weak ones, many will object that their moral beliefs derive from their Gods
- There is **nothing more** to morality **than** this
- There **simply isn't** a strong scriptural tradition in Christianity against abortion
- **Having done this** the vast majority of ethicists have concluded that abortion isn't generally morally problematic

1) This article was written by Abortion John Messerly on May 10, 2016, and appeared at Reason and Meaning. The source is https://reasonandmeaning.com/2016/05/10/ethicists-generally-agree-the-pro-life- arguments-are-worthless/

Abortion continues to make political news, but *a question rarely asked by politicians or other *interlocutors[2] is: what do professional ethicists think about abortion? If ethicists have reached a *consensus[3] about the morality or immorality of abortion, surely their conclusions should be important. And, as a professional ethicist myself, I can tell you that among ethicists *it is *exceedingly[4] rare to find *defenders[5] of *the view that abortion is murder. In fact, support for this anti-abortion position, *to the extent it exists at all, comes almost *exclusively[6] from the small percentage of philosophers who are *theists[7]. And even among theists, *opposition to abortion is far from *unanimous[8]. *Yet few seem to take notice.

To support the claim that the vast majority of ethicists reject the pro-life position, *consider the *disclaimer[9] that appears in the most *celebrated[10] anti-abortion *piece[11] in the philosophical ethics literature, Don Marquis' "Why Abortion Is Immoral." Marquis begins:

*The view that abortion is, with rare exceptions, seriously immoral has received little support in the recent philosophical literature. No doubt *most philosophers *affiliated[12] with secular *institutions of higher education[2)] believe that the anti-abortion position is either a symptom of irrational religious *dogma[13] or *a conclusion generated by seriously confused philosophical argument.

Marquis *concedes[14] that abortion isn't considered immoral according to most ethicists, *but why they not, for the most part, find

1. pro-life 낙태[낙태 합법화]에 반대하는
2. interlocutor 대화상대자
3. consensus 의견일치
4. exceedingly 대단히
5. defender 옹호자
6. exclusively 오로지
7. theist 유신론자
8. unanimous 만장일치의, 모두 의견이 같은
9. disclaimer 부인(행위), 거부
10. celebrated 유명한
11. piece 부분, 기사(글)
12. affiliate (더 큰 회사기관 등과) 제휴[연계]하다
13. dogma 신조
14. concede 인정하다

2) institutions of higher education 고등교육기관(대학).

abortion morally problematic? *Perhaps professional ethicists, who are *typically[15] non-religious philosophers, find nothing morally *objectionable[16] about abortion because they aren't religious. In other words, *if they were *devout[17] they would recognize abortion as a moral *abomination[18]. But we could easily *turn this around. Perhaps *religiously oriented[19] ethicists oppose abortion because they are religious. In other words, if they were not devout, they would see that abortion isn't morally problematic. So both religious and secular ethicists could claim that the other side *prejudges[20] the case.

However, it is *definitely[21] not the case that secular ethicists *care less about[22] life or morality than religious ethicists. Consider that *virtually[23] all moral philosophers believe that murder, theft, *torture[24], and lying are immoral because *cogent[25] arguments *underlie[26] such prohibitions. Oftentimes *there is little difference between the views of religious and secular ethicists regarding moral issues. Moreover, when there is disagreement among the two groups, perhaps the secular philosophers *are ahead of the ethical curve with their general acceptance of abortion, homosexuality, and certain forms of *euthanasia[27].

How then do we *adjudicate[28] disputes in the moral realm when ethicists, like ordinary people, start with different assumptions? *The key to answering this question is to emphasize reason and argument, the *hallmarks[29] of doing philosophical ethics. Both secular and religious individuals can participate in rational discourse to resolve

15. typically 보통, 일반적으로
16. objectionable 불쾌한
17. devout 독실한
18. abomination 혐오스러운 것
19. religiously oriented 종교지향의
20. prejudge 예단(속단)하다
21. definitely 분명히(틀림없이)
22. care about ~에 관심을 가지다
23. virtually 사실상, 거의
24. torture 고문
25. cogent 설득력 있는
26. underlie ~의 기저를 이루다
27. euthanasia 안락사
28. adjudicate 판결(판정)을 내리다
29. hallmark 특징(특질)

their disputes. In fact, *natural law moral theory[3] - the *dominant[30] ethical theory throughout the history of Christianity - *claims that morality is grounded in reason, which implies that what is right is supported by the best rational arguments. Natural law theorists argue that *by exercising the human reason their God has given them, they can understand what is right and wrong. *Thus secular and religious philosophers work in the same *arena[31], one where moral truths are those supported by the best reasons.

That ethicists emphasize rational discourse may be *counter-intuitive[32] in a society dominated by appeals to emotion, prejudice, faith, and group *loyalty[33]. But ethicists, secular and religious alike, try to *impartially[34] examine the arguments for and against moral *propositions[35] in order to determine where the weight of reason lies in the matter. Ethicists may not be perfect *umpires[36], and the truth about moral matters is often difficult to determine, but ethicists are trained to be impartial and *thorough[37] when analyzing arguments. Some are better at this than others, but when a *significant majority[38] agrees, it is probably because some arguments really are stronger than others.

Now you might wonder what makes ethicists better able to adjudicate between good and bad arguments than ordinary people. The answer is that professional ethicists are *schooled[39] in logic and the critical thinking skills demanded by those who carefully and

30. dominant 지배적인
31. arena 무대
32. counter-intuitive 직관에 반대되는
33. loyalty 충성
34. impartially 치우치지 않고, 편견 없이
35. proposition 문제, 과제
36. umpire 심판
37. thorough 빈틈없는, 철두철미한
38. significant majority 상당한 다수, 대다수
39. school 훈련시키다, 교육하다

3) natural law moral theory(윤리법, 도덕률, 자연법) 하느님이 인간 본성에 심어 준 도덕적 법칙의 총체로 인간이 본성적으로 부여받은 생활 규범의 총체를 말함.

40. conscientiously 양심적으로
41. take notice 주의(주목)하다
42. fervently 열렬하게
43. scrutiny 철저한 검토
44. impartial 공정한
45. expert 전문적인
46. object 반대하다, 이의를 제기하다

*conscientiously[40] examine arguments. They are also trained in the more abstract fields of *meta-ethics[4)], which considers the meaning of moral terms and concepts, as well as in ethical theory, which considers norms, standards, or criteria for moral conduct. Moreover, they *are familiar with the best philosophical arguments that have been advanced for and against moral propositions. *So they are in a good position to reject arguments that may influence those unfamiliar with favored positions.

All this education doesn't mean that *the majority of ethicists are right, so individuals who disagree with them may choose to follow their own conscience. But if the vast majority of ethicists agree about an ethics issue, we should *take notice[41]. *It might be that the reasons you give for your *fervently[42] held moral beliefs don't stand up to critical *scrutiny[43]. *Perhaps they can't be rationally defended as well as those reached after conscientious, informed, and *impartial[44] analysis. This doesn't mean that you should ignore your conscience and accept *expert[45] opinion, but if you are serious about a moral problem you should want to know the views of those who have thoroughly studied the issue.

At this point, you might *object[46] that there are no moral experts because ethics is relative to an individual's opinions or emotions. You might say that the experts have their opinion and you have yours, and that's the end of it. Perhaps our view of behaviors in the moral realm are similar to how we view carrots - some people like them

4) meta- '더 높은', '초월한'의 뜻을 나타냄.

and some don't. This theory is called personal *moral relativism[5]. However, *not only do most ethicists reject moral relativism, so must pro-lifers. After all, pro-lifers don't think that the moral prohibition against abortion is relative; they think it's absolute. They believe that there are good reasons why abortion is immoral and any rational person should accept those reasons. However, these reasons must be evaluated to see if they are really good ones; to see if they *convince[47] other *knowledgeable[48] persons. Yet so far, the pro-life arguments haven't persuaded many ethicists.

*Lacking good reasons or armed with weak ones, many will object that their moral beliefs derive from their Gods. *To base your ethical views on Gods you would need to know: 1) if Gods exist; 2) if they are good; 3) if they *issue good commands; 4) how to find the commands; and 5) the proper version and translation of the holy books issuing commands, or the right interpretation of a *revelation[49] of the commands, or the *legitimacy[50] of a church authority[51] issuing commands. Needless to say, *it is hard, if not impossible, to know any of this.

Consider just the interpretation problem. When does a *seemingly[52] straightforward command from a holy book like, "thou shalt not kill," apply? In self-defense? In war? Always? And to whom does it apply? To non-human animals? *Intelligent aliens[53]? Serial killers? All living things? The unborn? The brain-dead?

47. convince 납득시키다

48. knowledgeable 많이 아는, 식견이 있는

49. revelation 계시

50. legitimacy 합법성

51. church authority 교회 권위자

52. seemingly 외견상으로, 겉보기에는

53. intelligent aliens 지능이 있는 외계인

5) moral relativism(도덕적 상대주의) 시공간을 초월해 지켜야 할 도덕법칙은 없다고 보는 견해로 도덕적 상대주의에서는 보편적이며 불변하는 가치는 존재하지 않고, 한 사회 안에서도 개인의 행동을 규제할 어떤 근거도 없기 때문에 도덕문제에 관한 한 누구에게나 획일적으로 적용되는 규범은 없다는 점을 근본 입장으로 삼음.

54. adultery
간통

55. vision
(종교적인) 환영

56. revelation
계시

Religious commands such as “don’t kill,” “honor thy parents,” and “don’t commit *adultery[54]” are ambiguous. Difficulties also arise if we hear voices commanding us, or if we accept an institution’s authority. Why trust the voices in our heads, or institutional authorities?

For the sake of argument though, let’s assume: that there are Gods; that you know the true one; that your God issues good commands; that you *have access to those commands because you have found the right book or church, or had the right *vision[55], or heard the right voices; and that you interpret and understand the command correctly - even if they came from a book that has been translated from one language to another over thousands of years, or from a long-ago *revelation[56]. It is almost impossible that you are correct about all this, but for the sake of the argument let’s say that you are. However, even in this case, most philosophers would argue that you can’t base ethics on your God.

To understand why you can’t base ethics on Gods consider the question: what is the relationship between the Gods and their commands? A classic formulation of this relationship is called the *divine-command theory[6)]. According to divine command theory, things are right or wrong simply because the Gods command or forbid them. *There is nothing more to morality than this. It’s like a parent who says to a child: it’s right because I say so. To see how this

6) divine-command theory(신의 명령이론) 어떤 행동은 만일 신에 의해 명령을 받게 되념 도덕적으로 좋고 신에 의해 금지되면 도덕적으로 나쁘다고 주장하는 이론.

formulation of the relationship fails, consider a famous philosophical *conundrum[57]: "Are things right because the Gods command them, or do the Gods command them because they are right?"

If things are right simply because the Gods command them, then those commands are *arbitrary[58]. In that case, the Gods could have made their *commandments[59] backward! If divine *fiat[60] is enough to make something right, then the Gods could have commanded us to kill, lie, cheat, steal and commit adultery, and those behaviors would then be moral. But the Gods can't make something right if it's wrong. The Gods can't make torturing children morally acceptable simply by divine *decree[61], and that is the main reason why most Christian theologians reject divine command theory.

On the other hand, if the Gods command things because they are right, then there are reasons for the God's commands. On this view, the Gods, in their infinite wisdom and *benevolence[62], command things because they see certain commands as good for us. But if this is the case, then *there is some standard, norm or criteria by which good or bad are measured which is independent of the Gods. Thus all us, religious and secular alike, should be looking for the reasons that certain behaviors should be condemned or praised. Even the thoughtful believer should engage in philosophical ethics.

So either the Gods commands are without reason and therefore arbitrary, or they are rational according to some standard. This standard - say that *we would all be better off - is thus the reason we should be moral and that reason, not the Gods' authority, is what

57. conundrum 난문제, 수수께끼
58. arbitrary 임의적인, 제멋대로의
59. commandment 계명
60. fiat 명령, 지시
61. decree 칙령
62. benevolence 박애

63. supposedly 추정 상

64. preacher 전도사

65. mystic 신비주의자

66. inerrancy 잘못(틀림)이 없음

67. sacred scriptures 신성한 경전

68. unequivocally 모호하지 않게, 명백히

69. multiple 많은, 다수의

makes something right or wrong. The same is true for a *supposedly[63] authoritative book. Something isn't wrong simply because a book says so. There must be a reason that something is right or wrong, and if there isn't, then the book has no moral authority on the matter.

At this point, the believer might object that the Gods have reasons for their commands, but we can't know them. Yet if the ways of the Gods are really mysterious to us, what's the point of religion? If you can't know anything about the Gods or their commands, then why follow those commands, why have religion at all, why listen to the priest or *preacher[64]? If it's all a mystery, we should remain silent or become *mystics[65].

*In response, *the religious may say that, even though they don't know the reason for their God's commands, they must oppose abortion because of the **inerrancy[66] of their *sacred scriptures[67][7)] or church tradition. They might say that since the Bible and their church oppose abortion, that's good enough for them, *despite what moral philosophers say. But in fact, neither church authority nor Christian scripture *unequivocally[68] opposes abortion.

As for scriptures, they don't generally offer specific moral guidance. Moreover, most ancient scriptures survived as oral traditions before being written down; they have been translated *multiple[69] times; they *are open to multiple interpretations; and

7) inerrancy of their sacred scriptures (성서 무류설(無謬說)) 성서 내용은 과학적으로도 절대로 오류가 없다고 믿는 것.

they don't discuss many contemporary moral issues. Furthermore, the issue of abortion doesn't arise in the Christian scriptures except *tangentially.[70] *There are a few Biblical passages quoted by conservatives to support the anti-abortion position, the most well-known is in *Jeremiah[8]: "Before I formed you in the womb I knew you, and before you were born I *consecrated[71] you." But, as anyone who has examined this passage knows, the *sanctity[72] of *fetal[73] life isn't being discussed here. Rather, Jeremiah is asserting his authority as a *prophet[74]. This is a classic example of seeking support in holy books *for a position you already hold.

Many other Biblical passages point to the more liberal view of abortion. Three times in the Bible (Genesis 38:24; Leviticus 21:9; Deuteronomy 22:20–21) the death penalty is recommended for women who have sex *out-of-wedlock[75], even though killing the women would kill their *fetuses[76]. In *Exodus[9] 21 God prescribes death as the penalty for murder, whereas the penalty for causing a woman to *miscarry[77] is a *fine[78]. In the *Old Testament[10], the fetus doesn't seem to have personhood status, and the *New Testament[11] says nothing about abortion at all. *There simply isn't a strong scriptural tradition in Christianity against abortion.

70. tangentially 약간 스칠 정도로
71. consecrate (종교의식을 통해) 축성하다
72. sanctity 존엄성, 신성함
73. fetal 태아의
74. prophet 예언자
75. out-of-wedlock 혼외의
76. fetus 태아
77. miscarry 유산
78. fine 벌금

8) Jeremiah (성서) 예레미야 히브리의 예언자), 예레미야서(書)(구약 성서의 한 권).

9) Exodus (출애굽기) 구약성서의 한 책으로, '모세 5경' 또는 '율법서'의 제2서라고 하며, 내용은 이스라엘 백성이 이집트를 탈출한 기록.

10) Old Testament (구약성서) 유대교와 그리스도교가 함께 경전으로 인정하는 종교문서들로 본래 헤브라이어로 쓰여진 24권의 책들을 그리스어로 번역하면서 39권으로 재편집하였음.

11) New Testament (신약성서) 그리스도교 경전(經典) 중 4세기 로마 가톨릭 교회가 집대성한 정경(正經)으로 보통 '신약(새로운 약속이라는 뜻)으로 약칭됨. 예수그리스도의 언행을 기록한 4권의 복음서(마태오·마르코·루가·요한의 복음서), 그 제자들의 전도행각에 관한 기록(사도행전), 여러 사도들의 편지글(서간서) 및 예언서(요한의 묵시록) 등 27서(書)로 구성되어 있으며, 전부 그리스어로 쓰여 있음.

79. contraception
피임

80. distribute
분배하다,
나누어 퍼뜨리다

81. birth control
산아제한

82. condemnation
비난

83. zygote
접합체, 수정란

84. conception
수정

85. look to
기대를 걸다

86. superimpose
덧붙이다

There also is no strong church tradition against abortion. It is true that the Catholic Church has held for centuries that activities like *contraception[79] and abortion are immoral. Yet, while most pro-lifers don't consider those *distributing[80] *birth control[81] to be murderers, the Catholic Church and others do take the extreme view that abortion is murder. Where does such a strong *condemnation[82] come from? The history of the Catholic view isn't clear on the issue, but in the 13th century, the philosopher *Thomas Aquinas[12)] argued that the soul enters the body when the *zygote[83] has a human shape. Gradually, other Christian theologians argued that the soul enters the body a few days after *conception[84], although we don't exactly know why they believed this. But, given what we now know about fetal development today, if the Catholic Church's position remained consistent with the views of Aquinas, they should say that the soul doesn't enter the zygote for at least a month or two after conception. (Note also that there really is no moment of conception.)

Thus the anti-abortion position doesn't clearly follow from either scripture or church tradition. Instead what happens is that people already have moral views, and they then *look to[85] their religion for support. In other words, moral convictions aren't usually derived from scripture or church tradition so much as *superimposed[86] on them. (For example, American Christians used the Bible to both support and oppose slavery.) But even if the pro-life position did follow from a religious tradition, that would only be relevant for

12) Thomas Aquinas(1225~1274) 토마스 아퀴나스 이탈리아 출신의 학자.

religious believers. For the rest of us, and for many religious believers too, the best way to adjudicate our disputes without *resorting to[87] violence is to conscientiously examine the arguments for and against moral propositions by shining the light of reason upon them. *Having done this the vast majority of ethicists have concluded that abortion isn't generally morally problematic.

It also clearly follows that religious believers have no right to *impose[88] their views upon the rest of us. We live in a morally *pluralistic[89] society where informed by the *ethos[90] of the *Enlightenment[13)], we should reject attempts to impose *theocracy[91]. We should allow people to follow their conscience in moral matters - you can drink alcohol - as long as others aren't harmed - you shouldn't drink and drive. In philosophy of law, this is known as the *harm principle[14)]. Now if rational *argumentation[92] supported the view that a zygote is a full person, then we might have reason to *outlaw[93] abortion, *inasmuch as[94] abortion would harm another person. (I say might because the fact that something is a person doesn't necessarily imply that it is wrong to kill it, as defenders of war, self-defense, and capital punishment claim.)

But for now, the received view among ethicists is that the pro-life arguments fail, primarily *because the fetus satisfies few if any of the necessary and sufficient conditions for personhood. *The

87. resort to
~에 의지하다

88. impose
부과하다, 강요하다

89. pluralistic
다원론의

90. ethos
기풍(정신)

91. theocracy
신권정치

92. argumentation
논증

93. outlaw
불법화하다, 금하다

94. inasmuch as
~인 한, ~이므로

13) Enlightenment(계몽주의) 17세기 후반에 시작되어 18세기 프랑스에서 전성기를 이룬 사조로. 신(神)이 아닌 인간의 이성(理性)에 의해 의식이 형성되어야 한다는 사상이며, 프랑스혁명의 사상적 배경이 되었음.

14) harm principle(해악원리) 개인의 행동들은 오로지 다른 개인들에게 해를 입히는 것을 막기 위한 것으로 제한된다는 원리로 밀(John Stuart Mill)이 On Liverty에서 말함.

95. acorn
도토리

96. fertilized
수정된

97. rhetoric
미사여구

98. punitive
징벌을 위한

99. puritanical
청교도적인

100. hypocritical
위선적인

101. self-interested
자기 본위의, 이기적인

102. feign
가장하다

103. constituency
선거구민, 지지층

104. ploy
계책, 술책

105. garner
얻다, 모으다

106. unsuspecting
의심하지 않는

impartial view, backed by contemporary biology and philosophical argumentation, is that a zygote is a potential person. That doesn't mean it has no moral significance, but it does mean that it has less significance than an actual person. An *acorn[95] may become an oak tree, *but an oak tree it is not. You may believe that your God puts souls into newly *fertilized[96] eggs, thereby granting them full personhood, but that is a religious belief which isn't grounded in science or philosophical ethics.

As for American politics and abortion, no doubt much of the anti-abortion *rhetoric[97] in American society comes from a *punitive[98], *puritanical[99] desire to punish people for having sex. Moreover, many are *hypocritical[100] on the issue, simultaneously opposing abortion as well as the only proven ways of reducing it - good sex education and readily available birth control.

As for many (if not most) politicians, their public opposition is hypocritical and *self-interested[101]. Generally, they don't care about the issue - they care about the power and wealth derived from politics - *but they *feign[102] concern by throwing red meat to their *constituencies[103]. They use the issue as a *ploy[104] to *garner[105] support from the *unsuspecting[106]. These politicians may be pro-birth, but they aren't generally pro-life, *as evidenced by their opposition to policies that would support the things that children need most after birth like education, health-care, and economic opportunities.

But what politicians and many ordinary people clearly don't care about is whether their *fanatical[107] anti-abortion position is based on rational argumentation. And, according to most ethicists who have carefully examined the problem, it does not.

107. fanatical
광신(열광)적인

GRAMMAR

준동사(Verbals or Non-finite Verbs)

1. 준동사란?

정형동사(finite verbs)와는 달리 주어의 인칭과 성, 수에 따라 어형이 변하지 않으며 완전한 문장을 만드는데 반드시 필요한 술어동사(본동사)가 되지 못하는 동사들을 말한다. 그러나 준동사는 목적어나 보어를 수반할 수 있고, 부사의 수식을 받으며 완료형과 수동형을 갖는다는 점에서 정형동사와 비슷하다. 일반적으로 **부정사(infinitive), 동명사(gerund), 분사(participle)**를 묶어 준동사라 하는데 그 기능은 문맥에 따라 명사, 형용사, 부사의 역할을 한다.

	형태	기능
부정사	원형부정사(동사원형) to 부정사(to + 동사원형)	명사, 형용사, 부사
동명사	동사원형 + -ing	명사
분사	현재분사(동사원형 + -ing) 과거분사(동사원형 + -pp)	형용사, 부사

2. to 부정사

1) 명사적 용법

To study a foreign language is to open a window to your mind.

His ambition is to be a pilot.

I want to stay here all day.

2) 형용사적 용법

The ability to think and speak is peculiar to man.

3) 부사적 용법

Women are made to be loved, not to be loved.

He rose to be head of a college.

4) 독립부정사

To be frank with you, I don't agree with you on this matter.

5) 수동형 부정사: to + be + p.p

Women like to be loved.

6) 완료형 부정사: to + have + p.p

I'm happy to have had this talk with you.

3. 원형부정사(Bare Infinitive)

1) 조동사 다음에서: You cannot buy happiness with money.

2) 지각동사 다음에서: I saw your brother go out a moment ago.

3) 사역동사 다음에서: Don't let such a trivial matter come between us.

4) All, The best 등으로 시작하는 명사절이 주어로 사용된 문장의 보어에서:

All you have to do is pay me what you owe me.

5) but, except 다음에서: She did nothing but sob.

4. 부정사의 의미상의 주어

To see is to believe. (의미상의 주어는 일반적인 사람)
I expect to hear from her soon. (의미상의 주어는 I)
I want you to come early. (의미상의 주어는 you)
I have no friend to help me. (의미상의 주어는 friend)
I have no friend to help. (의미상의 주어는 I)

* 부정사의 의미상의 주어가 문장의 주어와 다를 때는 for + 목적격을 사용한다.
He is eager for me to come.
The rule was for women and men to sit apart.

PHRASES and STRUCTURES

* a question **rarely asked** by politicians or other interlocutors is:
정치가나 다른 대화상대자들에 의해 거의 질문되지 않는 것은 다음과 같다:
= a question **(which is) rarely asked** by politicians or other interlocutors is.
과거분사(asked) 앞에 관계대명사의 주격(which)과 be동사 생략

* **It** is exceedingly rare **to** find defenders of **the view that** abortion is murder.
낙태는 살인이라는 견해를 옹호하는 사람을 찾기는 대단히 드물다.
It ~ to 구문
that이하는 **the view**와 동격

* to the extent it exists at all
그것이 존재하는 한
= to the extent **(that)** it exists at all

* Opposition to abortion **is far from** unanimous.
낙태 반대는 의견이 전혀 일치하지 않는다.
be far from + 형용사 전혀 ~아니다

* Yet **few** seem to take notice. 그렇지만 주목 하는 사람은 거의 없는 것 같다.
few는 부정적으로 사용됨(거의 ~ 않다)

* Consider the disclaimer **that** appears in the most celebrated anti-abortion piece in the philosophical ethics literature.
철학적 윤리 문헌에서 가장 유명한 낙태반대 기사(글)에 나타나는 그 부정을 고려해라.
= Consider the disclaimer, **and it(the disclaimer)** appears in the most celebrated anti-abortion piece in the philosophical ethics literature.
주격 관계대명사 that = and + it(the disclaimer)

* **The view that** abortion is, with rare exceptions, seriously immoral **has received little** support in the recent philosophical literature.
낙태가, 드물게 예외가 있지만, 심각하게 비도덕적이라는 견해는 최근의 철학적 문헌에서 거

의 지지를 받지 못했다.

that이하는 **the view**와 동격이고, **the view**는 주어이고 **has received**는 동사임

little은 부정적으로 사용됨(거의 ~ 않다)

* **most philosophers** affiliated with secular institutions of higher education **believe** that ~

세속적인 고등교육기관과 관계가 있는 대부분의 철학자들은 that이하를 믿는다

= most philosophers **(who are) affiliated with** secular institutions of higher education believe that ~

과거분사(affiliated) 앞에 관계대명사의 주격(who)과 be동사 생략

주어는 most philosophers, 동사는 believe

be affiliated with ~ ~와 관계가 있다

* a conclusion **generated** by seriously confused philosophical argument

대단히 혼란스러운 철학적 주장에 의해 만들어진 결론

= a conclusion **(which is) generated** by seriously confused philosophical argument

과거분사(generated) 앞에 관계대명사의 주격(which)과 be동사 생략

* but why they not, for the most part, **find abortion** morally **problematic**?

그렇지만 그들은(윤리학자) 대개 왜 낙태를 도덕적으로 문제시하지 않는가?

for the most part 대개

find + 목적어 + 형용사 목적어를 ~라고 여기다

* Perhaps professional ethicists, **who** are typically non-religious philosophers, find nothing morally objectionable about abortion because they aren't religious.

아마도 전문적인 윤리학자들, 그런데 그들은 보통 종교적이지 않는 철학자들인데, 어떤 것도 낙태에 관해 도덕적으로 불쾌하다고 여기지 않을 것이다. 왜냐하면 그들이 종교적이지 않기 때문이다.

= Perhaps professional ethicists, **and they(ethicists)** are typically non-religious philosophers, find nothing morally objectionable about abortion because they aren't religious.

who = and + they(ethicists)

find + nothing + objectionable

* **If** they **were** devout they **would recognize** abortion **as** a moral abomination.

만일 그들이 독실한 신자라면 그들은 낙태를 도덕적으로 혐오스러운 것으로 인식할 것이다.

recognize A as B A를 B로 인식하다

가정법 과거로 사용됨

If + 주어 + were ~ , 주어 + would + 동사원형

* **turn this around** 이것을 돌리다, 상황을 역전시키다

* There is **little** difference between the views of religious and secular ethicists regarding moral issues.

도덕적 문제에 관해서 종교적 윤리학자와 세속적 윤리학자의 견해 사이에 차이가 거의 없다.

little은 부정적으로 해석함(거의 없다)

* **are ahead of** 보다 앞서 있다

* The key to answering this question is to emphasize reason and argument, the hallmarks of doing philosophical ethics.

이러한 질문에 답하는 것의 핵심은 이성과 주장을 강조하는 것인데, 그것들(이성과 주장)은 철학적 윤리를 행하는 것의 특징들이다.

= The key to answering this question is to emphasize reason and argument, **(and they are)** the hallmarks of doing philosophical ethics.

, = ~~and they are~~ (being)

* claims that morality is grounded in reason, **which** implies that what is right is supported by the best rational arguments

도덕성이 이성에 근거를 두고 있다고 주장하는데, 그 주장은 옳은 것은 최상의 이성적인 주장에 의해 지지를 받는다는 것을 함축한다

= claims that morality is grounded in reason, **and it(앞 문장)** implies that what is right is supported by the best rational arguments

which = and + it(앞 문장)

* by exercising the human reason their God has given them

그들의 신이 그들에게 주었던 인간의 이성을 실행함으로써

= by exercising the human reason **(which)** their God has given them

= by exercising the human reason, **and** their God has given them **it(human reason)**

목적격 관계대명사 which가 생략되어 있음
which = and + it(human reason)
give + 간접목적어 + 직접목적어

* Thus secular and religious philosophers work in the same arena, **one** where moral truths are those supported by the best reasons.
이와 같이 세속적이고 종교적인 철학자들은 같은 무대에서 일을 하는데, 그 무대는 도덕적 진실이 최상의 이성에 의해 지지를 받는 곳이다.
one = a arena = where 이하

* **are familiar with** ~ ~에 익숙하다, 잘 알다

* So they are in a good position to reject arguments **that** may influence **those** unfamiliar with favored positions.
그래서 그들은 주장들을 거부할 좋은 입장에 있는데, 주장들은 호감을 사고 있는 입장과는 익숙하지 않은 주장들에 영향을 미칠 수 있다.
= So they are in a good position to reject arguments, **and they(arguments)** may influence those(arguments) **(which are) unfamiliar** with favored positions.
주격 관계대명사 that = and they(arguments)
unfamiliar 앞에 관계대명사의 주격(which)과 be동사 생략
are in a good position 좋은 입장에 있다
are unfamiliar with ~ ~에 익숙하지 않다

* The majority of ethicists are right, so individuals **who** disagree with them may choose to follow their own conscience.
대다수의 윤리학자들은 옳고, 따라서 윤리학자들과 의견이 다른 개인들은 그들 자신의 양심을 따르기로 결심할 수도 있다.
= The majority of ethicists are right, so individuals, **and they(individuals)** disagree with them may choose to follow their own conscience.
who = and they(individuals)
choose + to + 동사원형 (~하려고) 결심하다

* It might be that the reasons you give for your fervently held moral beliefs don't stand up to critical scrutiny.
당신이 당신의 열렬하게 가지고 있는 도덕적 믿음에 대한 이유들이 비판적인 철저한 검토에

도 여전히 효력이 유지되지 않을 수 있다.

= It might be that the reasons **(which)** you give for your fervently held moral beliefs don't stand up to critical scrutiny.

= It might be that **<u>the reasons</u>, and** you give **them(reasons)** for your fervently held moral beliefs **<u>don't stand</u>** up to critical scrutiny.

목적격 관계대명사 which 생략 = and + them(reasons)

It은 that이하

that절 속에서 주어는 the reasons, 동사는 stand

stand up to (something) (~에도 여전히) 효력(유효성)이 유지되다

* Perhaps they can't be rationally defended as well as **those reached** after conscientious, informed, and impartial analysis.

아마도 **그것들(이유)**은 양심적인, 알려진, 그리고 공정한 분석 후에 도달된 것들(이유)만큼 잘 이성적으로 옹호될 수 없다.

= Perhaps they can't be rationally defended as well as **those(= reasons) (which are) reached** after conscientious, informed, and impartial analysis.

과거분사(reached) 앞에 관계대명사의 주격(which)과 be동사 생략

those = reasons

* Not only do most ethicists reject moral relativism, so must pro-lifers.

대부분의 윤리학자들이 도덕적 상대주의를 거부할 뿐만 아니라 낙태 반대론자들도 또한 그 것을 거부함에 틀림없다.

= Not only do most ethicists reject moral relativism, so pro-lifers must reject moral relativism.

so + 조동사 + 주어 구문

must 강한 추측 ~임에 틀림없다

* **Lacking** good reasons or **armed** with weak **ones**, many will object that their moral beliefs derive from their Gods.

많은 사람들은 좋은 이유들이 부족하거나 약한 이유들로 무장되어있기 때문에 많은 사람들은 그들의 도덕적 믿음이 그들의 신에게서 나온다는 것을 반대할 것이다.

= **Because many (people) lack** good reasons or **are armed** with weak **ones(reasons)**, they will object that their moral beliefs derive from their Gods.

Lacking(분사구문) = **~~Because many (people)~~ lack**

armed(분사구문) = ~~Because many (people) are~~(being) armed

* To **base** your ethical views **on** Gods
  당신의 윤리적 견해의 토대를 신에 두기 위해서는

* **issue good commands** 좋은 명령을 내리다

* **It** is hard, **if not** impossible, **to** know any of this.
  이것 중의 어떤 것도, 불가능하지는 않는다 하더라도, 알기가 어렵다.
  = It is hard, **(even) if (it is) not** impossible, to know any of this.
  if not = (even) if (it is) not
  It ~ to 구문

* **have access to ~** ~에 접근할 수 있다

* There is **nothing more** to morality **than** this.
  도덕에는 이보다 더한 것이 없다.
  There is **nothing more** dreadful **than** imagination without taste.
  무미건조한 상상력보다 끔찍한 것은 없다.

* There is some standard, norm or criteria **by which** good or bad are measured **which** is independent of the Gods.
  어떤 표준, 규범, 혹은 기준이 있고, 그것(어떤 표준, 규범, 혹은 기준)에 의해 선이나 악이 측정되는데, 그것은 신과는 독립적이다(관련이 없다).
  = There is some standard, norm or criteria, **and** good or bad are measured **by it(some standard, norm or criteria), and it(some standard, norm or criteria)** is independent of the Gods.
  by which = and + by it(some standard, norm or criteria)
  which = and + it(some standard, norm or criteria)

* **We would all be better off**. 우리 모두는 잘 살 것이다.

* **In response** 이에 대응해서

* **the religious** 종교적인 사람들

* **despite what** moral philosophers say

도덕적 철학자들이 말하는 것에도 불구하고

= in spite of what moral philosophers say

what은 선행사를 포함하는 관계대명사

* **are open to** ~ ~의 여지가 있다

* There are **a few** Biblical passages **quoted** by conservatives to support the anti-abortion position.

보수주의자들에 의해 인용되는 몇몇 성서의 구절이 있는데, 그것들은 낙태반대 입장을 지지하기 위한 것이다.

= There are a few Biblical passages **(which are) quoted** by conservatives to support the anti-abortion position.

과거분사(quoted) 앞에 관계대명사의 주격(which)과 be동사 생략

* for a position you already hold

당신이 이미 가지고 있는 입장에 대해

= for a position **(which)** you already hold

= for a position, **and** you already hold **it(position)**

목적격 관계대명사 which 생략 = and + it(position)

* There **simply** isn**'t** a strong scriptural tradition in Christianity against abortion.

기독교에서 낙태를 반대하는 강한 성서상의 전통은 전혀 없다.

simply ~ not 전혀 없다(아니다)

* **Having done** this the vast majority of ethicists have concluded that abortion isn't generally morally problematic.

이것을 하고 난 후 대다수의 윤리학자들은 낙태가 일반적으로 도덕적으로 문제가 되지 않는다고 결론을 내렸다.

= **After they have** done this, the vast majority of ethicists have concluded that abortion isn't generally morally problematic.

Having done(분사구문) = ~~After they~~ have done

* because the fetus satisfies **few** if any of the necessary and sufficient conditions for

personhood
태아가 인간성에 대한 필요충분조건들이 있다하더라도 거의 충족하지 않기 때문에
= because the fetus satisfies few **(even) if (there is)** any of the necessary and sufficient conditions for personhood
few는 부정적으로 사용됨(거의 ~ 않다)

* The impartial view, **backed** by contemporary biology and philosophical argumentation,
공평한 견해는, 현대 생물학과 철학적 논증에 의해 뒷받침되는데,
= The impartial view, **(and it(the view) is) backed** by contemporary biology and philosophical argumentation
backed(분사구문) = ~~and it(the view) is~~(being) backed

* but an oak tree it is not
그러나 그것(도토리)은 참나무는 아니다
= but it(the acorn) is not an oak tree

* but they feign concern by **throwing red meat** to their constituencies
하지만 그들은 그들의 지지자들에게 붉은 고기를 던짐으로써(지지자들의 요구를 들어줌으로써) 걱정을 하는 척 한다
throwing red meat (정치적) 지지자들의 요구를 들어주다, 만족시키다

* as **evidenced** by their opposition to policies **that** would support the things **that** children need most after birth like education, health-care, and economic opportunities
정책들에 대한 그들의 반대에 의해서 입증되었듯이, 그런데 그 정책들은 그것들을 지원해 줄 것인데, 아이들은 교육, 건강관리, 그리고 경제적인 기회와 같이 출생 후에 그것들을 가장 필요로 한다
= as **(it is) evidenced** by their opposition to policies, **and they(policies)** would support the things, and children need **them(things)** most after birth like education, health-care, and economic opportunities
evidenced = ~~it was~~(being) evidenced(분사구문)
주격 관계대명사 that = and + they(policies)
목적격 관계대명사 that = and + them(things)

Unit 9

The Fourth Industrial Revolution: what it means, how to respond[1)]

WARMING UP

- The transformation will be unlike anything humankind has experienced before
- Impressive progress has been made in AI in recent years, **driven** by exponential increases in computing power
- The Fourth Industrial Revolution has the potential **to raise** global income levels and **improve** the quality of life for populations around the world
- They can also create and propagate unrealistic expectations as to **what** constitutes success for an individual or a group, as well as offer opportunities **for** extreme ideas and ideologies **to** spread
- Technology has **made possible** new products and services **that** increase the efficiency and pleasure of our personal lives
- New patterns of consumer behavior **force** companies **to adapt** the way they design, market, and deliver products and services

1) This article was written by Klaus Schwab, who is Founder and Executive Chairman of the World Economic Forum. The source is https://www.weforum.org/agenda/2016/01/the-fourth-industrial-revolution-what-it-means-and-how-to-respond/

*We stand on the brink of a technological revolution that will fundamentally alter the way we live, work, and relate to one another. In its *scale[1], scope, and complexity, *the *transformation[2] will be unlike anything humankind has experienced before. We do not yet know just how it will *unfold[3], but one thing is clear: the response to it must be *integrated[4] and *comprehensive[5], *involving all *stakeholders[6] of the global *polity[7], from the public and private sectors to *academia[8] and civil society.

The First Industrial Revolution used water and steam power to *mechanize[9] production. The Second used electric power to create mass production. The Third used electronics and information technology to *automate[10] production. Now a Fourth Industrial Revolution is building on the Third, the digital revolution that has been occurring since the middle of the last century. *It is characterized by a fusion of technologies that is *blurring[11] the lines between the physical, digital, and biological *spheres[12].

There are three reasons why today's transformations represent not merely a *prolongation[13] of the Third Industrial Revolution but rather the arrival of a Fourth and *distinct[14] one: *velocity[15], scope, and systems impact. The speed of current *breakthroughs[16] has no historical precedent. When compared with previous industrial revolutions, the Fourth is evolving at an *exponential[17] rather than a linear pace. Moreover, it is *disrupting[18] almost every industry in every country. And the breadth and depth of these changes *herald[19] the transformation of entire systems of production, management, and

1. scale
규모(범위)
2. transformation
변화
3. unfold
펼쳐지다
4. integrate
통합시키다
5. comprehensive
포괄적인
6. stakeholder
이해당사자
7. polity
정치적 조직체
8. academia
학계
9. mechanize
기계화하다
10. automate
자동화하다
11. blur
흐릿하게 하다
12. sphere
영역
13. prolongation
연장
14. distinct
뚜렷이 구별되는
15. velocity
속도
16. breakthrough
돌파구
17. exponential
기하급수적인
18. disrupt
방해하다, 지장을 주다
19. herald
예고하다
(도래를 알리다)

20. multiply 크게 증가하다
21. emerging 최근 생겨난
22. virtual 가상의, 컴퓨터를 이용한
23. fabrication 제조, 제작
24. interact 상호작용을 하다
25. additive manufacturing 3차원 인쇄 = 3D printing
26. synthetic biology 합성생물학
27. symbiosis 공생
28. microorganism 미생물

governance.

The possibilities of billions of people connected by mobile devices, with unprecedented processing power, storage capacity, and access to knowledge, are unlimited. And these possibilities will be *multiplied[20] by *emerging[21] technology breakthroughs in fields such as artificial intelligence, robotics, the Internet of Things, autonomous vehicles, 3-D printing, nanotechnology, biotechnology, materials science, energy storage, and quantum computing.

Already, artificial intelligence is all around us, from self-driving cars and drones to *virtual[22] assistants and software that translate or invest. Impressive progress has been made in AI in recent years, *driven by exponential increases in computing power and by the availability of vast amounts of data, from software used to discover new drugs to algorithms used to predict our cultural interests. Digital *fabrication[23] technologies, meanwhile, are *interacting[24] with the biological world *on a daily basis. Engineers, designers, and architects are combining computational design, *additive manufacturing[25], materials engineering, and *synthetic biology[26] to pioneer a *symbiosis[27] between *microorganisms[28], our bodies, *the products we consume, and even the buildings we inhabit.

Challenges and opportunities

Like the revolutions that preceded it, *the Fourth Industrial Revolution has the potential to raise global income levels and improve the quality of life for populations around the world. *To date, those who have gained the most from it have been consumers able to *afford[29] and access the digital world; *technology has made possible new products and services that increase the efficiency and pleasure of our personal lives. Ordering a cab, *booking[30] a flight, buying a product, making a payment, listening to music, watching a film, or playing a game - any of these can now be done *remotely[31].

In the future, technological innovation will also lead to a supply-side miracle, with long-term *gains[32] in efficiency and productivity. Transportation and communication costs will drop, *logistics[33] and global supply chains will become more effective, and the cost of trade will diminish, all of which will open new markets and drive economic growth.

At the same time, as the economists Erik Brynjolfsson and Andrew McAfee have pointed out, the revolution could yield greater *inequality[34], particularly in its potential to disrupt labor markets. As automation substitutes for labor across the entire economy, the *net[35] *displacement[36] of workers by machines might *exacerbate[37] the gap between *returns[38] to capital and returns to labor. On the other hand, it is also possible that the displacement of workers by technology will, *in aggregate, result in a net increase in safe and *rewarding[39] jobs.

*We cannot foresee at this point which scenario is likely to emerge, and history suggests that the outcome is likely to be some combination of the two. However, I am convinced of one thing - that

29. afford
~할 여유가 있다

30. book
예약하다

31. remotely
원격으로

32. gains
이득

33. logistics
물류

34. inequality
불평등

35. net
순-, 실-

36. displacement
이동, 해직

37. exacerbate
악화시키다

38. returns
수익

39. rewarding
돈을 많이 버는

40. segregate 분리하다, 차별하다
41. beneficiary 수혜자
42. shareholder 주주
43. stagnate 침체되다
44. hollowing 산업공동화
45. disillusioned 환멸을 느낀
46. pervasive 만연하는
47. recipe 방안, 비결
48. malaise 불안(만)감
49. dereliction 태만, 포기
50. discontent 불만
51. fuel 부채질하다, 가속화하다
52. pervasiveness 만연

in the future, talent, more than capital, will represent the critical factor of production. *This will give rise to a job market increasingly *segregated[40] into "low-skill/low-pay" and "high-skill/high-pay" segments, which in turn will lead to an increase in social tensions.

In addition to being a key economic concern, inequality represents the greatest societal concern associated with the Fourth Industrial Revolution. The largest *beneficiaries[41] of innovation tend to be the providers of intellectual and physical capital - the innovators, *shareholders[42], and investors - which explains the rising gap in wealth between those dependent on capital versus labor. Technology is therefore one of the main reasons why incomes have *stagnated[43], or even decreased, for a majority of the population in high-income countries: the demand for highly skilled workers has increased while the demand for workers with less education and lower skills has decreased. The result is a job market with a strong demand at the high and low ends, but a *hollowing[44] out of the middle.

This helps explain why so many workers are *disillusioned[45] and fearful that their own real incomes and those of their children will continue to stagnate. It also helps explain why middle classes around the world are increasingly experiencing a *pervasive[46] sense of dissatisfaction and unfairness. A winner-takes-all economy that offers only limited access to the middle class is a *recipe[47] for democratic *malaise[48] and *dereliction[49].

*Discontent[50] can also be *fueled[51] by the *pervasiveness[52] of digital technologies and the dynamics of information sharing typified by social media. More than 30 percent of the global population now uses social media platforms to connect, learn, and share information. In an ideal world, these interactions would provide an opportunity for cross-cultural understanding and *cohesion[53]. However, *they can also create and *propagate[54] unrealistic expectations as to what constitutes success for an individual or a group, as well as offer opportunities for extreme ideas and ideologies to spread.

The impact on business

An underlying theme in my conversations with global *CEOs[55] and *senior business executives[56] is that the *acceleration[57] of innovation and the *velocity[58] of *disruption[59] are hard to comprehend or anticipate and that these *drivers[60] constitute a source of constant surprise, *even for the best connected and most well informed. Indeed, across all industries, *there is clear evidence that the technologies that *underpin[61] the Fourth Industrial Revolution are having a major impact on businesses.

On the supply side, many industries are seeing the introduction of new technologies that create entirely new ways of serving existing needs and *significantly[62] disrupt existing industry value chains. Disruption is also flowing from *agile[63], innovative competitors who, thanks to access to global digital platforms for research, development, marketing, sales, and distribution, can *oust[64] *well-established[65] *incumbents[66] faster than ever *by improving the quality, speed, or price at which value is *delivered[67].

53. cohesion
화합

54. propagate
전파하다

55. CEO
최고경영자
(=chief executive officer)

56. senior business executive
고위경영진

57. acceleration
가속

58. velocity
속도

59. disruption
붕괴

60. driver
추진요인, 동인

61. underpin
뒷받침하다

62. significantly
상당히

63. agile
민첩한

64. oust
몰아내다, 쫓아내다

65. well-established
확고부동한, 안정된

66. incumbent
재임자

67. deliver
내놓다, 산출하다

68. engagement 참여

69. technology-enabled 기술이 가능한

70. render (어떤 상태가 되게) 만들다[하다] (=make)

71. product enhancement 제품고도화(향상)

72. collaborative 공동의

73. organizational 조직의

74. epicenter 중심점

75. enhance 높이다, 향상시키다

76. durable 오래가는, 내구성이 있는

77. resilient 회복력 있는

78. analytics 분석정보

Major shifts on the demand side are also occurring, as growing transparency, consumer *engagement[68], and *new patterns of consumer behavior (increasingly built upon access to mobile networks and data) force companies to adapt the way they design, market, and deliver products and services.

A key trend is the development of *technology-enabled[69] platforms that combine both demand and supply to disrupt existing industry structures, such as those we see within the "sharing" or "on demand" economy. These technology platforms, *rendered[70] easy to use by the smartphone, convene people, assets, and data - thus creating entirely new ways of consuming goods and services in the process. In addition, they lower the barriers for businesses and individuals to create wealth, altering the personal and professional environments of workers. These new platform businesses are rapidly multiplying into many new services, ranging from laundry to shopping, from chores to parking, from massages to travel.

On the whole, *there are four main effects that the Fourth Industrial Revolution has on business - on customer expectations, on *product enhancement[71], on *collaborative[72] innovation, and on *organizational[73] forms. Whether consumers or businesses, customers are increasingly at the *epicenter[74] of the economy, which *is all about improving how customers are served. Physical products and services, moreover, can now be *enhanced[75] with digital capabilities that increase their value. New technologies make assets more *durable[76] and *resilient[77], while data and *analytics[78] are transforming how they are maintained. A world of customer experiences, data-based services, and *asset performance[79] through analytics, meanwhile, requires new forms of collaboration, *particularly given the speed at which innovation and disruption are taking place. And the emergence of global platforms and other new business models, finally, means that talent, culture, and organizational forms will have to be rethought.

*Overall[80], the *inexorable[81] shift from simple digitization (the Third Industrial Revolution) to innovation based on combinations of technologies (the Fourth Industrial Revolution) is forcing companies to reexamine the way they do business. The *bottom line[82], however, is the same: business leaders and senior executives need to understand their changing environment, challenge the assumptions of their operating teams, and *relentlessly[83] and continuously innovate.

The impact on government

As the physical, digital, and biological worlds continue to *converge[84], new technologies and platforms will increasingly enable citizens to engage with governments, voice their opinions, *coordinate[85] their efforts, and even *circumvent[86] the supervision of *public authorities[87]. Simultaneously, governments will gain new technological powers to increase their control over *populations[88], based on pervasive *surveillance[89] systems and the ability to control digital infrastructure. On the whole, however, governments will

79. asset performance 자산실적
80. overall 종합적으로
81. inexorable 멈출 수 없는, 거침없는
82. bottom line 핵심, 요점
83. relentlessly 가차 없이
84. converge 모이다
85. coordinate 조정하다
86. circumvent 피하다
87. public authorities 공공기관
88. population 주민
89. surveillance 감시

90. engagement
참여

91. policymaking
정책입안

92. decentralization
분권화

93. competitive edge
경쟁우위

94. regulation
규제

95. decision-making
의사결정

96. feasible
실현가능한

97. regulator
규제기관, 담당자

98. cope
대처하다

increasingly face pressure to change their current approach to public *engagement[90] and *policymaking[91], as their central role of conducting policy diminishes owing to new sources of competition and the redistribution and *decentralization[92] of power that new technologies make possible.

Ultimately, the ability of government systems and public authorities to adapt will determine their survival. *If they prove capable of embracing a world of disruptive change, subjecting their structures to the levels of transparency and efficiency that will enable them to maintain their *competitive edge,[93] they will endure. If they cannot evolve, they will face increasing trouble.

This will be particularly true in the realm of *regulation[94]. Current systems of public policy and decision-making[95] evolved alongside the Second Industrial Revolution, when decision-makers had time to study a specific issue and develop the necessary response or appropriate regulatory framework. The whole process was designed to be linear and mechanistic, following a strict "top down" approach.

But such an approach is no longer *feasible[96]. Given the Fourth Industrial Revolution's rapid pace of change and broad impacts, *legislators and *regulators[97] are being challenged to an unprecedented degree and for the most part are proving unable to *cope[98].

How, then, can they preserve the interest of the consumers and the public *at large while continuing to support innovation and technological development? By embracing "agile" governance, just as the *private sector[99] has increasingly adopted agile responses to software development and business operations more generally. This means regulators must continuously adapt to a new, fast-changing environment, *reinventing[100] themselves so they can truly understand what it is they are regulating. To do so, governments and regulatory *agencies[101] will need to collaborate closely with business and civil society.

The Fourth Industrial Revolution will also *profoundly[102] impact the nature of national and international security, affecting both the probability and the nature of conflict. The history of *warfare[103] and international security is the history of technological innovation, and today is no exception. Modern conflicts involving states are increasingly "hybrid" in nature, combining traditional battlefield techniques with elements previously associated with *nonstate[104] actors. The distinction between war and peace, *combatant[105] and noncombatant, and even violence and nonviolence (think cyberwarfare) is becoming *uncomfortably[106] *blurry[107].

As this process takes place and new technologies such as autonomous or biological weapons become easier to use, individuals and small groups will increasingly join states in being capable of causing mass harm. This new *vulnerability[108] will lead to new fears. But at the same time, advances in technology will create the potential to reduce the scale or impact of violence, through the development of new modes of protection, for example, or greater precision in targeting.

99. private sector
민간부문

100. reinvent
다른 모습을
보여주다

101. agency
기관

102. profoundly
깊이

103. warfare
전투, 전쟁

104. nonstate
비국가의(국제 관계
의 영향을 미치지 않
는)

105. combatant
전투원

106. uncomfortably
불편하게

107. blurry
흐릿한

108. vulnerability
취약성

109. nurture
발전시키다

110. augmentation
증가

111. early adopter
얼리 어답터 (남들보다 먼저 신제품을 사서 써 보는 사람)

112. inexorable
거침없는

113. quintessential
본질적인

114. compassion
동정

115. track
추적하다

116. connectivity
연결

117. intensify
심해지다

The impact on people

The Fourth Industrial Revolution, finally, will change not only what we do but also who we are. It will affect our identity and all the issues associated with it: our sense of privacy, our notions of ownership, our consumption patterns, *the time we devote to work and leisure, and how we develop our careers, cultivate our skills, meet people, and *nurture[109] relationships. It is already changing our health and leading to a "quantified" self, and sooner than we think it may lead to human *augmentation[110]. The list is endless because it is bound only by our imagination.

I am a great enthusiast and *early adopter[111] of technology, but sometimes I wonder whether the *inexorable[112] integration of technology in our lives could diminish some of our *quintessential[113] human capacities, such as *compassion[114] and cooperation. Our relationship with our smartphones is *a case in point. Constant connection may deprive us of one of life's most important assets: the time to pause, reflect, and engage in meaningful conversation.

One of the greatest individual challenges posed by new information technologies is privacy. We instinctively understand why it is so essential, yet the *tracking[115] and sharing of information about us is a crucial part of the new *connectivity[116]. Debates about fundamental issues such as the impact on our inner lives of the loss of control over our data will only *intensify[117] in the years ahead. Similarly, the revolutions occurring in biotechnology and AI, which are redefining what it means to be human by pushing back the current *thresholds[118] of *life span[119], health, cognition, and capabilities, will compel us to redefine our moral and ethical boundaries.

Shaping the future

*Neither technology nor the disruption that comes with it is an *exogenous[120] force over which humans have no control. All of us are responsible for guiding its evolution, in the decisions we make on a daily basis as citizens, consumers, and investors. *We should thus grasp the opportunity and power we have to shape the Fourth Industrial Revolution and direct it toward a future that reflects our common objectives and values.

To do this, however, we must develop a comprehensive and globally shared view of how technology is affecting our lives and reshaping our economic, social, cultural, and human environments. There has never been a time of greater promise, or one of greater potential *peril[121]. Today's decision-makers, however, are too often trapped in traditional, linear thinking, or too absorbed by the multiple crises demanding their attention, to think *strategically[122] about the forces of disruption and innovation shaping our future.

*In the end, it all *comes down to people and values. We need to shape a future that works for all of us by putting people first and *empowering[123] them. In its most *pessimistic[124], *dehumanized[125] form, the Fourth Industrial Revolution may indeed have the potential to "robotize" humanity and thus to deprive us of our heart and soul.

118. threshold 기준치
119. life span 수명
120. exogenous 외인성의
121. peril 위험
122. strategically 전략적으로
123. empower 권한을 주다
124. pessimistic 비관적인
125. dehumanized 비인간적인

126. complement
보완물

127. empathy
공감

128. stewardship
관리

129. collective
집단의

130. prevail
이기다

But as a *complement[126] to the best parts of human nature - creativity, *empathy[127], *stewardship[128] - it can also lift humanity into a new *collective[129] and moral consciousness based on a shared sense of destiny. It *is incumbent on us all to make sure the latter *prevails[130].

GRAMMAR

동명사

동명사는 명사적 특성과 동사적 특성을 갖는다.

1. 명사적 특성

관사, 소유격, 지시형용사 등을 붙일 수 있다.

His handling of the situation was mastery.
The writing of letters is good excercise in English composition.

2. 동사적 특성

부사(구)의 수식을 받으며 목적어를 수반할 수 있다. 수동형과 완료형을 만들 수 있다.

He began reading slowly and in a clear voice.
I would appreciate your keeping it a secret.

> He was arrested for the stealing of horses. (명사적 동명사, of가 사용됨)
> *the stealing horses.
> *stealing of horses.
> stealing horses. (동사적 동명사)

3. 동명사의 의미상의 주어

I am fond of fishing. (의미상의 주어는 문장의 주어와 일치: I)

의미상의 주어가 문장의 주어와 일치하지 않을 때는 소유격이 사용된다. 목적격도 사용될 수 있지만 구어체, 비격식체에서 사용된다.

I am fond of fishing. (의미상의 주어는 문장의 주어와 일치: I)

PHRASES and STRUCTURES

* We stand **on the brink of** a technological revolution **that** will fundamentally alter the way we live, work, and relate to one another.

우리는 기술혁명의 바로 직전에 서있는데 그 기술혁명은 우리가 살고, 일하고, 서로서로 관련짓는 방식을 근본적으로 바꿀 것이다.

= We stand on the brink of a technological revolution, **and it(the technological revolution)** will fundamentally alter the way we live, work, and relate to one another.

on the brink of = on the verge of ~의 직전에

주격 관계대명사 that = and + it(the technological revolution)

* The transformation will be unlike anything humankind has experienced before.

그 변화는 인류가 이전에 경험했던 어떤 것과도 다를 것이다.

= The transformation will be unlike anything **(that)** humankind has experienced before.

= The transformation will be unlike anything, **and** humankind has experienced **it(anything)** before.

목적격 관계대명사 that 생략 = and + it(anything)

* **involving** all stakeholders of the global polity

그런데 그것은 세계 정치조직체의 모든 이해당사들을 포함한다

= and it involves all stakeholders of the global polity

involving(분사구문) = ~~and it~~ involves

* It is characterized by a fusion of technologies **that** is blurring the lines between the physical, digital, and biological spheres.

그것(4차 산업혁명)은 기술의 융합으로 특징지어지는데, 기술의 융합은 물리적, 디지털과 생물학적 영역들 사이의 경계를 흐릿하게 하고 있다.

= It is characterized by a fusion of technologies, **and it(the fusion)** is blurring the lines between the physical, digital, and biological spheres.

주격 관계대명사 that = and + it(the fusion)

* **driven** by exponential increases in computing power
인상적인 진척은 연산 능력에서 기하급수적인 증가에 의해 추진되었다
= (and it(impressive progress) was) driven by exponential increases in computing power
driven(분사구문) = ~~and it(impressive progress) was~~(being) driven

* **on a daily basis** 매일

* the products we consume, and even the buildings we inhabit
우리가 소비하는 제품, 심지어 우리가 살고 있는 건물
= the products **(which)** we consume, and even the buildings **(which)** we inhabit
= the products, **and** we consume **them(the products)**, and even the buildings, **and** we inhabit **them(the buildings)**
목적격 관계대명사 which 생략 = and + them(the products)
목적격 관계대명사 which 생략 = and + them(the buildings)

* The Fourth Industrial Revolution has the potential **to raise** global income levels and **improve** the quality of life for populations around the world.
4차 산업혁명은 세계의 수입 수준을 올리고 전 세계의 인구의 삶의 질을 향상시킬 잠재성을 가진다.
to raise, and improve는 the potential을 수식하는 to부정사의 형용사적 용법

* **To date**, those who have gained the most from it have been consumers able to afford and access the digital world.
지금까지 그것(4차 산업혁명)으로부터 가장 많은 것을 얻었던 사람들은 디지털 세계에 접근하고 감당할 수 있었던 소비자들이었다.
= **To date**, those who have gained the most from it have been consumers **(who were)** able to afford and access the digital world.
to date 지금까지
형용사(able) 앞에 관계대명사의 주격(who)과 be동사가 생략됨

* Technology has made possible new products and services **that** increase the efficiency and pleasure of our personal lives.
기술은 새로운 제품과 서비스가 가능하도록 해 주었는데, 그것들은 우리의 개인의 삶의 즐

거움과 효율성을 증가시킨다.

= Technology has **made possible** new products and services, **and they(new products and services)** increase the efficiency and pleasure of our personal lives.

주격 관계대명사 that = and + they(new products and services)

make + 목적어 + 형용사 목적어가 ~하게 하다

* **in aggregate** 전체적으로

* We cannot foresee at this point **which scenario** is likely to emerge.

우리는 이 시점에서 어떤 시나리오가 나올 것 같은지를 예측할 수 없다.

which는 scenario를 수식하는 의문형용사(어떤)로 사용됨

be likely to ~ ~할 것 같다

* This will give rise to a job market increasingly **segregated** into "low-skill/low-pay" and "high-skill/high-pay" segments, **which** in turn will lead to an increase in social tensions.

이것은 "저기술/저임금"과 "고기술/고임금" 부분으로 점점 차별되는 취업시장을 낳게 될 것이고, 그것은 결국 사회적 긴장의 증가로 이끌 것이다.

= This will **give rise to** a job market increasingly **(which is) segregated** into "low-skill/low-pay" and "high-skill/high-pay" segments, **and it(앞 문장) in turn** will lead to an increase in social tensions

과거분사(segregated) 앞에 관계대명사의 주격(which)과 be동사가 생략됨

which = and + it(앞 문장)

give rise to ~ 낳다, ~이 생기게 하다

in turn 결국

* They can also create and propagate unrealistic expectations **as to what** constitutes success for an individual or a group, as well as offer opportunities for extreme ideas and ideologies to spread.

그들은 또한 개인이나 집단의 성공을 이루는 것에 관한 비현실적인 기대를 만들어내고 전파할 수 있으며 그뿐만 아니라 극단적인 이념과 이데올로기가 전파할 기회를 제공할 수 있다.

as to ~ ~에 관한

what은 선행사를 포함하는 관계대명사

* even for **the** best **connected** and most well **informed**
  최상으로 관련이 있고 아주 정보가 많은 사람들조차도
  the + 형용사 = ~한 사람들

* There is clear **evidence that** the technologies **that** underpin the Fourth Industrial Revolution are having a major impact on businesses.
  4차 산업혁명을 뒷받침하는 기술들이 비지니스에 중대한 영향을 미치고 있다는 분명한 증거가 있다.
  = There is clear evidence that the technologies, **and they(technologies)** underpin the Fourth Industrial Revolution are having a major impact on businesses.
  evidence와 that절은 동격(~라는 증거)
  주격 관계대명사 that = and + they(technologies)

* by improving the quality, speed, or price **at which** value is delivered
  가치가 산출되는 질, 속도, 가격을 개선시킴으로써
  = by improving the quality, speed, or price, **and** value is delivered **at them(the quality, speed, or price)**
  at which = and + at them(the quality, speed, or price)

* New patterns of consumer behavior (increasingly built upon access to mobile networks and data) **force** companies **to adapt** the way they design, market, and deliver products and services.
  소비자 행동의 새로운 유형은 (점점 모바일 망과 데이터의 접근에 기반을 두고) 기업으로 하여금 제품과 서비스를 고안하고, 시장에 내놓고, 제공하는 방식을 맞추도록 강요한다.
  force + 목적어 + to + 동사원형 목적어가 ~하도록 강요하다

* There are four main effects **that** the Fourth Industrial Revolution has on business.
  4차 산업혁명이 비즈니스에 미친 네 가지 주요한 영향들이 있다.
  = There are four main effects, **and** the Fourth Industrial Revolution has **them(effects)** on business.
  목적격 관계대명사 that = and + them(effects)

* **is all about** ~ ~이 전부다

* particularly **given** the speed at which innovation and disruption are taking place
특히 혁신과 붕괴가 일어나고 있는 속도를 고려해 볼 때
given ~ ~을 고려해 볼 때

* If they prove capable of embracing a world of disruptive change, **subjecting their structures to** the levels of transparency and efficiency **that** will enable them to maintain their competitive edge, they will endure.
만일 그들(정부제도와 공공기관)이 파괴적인 변화의 세계를 포용할 수 있고 그들의 구조를 투명하고 효율적인 단계가 되게 만들 수 있게 된다면, 그런데 그 투명하고 효율적인 단계는 그들로 하여금 그들의 경쟁우위를 유지할 수 있게 해 줄 것인데, 그들은 지속될 것이다.
= If they **prove capable** of embracing a world of disruptive change, subjecting their structures to the levels of transparency and efficiency, **and they(levels)** will enable them to maintain their competitive edge, they will endure.
prove + (to be) + 형용사 ~이 되다
The experiment proved (to be) successful. 그 실험은 성공적이었다.
subject A to B A로 하여금 B를 당하게(겪게) 만들다
주격 관계대명사 that = and + they(levels)

* Legislators and regulators are being challenged to an unprecedented degree and for the most part are proving unable to cope.
입법자와 규제기관들이 전례가 없을 정도로 도전을 받고 있으며 대게 대처할 수 없게 되어가고 있다.
= Legislators and regulators are being challenged to an unprecedented degree and for the most part are **proving (to be) unable** to cope.
to an unprecedented degree 전례가 없을 정도로
for the most part 대게, 보통
prove + (to be) + 형용사 ~이 되다

* **at large** 전체적인

* the time we devote to work and leisure
우리가 일과 여가에 쏟는(보내는) 시간
= the time **(which)** we devote to work and leisure
= the time, **and** we devote **it(the time)** to work and leisure

목적격 관계대명사 which 생략 = and + it(the time)

* **a case in point** (논의 중인 문제·상황 등에) 딱 들어맞는 사례

* Neither technology nor the disruption that comes with it is an exogenous force **over which** humans have no control.
기술도 기술과 함께 오는 붕괴도 인간이 통제하지 못하는 외인적인 힘이 아니다.
= Neither technology nor the disruption that comes with it **is** an exogenous force, **and** humans have no control **over it(force)**.
over which = and + over it(force)
is가 본동사임
have no control over ~ 어떻게 할 수 없다

* We should thus grasp the opportunity and power we have to shape the Fourth Industrial Revolution and direct it toward a future that reflects our common objectives and values.
따라서 우리는 4차 산업혁명을 형성하고 우리의 공통의 목적과 가치를 반영하는 미래로 4차 산업혁명이 방향을 잡아가도록 하기 위해 우리가 가지고 있는 기회와 힘을 잡아야 한다.
= We should thus grasp the opportunity and power **(which)** we have to shape the Fourth Industrial Revolution and direct it toward a future **that** reflects our common objectives and values.
= We should thus grasp the opportunity and power, **and** we have **them(opportunity and power)** to shape the Fourth Industrial Revolution and direct it toward a future, **and it(future)** reflects our common objectives and values.
목적격 관계대명사 which 생략 = and + them(opportunity and power)
주격 관계대명사 that = and + it(future)
to shape to부정사의 목적(~하기 위해)

* **In the end** 결국

* **comes down to** ~ 결국 ~이 되다, ~에 이르다

* **is incumbent on** ~ ~의 의무가 있다

Unit 10

Where AI and ethics meet[1]

WARMING UP

- A paper in Nature Machine *Intelligence* **throws a spanner** in the works by claiming that such high principles, **while laudable**, will not give us the ethical AI society we need
- The field of AI ethics is generally **broken into** two areas:
- A robot may not injure a human being, or, through inaction, **allow** a human being **to come** to harm
- They have nonetheless **informed** the real-world field **of** AI ethics
- The film adaptation of I, Robot was released, **featuring** an AI whose interpretation of the three laws led to a plan to dominate human beings in order to save us from ourselves
- AI research is obviously a far younger field, **devoid** of these rich historical opportunities to learn

1) This article was written by Stephen Fleischfresser, who is a lecturer at the University of Melbourne's Trinity College and holds a PhD in the History and Philosophy of Science. The source is https://cosmosmagazine.com/society/where-ai-and-ethics-meet

*Given a *swell[1] of *dire[2] warnings about the future of artificial intelligence over the last few years, the field of AI ethics has become a *hive[3] of activity.

These warnings come from *a variety of experts such as Oxford University's Nick Bostrom, but also from more *public figures[4] such as Elon Musk and the *late[5] Stephen Hawking. *The picture they paint is *bleak[6].

In response, many have *dreamed up[7] sets of principles to guide AI researchers and help them negotiate the *maze[8] of human morality and ethics. Now, a paper in Nature Machine Intelligence *throws a spanner in the works by claiming that *such high principles, while *laudable[9], will not give us the ethical AI society we need.

The field of AI ethics *is generally broken into two areas: *one concerning the ethics guiding humans who develop AIs, and the other machine ethics, guiding the moral behaviour of the AIs or robots themselves. However, the two areas are not so easily separated.

Machine ethics has a long history. In 1950 the great science fiction writer Isaac Asimov clearly *articulated[10] his now famous "three laws of robotics" in his work I, Robot, and proposed them as such:

1. A robot may not injure a human being, or, through *inaction[11], *allow a human being to come to harm.

2. *A robot must obey the orders given it by human beings except where such orders would conflict with the First Law.

1. swell
증가, 팽창

2. dire
끔찍한, 무서운

3. hive
벌집, 중심지

4. public figure
유명인사

5. late
고인이 된, 죽은

6. bleak
암울한, 절망적인

7. dream up
생각해 내다

8. maze
미로, 종잡을 수 없이 복잡한 것

9. laudable
칭찬할 만한

10. articulate
분명히 표현하다

11. inaction
무활동, 나태함

12. zeroth
영차의

13. musing
사색

14. ensure
보장하다

15. turn on
반항하다, 대들다

16. safety feature
안전장치

17. benevolent
자애로운

18. wanting
부족한

19. adaptation
각색

20. release
공개하다, 발표하다

21. feature
주연시키다

22. highlight
강조하다

23. flaw
결함(점)

24. proponent
지지자

25. hopelessly
절망적으로

3. A robot must protect its own existence as long as such protection does not conflict with the First or Second Law.

Later a "*zeroth[12]" law was added: A robot may not harm humanity, or, by inaction, allow humanity to come to harm.

These laws together were Asimov's (and editor John W Campbell's) *musing[13] on how to *ensure[14] an artificially intelligent system would not *turn on[15] its creators: a *safety feature[16] designed to produce friendly and *benevolent[17] robots.

Asimov explored the limits of the three laws in numerous writings, *often finding them *wanting[18]. While the laws were a literary device, *they have nonetheless informed the real-world field of AI ethics.

In 2004, the film *adaptation[19] of *I, Robot* was *released[20], *featuring[21] an AI whose interpretation of the three laws led to a plan to dominate human beings in order to save us from ourselves.

To *highlight[22] the *flaws[23] in the ethical principles of the three laws, an organization called the Singularity Institute for Artificial Intelligence (now the Machine Intelligence Research Institute), *headed up by the American AI researcher Eliezer Yudkowsky, started an online project called Three Laws Unsafe. Yudkowsky, an early theorist of the dangers of super-intelligent AI and *proponent[24] of the idea of Friendly AI, argued that such principles would be *hopelessly[25] simplistic *if AI ever developed to the stage depicted in Asimov's fictions.

Despite widespread recognition of the *drawbacks[26] of the three laws, many organizations, from private companies to governments, nonetheless *persisted with[27] projects to develop principle-based systems of AI ethics, with one paper listing "84 documents containing ethical principles or guidelines for AI" that have been published *to date.

This continued focus on ethical principles is partly because, while the three laws were designed to govern AI behaviour alone, principles of AI ethics apply to AI researchers as well as the intelligences that they develop. The ethical behaviour of AI is, in part, a reflection of the ethical behaviour of those that design and *implement[28] them, and because of this, the two areas of AI ethics are *inextricably[29] bound to one another.

AI development needs strong moral guidance *if we are to avoid some of the more *catastrophic[30] scenarios *envisaged[31] by AI critics.

A *review[32] published last year by AI4People, an *initiative[33] of the international *non-profit[34] organization Atomium-European Institute for Science, Media and Democracy, reports that many of these projects have developed sets of principles that closely resemble those in medical ethics: beneficence (do only good), *nonmaleficence[35] (do no harm), autonomy (the power of humans to make individual decisions), and justice.

This *convergence[36], for some, lends a great deal of *credibility[37] to these as possible guiding principles for the development of AIs in the future.

26. drawback 결점, 문제점
27. persist with 집요하게 계속하다
28. implement 이행하다
29. inextricably 불가분하게
30. catastrophic 비극적인, 파멸의
31. envisage 예상(상상)하다
32. review 보고서
33. initiative (특정한 문제 해결·목적 달성을 위한 새로운) 계획
34. non-profit 비영리의
35. nonmaleficence 해악금지
36. convergence 집합점
37. credibility 신뢰성

38. predictive analytic 예측분석
39. principlism 원리주의
40. promising 유망한, 조짐이 좋은
41. undermine 약화시키다
42. efficacy 효력
43. fiduciary 신탁의
44. defining 본질적 의미를 규정하는
45. practitioner (전문직 종사자, 특히) 의사
46. deployment 배치
47. align 정렬하다, 한 줄로 하다

However, Brent Mittelstadt of the Oxford Internet Institute and the British Government's Alan Turing Institute – an ethicist whose research concerns primarily digital ethics in relation to algorithms, machine learning, artificial intelligence, *predictive analytics[38], Big Data and medical expert systems – now argues that such an approach, called "*principlism[39]", is not as *promising[40] as it might look.

*Mittelstadt suggests significant differences between the fields of medicine and AI research that may well *undermine[41] the *efficacy[42] of the former's ethical principles in the context of the latter.

His first argument concerns common aims and *fiduciary[43] duties, *the duties in which trusted professionals, such as doctors, place other's interests above their own. Medicine is clearly bound together by the common aim of promoting the health and well-being of patients and Mittelstadt argues that it is a "*defining[44] quality of a profession for its *practitioners[45] to be part of a 'moral community' with common aims, values and training".

For the field of AI research, however, the same cannot be said. "AI is largely developed by the private sector for *deployment[46] in public (for example, criminal sentencing) and private (for example, insurance) contexts," Mittelstadt writes. "The fundamental aims of developers, users and affected parties do not necessarily *align[47]."

Similarly, the fiduciary duties of the professions and their mechanisms of governance are absent in private AI research.

"*AI developers do not *commit[48] to public service, which in other professions requires practitioners to *uphold[49] public interests in the face of competing business or *managerial[50] interests," he writes. In AI research, "public interests are not granted *primacy[51] over commercial interests".

In a related point, Mittelstadt argues that *while medicine has a professional culture that *lays out[52] the necessary moral *obligations[53] and virtues stretching back to the physicians of ancient Greece, "AI development does not have a comparable history, homogeneous professional culture and identity, or similarly developed professional ethics frameworks".

*Medicine has had a long time over which to learn from its mistakes and the shortcomings of the minimal guidance provided by the Hippocratic tradition. In response, it has *codified[54] appropriate conduct into modern principlism which provides fuller and more satisfactory ethical guidance.

*AI research is obviously a far younger field, devoid of these rich historical opportunities to learn. Further complicating the issue is that the context of application for medicine is comparatively narrow, whereas "AI can in principle be *deployed[55] in any context involving human *expertise[56]", leading it to be radically *multidisciplinary[57] and *interdisciplinary[58], with researchers coming from "varied *disciplines[59] and professional backgrounds, which have *incongruous[60] histories, cultures, incentive structures and moral obligations".

48. commit
전념하다

49. uphold
유지시키다,
옹호하다

50. managerial
경영의

51. primacy
으뜸

52. lay out
펼치다, 제시하다

53. obligation
의무

54. codify
성문화하다

55. deploy
배치하다

56. expertise
전문지식(기술)

57. multidisciplinary
여러 학문분야에 걸친

58. interdisciplinary
학제간의

59. discipline
지식분야

60. incongruous
어울리지 않는

61. extraordinarily 엄청나게
62. point to 가리키다, 들먹이다
63. accountability 책임, 의무
64. draws on 의지하다
65. code 법규
66. commitment 전념
67. self-regulatory 자기규제의
68. normative 규범적인
69. binding 법적 구속력이 있는

This makes it *extraordinarily[61] difficult to develop anything other than "broadly acceptable principles to guide the people and processes responsible for the development, deployment and governance of AI across radically different contexts of use". The problem, says Mittelstadt, is translating these into actual good practice. "At this level of abstraction," he warns, "meaningful guidance may be impossible."

Finally, the author *points to[62] "the relative lack of legal and professional *accountability[63] mechanisms" within AI research. Where medicine has numerous layers of legal and professional protections to uphold professional standards, such things are largely absent in AI development. Mittelstadt *draws on[64] research showing that *codes[65] of ethics do not themselves result in ethical behaviour, without those codes being "embedded in organizational culture and actively enforced".

"This is a problem," he writes. "Serious, long-term *commitment[66] to *self-regulatory[67] frameworks cannot be *taken for granted."

All of this together leads Mittelstadt to conclude: "We must therefore hesitate to celebrate consensus around high-level principles that hide deep political and *normative[68] disagreement."

Instead he argues that AI research needs to develop *binding[69] and highly visible accountability structures" at the organizational level, as well as encouraging actual ethical practice in the field to inform higher level principles, rather than relying solely on top-down principlism. Similarly, he advocates a focus on organizational ethics rather than professional ethics, while simultaneously calling for the *professionalization[70] of AI development, partly through the licensing of developers of high-risk AI.

His final suggestion for the future of AI ethics is to *exhort[71] AI researchers not to treat ethical issues as design problems to be "solved". "It is foolish to assume," he writes, "that very old and complex normative questions can be solved with technical *fixes[72] or good design alone."

Instead, he writes that "*intractable[73] principled disagreements should be expected and welcomed, as they reflect both serious ethical consideration and diversity of thought. They do not represent failure, and do not need to be 'solved'. Ethics is a process, not a *destination[74]. The real work of AI ethics begins now: to translate and implement our lofty principles, and in doing so to begin to understand the real ethical challenges of AI."

70. professionalization 전문화
71. exhort 촉구하다
72. fix 해결책
73. intractable 아주 다루기 힘든
74. destination 종착지

GRAMMAR

분사

1. 형태

1) 현재분사
동사원형 + ing

2) 과거분사
동사원형 + ed

2. 분사는 형용사나 부사의 역할을 한다

A rolling stone gathers no moss.(형용사)
Children brought up in the country are not always healthier than those brought up in cities.(형용사)

3. 분사가 보어로 사용된다

He stood leaning against at the gate.(주격보어)
He sat buried in thought.(주격보어)
The mystery remains unsettled.(주격보어)
I found him lying on the floor.(목적격보어)
I am sorry to have kept you waiting.(목적격보어)
I could not make myself understood.(목적격보어)

4. 분사구문

분사(동사원형+-ing)가 접속사+주어+술어동사를 대신하는 부사구로 사용되는데 이러한 구를 분사구문이라 한다. 분사구문은 문맥에 따라 시간, 이유, 양보, 조건, 부대상황 등의 뜻을 갖는다.

1) 이유

Feeling tired, I went to bed early.(= because I felt tired)

Not having a car, she finds it difficult to get around.

(= because he doesn't have a car)

2) 양보

Sitting(=Though I am sitting) here in the sun, I still feel cold.

(여기 햇빛 속에 앉아 있어도 여전히 춥게 느껴진다)

3) 부대상황

Smiling brightly, she extended her hand.

(= She smiled brightly and extended her hand)

(그녀는 밝게 웃으며 그녀의 손을 내밀었다)

4)조건

Smiling at others, you will be smiled at by them.(= if you smile at ...)

(다른 사람들에게 웃으면 다른 사람들도 너에게 웃을 것이다)

5. 독립분사구문

분사구문의 의미상의 주어가 주절의 주어와 같지 않을 때의 분사구문을 말한다.

We'll leave tomorrow, the weather permitting.(We ≠the weather)

(날씨가 허용한다면 내일 우리는 떠날 것이다)

6. 비인칭 독립분사구문

분사구문의 주어가 주절의 주어와 일치하지 않는데도 분사구문의 주어가 탈락된 관용적인 분사구문을 말한다.

Generally speaking(= If we speak generally), man is stronger than woman.

7. 완료형 분사구문

다른 행위 이전에 한 행위가 일어날 때는 첫 번째 행위에 대해 having + done을 사용한다:

Having found a hotel, we looked for someplace to have dinner.

(호텔을 찾고 나서 우리는 저녁 먹을 장소를 찾았다)

after +-ing를 사용할 수도 있다.

After finishing her work, she went home.

PHRASES and STRUCTURES

* **Given** a swell of dire warnings
무서운 경고의 증가를 고려해 볼 때
given ~ ~을 고려해 볼 때

* **a variety of** 여러 가지의

* The picture they paint is bleak.
그들이 그리는 그림은 암울하다.
= The picture **(which)** they paint is bleak.
= The picture, **and** they paint **it(the picture)** is bleak.
목적격 관계대명사 which 생략 = and + it(the time)

* **throws a spanner in the works** (계획이나 일의 진행을) 방해하다, 망치다

* Such high principles, **while laudable**, will not give us the ethical AI society we need.
그런 고상한 원칙들은 칭찬할만하지만 우리가 필요로 하는 윤리적인 인공지능사회를 우리에게 주지 않을 것이다.
= Such high principles, **while (they are) laudable**, will not give us the ethical AI society **(which)** we need.
= Such high principles, while (they are) laudable, will not give us the ethical AI society, **and** we need **it(the society)**.
while laudable = while ~~they are~~(being) laudable
목적격 관계대명사 which 생략 = and + it(the society)

* **is generally broken into two areas** 일반적으로 두 영역으로 나누어진다

* **one** concerning the ethics guiding humans **who** develop AIs, and **the other** machine ethics, **guiding** the moral behaviour of the AIs or robots themselves
하나는 AI를 개발하는 인간을 인도하는 윤리와 관련이 있는 것이고, 다른 하나는 기계 윤리

인데 그것은 AI나 로봇 자체의 도덕적 행동을 인도하는 것이다
= one concerning the ethics guiding humans, **and they(humans)** develop AIs, and the other machine ethics, **and it(machine ethics) guides** the moral behaviour of the AIs or robots themselves
one ~, the other ~ (두 개 중) 하나는 ~이고, 다른 하나는 ~이다
who = and + they(humans)
guiding(분사구문) = ~~and it(machine ethics)~~ guides

* **allow** a human being **to come** to harm
인간이 다치도록 하다
allow + 목적어 + to + 동사원형 목적어가 ~을 하도록 허락하다
come to harm 다치다

* A robot must obey the orders **given** it by human beings.
로봇은 인간에 의해 로봇에 주어진 명령을 따라야 한다.
= A robot must obey the orders **(which are) given** it by human beings.
과거분사(given) 앞에 관계대명사의 주격(which)과 be동사 생략

* often **finding** them **wanting**
그는 종종 그 제한들이 부족하다고 여겼다
= **and he often found** them wanting
find + 목적어 + 형용사 목적어가 ~라고 여기다

* They have nonetheless **informed** the real-world field **of** AI ethics.
그럼에도 불구하고 그 원칙들은 실제 현장에 AI 윤리를 알렸다.
inform A of B A에게 B를 알리다

* **featuring** an AI **whose** interpretation of the three laws led to a plan to dominate human beings in order to save us from ourselves
그 영화는 AI를 주연으로 하고 있는데 세 가지 원칙들에 대한 AI의 해석은 우리자신으로부터 우리를 구하기 위하여 인간을 지배하는 계획으로 이어졌다
= **and it(the film) featured** an AI, **and its(AI)** interpretation of the three laws led to a plan to dominate human beings in order to save us from ourselves
featuring(분사구문) = ~~and it(the film)~~ featured

whose = and + its(AI)
lead to ~ ~로 이어지다

* **headed up** by the American AI researcher Eliezer Yudkowsky
그런데 그 기관은 미국의 AI 연구자 엘리제르 유도스키에 의해 지휘를 받았는데
= **(and it(the organization) was) headed up** by the American AI researcher Eliezer Yudkowsky
headed up(분사구문) = ~~and it(the organization) was~~(being) headed up
head up ~ ~의 우두머리가 되다, ~을 지휘하다

* if AI ever developed to the stage **depicted** in Asimov's fictions
만일 AI가 아시모프의 소설에서 그려진 단계까지 발전하게 되면
= if AI ever developed to the stage **(which was) depicted in Asimov's fictions**
= 과거분사(depicted) 앞에 관계대명사의 주격(which)과 be동사 생략

* **to date** 지금까지

* if we are to avoid some of the more catastrophic scenarios **envisaged** by AI critics
만일 우리가 AI비판자들에 의해 예상되는 몇 가지 더 비극적인 시나리오를 피하려고 한다면
= if we are to avoid some of the more catastrophic scenarios **(which are) envisaged** by AI critics
= if we are to avoid some of the more catastrophic scenarios, **and they(scenarios) are envisaged** by AI critics
= 과거분사(envisaged) 앞에 관계대명사의 주격(which)과 be동사 생략

* Mittelstadt suggests significant differences between the fields of medicine and AI research **that** may well undermine the efficacy of the former's ethical principles in the context of the latter.
미틀스타트는 의학과 AI 연구 분야 사이의 중요한 차이를 제안하는데, 그 차이들은 아마 후자(AI)의 환경에서 전자(의학)의 윤리적 원칙들의 효력을 약화시킬 것이다 .
= Mittelstadt suggests significant differences between the fields of medicine and AI research, **and they(differences)** may well undermine the efficacy of the former's ethical principles in the context of the latter.
주격 관계대명사 that = and + they(differences)

may well 아마 ~일 것이다

* fiduciary duties, the duties **in which** trusted professionals, such as doctors, **place other's interests above their own**

신탁의무, 그런데 그것들은 의무인데, 그 의무 속에서 의사와 같은 신뢰를 받는 전문가들은 자신의 이익보다 남의 이익을 우선시한다

= fiduciary duties, **(and they are)** the duties, **and in them(duties)**, trusted professionals, such as doctors, place other's interests above their own

,는 동격으로 사용됨

in which = and + in them(duties)

place other's interests above their own

그들 자신의 이익보다 다른 사람의 이익을 우선시하다

* AI developers do not commit to public service, **which** in other professions requires practitioners to uphold public interests in the face of competing business or managerial interests.

AI 개발자들은 공적 서비스에 전념하지 않는데, 다른 전문직에서 공적인 서비스는 의사들이 경쟁 기업이나 경영이익 앞에서 공익을 유지하도록 요구한다.

= AI developers do not commit to public service, **and it(public service)** (in other professions) requires practitioners to uphold public interests in the face of competing business or managerial interests.

which = and + it(public service)

require + 목적어 + to + 동사원형 목적어가 ~하기를 요구하다

* while medicine has a professional culture **that** lays out the necessary moral obligations and virtues **stretching** back to the physicians of ancient Greece

의학이 전문적인 문화를 가지고 있지만, 그 문화는 필수적인 도덕적 의무와 미덕을 제시하는데 그것은 고대 그리스의 의사까지 거슬러 올라간다

= while medicine has a professional culture, **and it(culture)** lays out the necessary moral obligations and virtues, **and it(culture) stretches** back to the physicians of ancient Greece

주격 관계대명사 that = and + it(culture)

stretching(분사구문) = ~~and it(culture)~~ stretches

stretching back to ~ ~로 거슬러 올라가는

* Medicine has had a long time **over which** to learn from its mistakes and the shortcomings of the minimal guidance **provided** by the Hippocratic tradition.
의학은 오랜 시간을 가져 왔고 그 시간에 걸쳐 그 최소한의 가르침의 실수와 단점에서 배웠는데 그 최소한의 가르침은 히포크라테스 전통에 의해 제공된 것이다.
= Medicine has had a long time, **and over it(time)** to learn from its mistakes and the shortcomings of the minimal guidance **(which was) provided** by the Hippocratic tradition.
= Medicine has had a long time, **and over it(time)** to learn from its mistakes and the shortcomings of the minimal guidance, **and it(guidance) was provided** by the Hippocratic tradition.
over which = and + over it(time)
과거분사(provided) 앞에서 관계대명사의 주격과 be동사 생략 = (which was) provided
= ~~and it(guidance) was~~(being) provided

* AI research is obviously a far younger field, devoid of these rich historical opportunities to learn.
AI 연구는 분명히 훨씬 더 젊은 분야인데, 이런 것들을 배울 풍부한 역사적 기회가 없다.
= AI research is obviously a far younger field, **(and it(field) is) devoid** of these rich historical opportunities to learn.
devoid = ~~and it(field) is~~(being) devoid
be devoid of ~ ~이 없는
far는 비교급(younger)을 강조함 훨씬

* **taken for granted** 당연한 일로 여기다, 대수롭지 않게 여기다

Unit 11

How the Language You Speak Influences the Way You Think[1)]

WARMING UP

- These unique assets **make** us by far the most **adaptable** of all animals
- The faculty of language is **so** fundamental to the human condition **that** we take it completely for granted
- **Taken** at face value, that seems too strong a claim
- This redoubling is **more** a feature of the spoken **than** the written word
- **It stands to reason that** Turkish speakers have to pay more attention to evidentiality
- Language is also **made up of** all sorts of metaphors
- **Thinking** differently about space, they seem to think differently about time as well
- It has been said that when an old man dies, a library **burns to the ground**

1) This article was written by Neel Burton M.D. The source is https://www.psychologytoday.com/us/blog/hide-and-seek/201808/how-the-language-you-speak-influences-the-way-you-think

Time *heaved a gentle sigh as the wind swept through the willows. Communication does not require language, and many animals communicate effectively by other means and modes. However, *language is closely associated with symbolism, and so with conceptual thought and creativity. *These unique assets make us by far the most adaptable of all animals and enable us to *engage in[1] highly abstract *pursuits[2] such as art, science, and philosophy that define us as human beings.

Here's a thought experiment. *Imagine what it would be like to live without language - not without the ability to speak, but without an actual language. *Given the choice, would you rather lose the *faculty of sight[3] or the faculty of language? This is probably the first time that you have been faced with this question: *the faculty of language is so fundamental to the human condition that, unlike the faculty of sight, we take it completely for granted.

The *ostensible[4] purpose of language is to transmit thoughts from one *mind[5] to another. Language represents thought, but does it also determine thought?

*Wittgenstein[2)] famously wrote that 'the limits of my language *stand for the limits of my world'. *Taken at face value, that seems too strong a claim. There are over 7,000 languages in the world - with, *by some estimates, one dying out every two weeks or so. The number of basic colour terms varies quite considerably from one language to another. Dani, spoken in New Guinea, and Bassa, spoken

1. engage in
참여하게 하다

2. pursuit
활동, 추구

3. faculty of sight
시력

4. ostensible
표면상의

5. mind
사람

2) Wittgenstein(1889~1951) 오스트리아 태생의 영국 철학자.

6. subtly
미묘하게

7. equivalent
상당(대응)하는 것

8. yearning
갈망

9. conjure up
생각해내다

10. nay
아니다(no)

11. lore
(특정 주제에 대한) 구전 지식

12. anatomy
해부학, 몸

in Liberia and Sierra Leone, each have *no more than two colour terms, one for dark/cool colours and the other for light/warm colours. But, obviously, speakers of Dani and Bassa are able to perceive and think about more than just two colours.

More *subtly[6], there is no English *equivalent[7] for the German word Sehnsucht, which denotes dissatisfaction with reality and *yearning[8] for a richer, 'realer' ideal. But despite lacking the word, *Walt Whitman[3)] was clearly able to *conjure up[9] both the concept and the emotion: *Is it a dream? *Nay[10], but the lack of it the dream, And, failing it, life's *lore[11] and wealth a dream, And all the world a dream.*

*The English language has a word for children who have lost their parents(orphan), and a word for spouses who have lost their spouse(widow or widower), but no word for parents who have lost a child. This may mean that parents who have lost a child are less likely to enter our minds, but not that they cannot enter our minds or that we cannot conceive of them. *We often think about or remember things that cannot be put into words, such as the smell and taste of a mango, the dawn chorus of the birds, or the contours of a lover's face or other part of their *anatomy[12]. Animals and pre-linguistic babies must surely have thoughts, even though they have no language.

*If language does not determine thought, how, if at all, does it interact with thought? Russian, Greek, and many other languages

3) Walt Whitman(1819~1892) 미국의 시인.

have two words for blue, one for lighter shades and the other for darker shades–goluboy and siniy in Russian, and ghalazio and ble in Greek. A study found that, compared to English speakers, Russian speakers were quicker to *discriminate[13] between shades of goluboy and siniy, but not shades of goluboy or shades of siniy. Conversely, another study found that Greek speakers who had lived in the U.K. for a long time see ghalazio and ble as more similar than Greek speakers living in Greece. By creating *categories[14], by *carving up[15] the world, language enhances cognition.

*In contrast to modern Greek, Ancient Greek, *in common with many ancient languages, has no specific word for blue, *leaving *Homer[4)] to speak of 'the wine-dark sea'. But the Ancient Greeks did have several words for 'love', *including *philia, eros, storge*, and agape, each one referring to a different type or concept of love. This means that the Ancient Greeks could speak more precisely about love, but does it also mean that they could think more precisely about love, and, as a result, have more *fulfilled[16] *love lives[17]? Or perhaps they had more words for love because they had more fulfilled love lives *in the first place, or, more *prosaically[18], because their culture and society placed more emphasis on the different *bonds[19] that can exist between people, and on the various duties and expectations that *attend[20], or attended, to those bonds.

Philosophers and *academics[21] sometimes *make up[22] words to help them talk and think about an issue. In the Phaedrus, Plato

13. discriminate 식별하다, 구별하다
14. category 범주
15. carve up 분할하다
16. fulfilled 성취감을 느끼는
17. love life 애정생활
18. prosaically 평범하게, 단조롭게
19. bond 유대, 끈
20. attend to 정성을 들이다
21. academics 학자
22. make up 지어(만들어) 내다

4) Homer 고대 그리스의 시인, *Iliad and Odyssey*의 작가.

23. rhetoric
수사학

24. invariably
변함없이, 언제나

25. evolve
발달시키다

26. jargon
(특정 분야의 전문·특수) 용어

27. scaffolding
(건축공사장의) 비계, 발판

28. syncretic
혼합적인

29. echo
그대로 따라하다

30. proposition
명제

31. nuanced
미묘한

32. particularity
독특함

33. subconsciously
잠재의식적으로

coined the word psychagogia, the art of leading souls, to characterize *rhetoric[23] - another word that he invented. Every field of human endeavor *invariably[24] *evolves[25] its own specialized *jargon[26]. There seems to be an important relationship between language and thought: I often speak - or write, as I am doing right now - to define or refine my thinking on a particular topic, and *language is the *scaffolding[27] by which I arrive at my more subtle or *syncretic[28] thoughts.

While we're talking dead languages, it may come as a surprise that Latin has no direct translations for yes and no. Instead, one either *echoes[29] the verb in the question (in affirmative or negative) or expresses one's feelings about the truth value of the *proposition[30] with adverbs such as certe, fortasse, nimirum, plane, vero, etiam, sane, minime... This may have led to more *nuanced[31] thinking, as well as greater interpersonal engagement, though it must have been a nightmare for teens.

As I argue in my new book, Hypersanity: Thinking Beyond Thinking, *much of the *particularity[32] of a language is extra-lexical, built into the syntax and grammar of the language and virtually invisible to native speakers. English, for example, restricts the use of the present perfect tense ('has been', 'has read') to subjects who are still alive, marking a sharp grammatical divide between the living and the dead, and, *by extension, between life and death. But of course, as an English speaker, you already knew that, at least *subconsciously[33]. Language is full of built-in assumptions and *prejudices[34].

Here's another, more *substantial[35] example: When describing accidental events, English speakers tend to emphasize the agent ('I fired the gun') more than, say, speakers of Spanish or Japanese, who prefer to omit the agent ('the gun went off'). One study found that, as a result, English speakers are more likely to remember the agents of accidental events - and, I *surmise[36], to *attach blame.

Some languages seem more *egocentric[37] than others. *Many languages *forgo[38] the *explicit[39] use of the personal pronoun, which is instead built into the verb. For example, 'I want' in Spanish is simply quiero. English in contrast requires the explicit use of the personal pronoun in all cases. As does French. What's more, French speakers often *redouble[40] on the personal pronoun, as in Moi, je pense que… ('Me, I think that') with the stress on the moi. Sometimes, they also redouble on other personal pronouns, Et toi, qu'en penses-tu? ('And you, what do you think about it?'). But redoubling on the first personal pronoun is much more common: Bon aller, moi j'en ai marre hein ('Whatever, I'm fed up me'). *This redoubling is more a feature of the spoken than the written word, and, depending on context, can serve to emphasize or simply acknowledge a difference of opinion. *Equivalent[41] forms in English are more *strained[42] and *recondite[43], and less often used, for example, 'Well, as for me, I think that…' The redoubling, in French, on the first-person personal pronoun seems to *inject[44] drama into a conversation, as though the speaker were acting out her own part, or

34. prejudice
편견

35. substantial
실체가 있는, 실질적인

36. surmise
추측하다

37. egocentric
자기중심적인

38. forgo
포기하다

39. explicit
명시적인, 노골적인

40. redouble
배가하다

41. equivalent
동등한

42. strained
부자연스러운

43. recondite
잘 알려지지 않은

44. inject
주입하다, 더하다

45. play up
강조하다

46. separateness
분리, 개별적임

47. evidentiality
증거성

48. sense perception 감각 인식

49. testimony
증언

50. inference
추론

51. ongoing
계속 진행 중인

52. permanent
영구적인

53. address
호칭

54. intimate
절친한 친구

55. inferior
아랫사람, 하급자

56. downright
완전한

57. rudeness
버릇없음, 무례함

58. archaic
구식의, 낡은

59. Aboriginal
호주원주민의

*playing up[45] her difference and *separateness[46].

In English, verbs express tense, that is, time relative to the moment of speaking. In Turkish, they also express the source of the information (*evidentiality[47]) - whether the information is direct, acquired through *sense perception[48]; or indirect, acquired by *testimony[49] or *inference[50]. In Russian, they include information about completion, with (to simplify) the perfective aspect used for completed actions and the imperfective aspect for *ongoing[51] or habitual actions. Spanish, on the other hand, emphasizes modes of being, with two verbs for 'to be' - *ser*, to indicate *permanent[52] or lasting attributes, and estar, to indicate temporary states and locations. Like many languages, Spanish has more than one mode of second-person *address[53]: *tú* for *intimates[54] and social *inferiors[55], and *usted* for strangers and social superiors, equivalent to *tu* and vous in French, and *tu* and *lei* in Italian. There used to be a similar distinction in English, with *thou* used to express intimacy, familiarity, or *downright[56] *rudeness[57] - but because it is *archaic[58], many people now think of it as more formal than 'you'. *It stands to reason that, compared to English speakers, Turkish speakers have to pay more attention to evidentiality, Russian speakers to completion, and Spanish speakers to modes of being and social relations.

In many languages, nouns are divided into masculine and feminine. In German, there is a third, neutral class of nouns. In Dyribal, an *Aboriginal[59] language, there are four noun classes, including one for women, water, fire, violence, and exceptional animals - or, *as *George Lakoff[5] put it, 'women, fire, and dangerous things'. Researchers asked speakers of German and Spanish to describe objects with opposite gender assignments in these two languages and found that their descriptions *conformed to[60] gender *stereotypes[61], even when the testing took place in English. For example, German speakers described bridges (feminine in German, *die Brücke*) as beautiful, elegant, *fragile[62], peaceful, pretty, and *slender[63], whereas Spanish speakers described bridges (masculine in Spanish, *el Puente*) as big, dangerous, long, strong, *sturdy[64], and *towering[65].

Another study looking at the artistic *personification[66] of abstract concepts such as love, justice, and time found that, in 78% of cases, the gender of the concept in the artist's language predicted the gender of the personification, and that this pattern held even for uncommon *allegories[67] such as *geometry[68], necessity, and silence. Compared to a French or Spanish artist, a German artist is far more likely to paint death (*der Tod, la mort, la muerte*) or victory (*der Sieg, la Victoire, la Victoria*) as a man - though all artists, or at least all European artists, tend to paint death in *skeletal[69] form. Grammar, it seems, can directly and *radically[70] influence thought, perception, and action.

It is often said that, by de-emphasizing them, language *perpetuates[71] *biases[72] against women. For example, many writers in English continue to use 'mankind' to talk about humankind, and 'he' for 'he

60. conform to
~에 따르다

61. stereotype
고정관념,
정형화된 생각

62. fragile
허약한

63. slender
날씬한

64. sturdy
튼튼한

65. towering
우뚝 솟은

66. personification
의인화

67. allegory
우화

68. geometry
기하학

69. skeletal
뼈대의, 골격의

70. radically
근본적으로

71. perpetuate
영속시키다, 영구화하다

72. bias
편견

5) George P. Lakoff(1941 ~) 미국의 인지 언어학자.

or she'. Similarly, many languages use masculine plural pronouns to refer to groups of people with at least one man. If 100 women turn up with a baby in a *pram[73], and that baby happens to be male, French grammar dictates the use of the masculine plural *ils: ils sont arrivés, 'they have arrived',* 'they have arrived'.

Language changes as attitudes change, and sometimes politicians, pressure groups, and others attempt to change the language to change the attitudes - but, on the whole, *language, or at least grammar, serves to preserve the *status quo[74], to *crystallize[75] the order and culture that it reflects.

Language *is also made up of all sorts of metaphors. In English and Swedish, people tend to speak of time in terms of distance: 'I won't be long'; 'Let's look at the weather for the week ahead'; 'his drinking *caught up with him'. But in Spanish or Greek, people tend to speak of time in terms of size or volume - for example, in Spanish, hacemos una pequeña pausa('let's have a small break') rather than corta pausa('short break'). More generally, mucho tiempo('much time') is preferred to largo tiempo('long time'), and, in Greek, poli ora to makry kroniko diastima. *And guess what? According to a recent study of fully bilingual Spanish-Swedish speakers, the language used to *estimate[76] the duration of events alters the speaker's perception of the relative *passage[77] of time.

But *all in all, with perhaps a couple of exceptions, European languages do not differ *dramatically[78] from one another. To talk about space, speakers of Kuuk Thaayorre, an Aboriginal language,

73. pram
유모차

74. status quo
현재의 상황

75. crystallize
확고히 하다

76. estimate
추정하다, 판단하다

77. passage
경과

78. dramatically
극적으로, 급격히

use 16 words for absolute *cardinal[79] directions instead of relative references such as 'right in front of you', 'to the right', and 'over there'. As a result, even children are always aware of the exact direction in which they are facing. When asked to arrange a sequence of picture cards in temporal order, English speakers arrange the cards from left to right, whereas Hebrew speakers tend to arrange them from right to left. But speakers of Kuuk Thaayorre *consistently[80] arrange them from east to west, which is left to right if they are facing south, and right to left if they are facing north. *Thinking differently about space, they seem to think differently about time as well.

Language may not determine thought, but it focuses perception and attention on particular aspects of reality, structures and enhances cognitive processes, and even *to some extent *regulates[81] social relationships. *Our language reflects and at the same time shapes our thoughts and, *ultimately[82], our culture, which in turn shapes our thoughts and language. There is no equivalent in English of the Portuguese word saudade, which refers to the love and longing for someone or something that has been lost and may never be *regained[83]. The rise of saudade *coincided with[84] the decline of Portugal and the *yen[85] for its imperial *heyday[86], a yen so strong as to have written itself into the *national anthem[87]: Levantai hoje de novo o esplendor de Portugal ('Let us once again lift up the splendour of Portugal'). The three *threads[88] of language, thought, and culture are so tightly woven that they cannot be *prised apart[89].

79. cardinal 가장 중요한 (기본적인)
80. consistently 일관되게, 항상
81. regulate 규제하다
82. ultimately 궁극적으로, 결국
83. regain 되찾다, 회복하다
84. coincide with ~와 동시에 일어나다
85. yen 열망, 동경
86. heyday 전성기
87. national anthem 국가
88. thread 실, 가닥
89. prise apart 갈라놓다

It has been said that when an old man dies, *a library burns to the ground. But when a language dies, *it is a whole world that comes to an end.

GRAMMAR

조동사(Auxiliary Verbs)

조동사(Auxiliary 혹은 helping verb)는 본동사(main verb)를 도와서 본동사만으로는 나타내기 어려운 여러 가지 문법형식(예를 들어 부정문, 의문문, 진행상, 완료상, 수동태 등)과 의미(예를 들어 가능, 허가, 의무, 가능성 등)를 나타내기 위해 사용되는 단어를 말한다. 따라서 조동사의 유형은 다음과 같이 크게 두 가지로 나눌 수 있다.

1. 구조적 조동사(Structural Auxiliaries)

1) 의문문, 부정문을 만드는 조동사: do(does, did)

2) 진행상을 만드는 조동사: be(is, am, are, was, were)

3) 완료상을 만드는 조동사: have(has, had)

4) 수동태를 만드는 조동사: be(is, am, are, was, are)

2. 서법조동사(Modal Auxiliaries)

can/could, may/might, must, will/would, shall/should, ought to, need, dare, used to, be able to, have to, be about to, be going to, be likely to, be supposed to, be obliged to, be willing to, be due to, 등

동사	의미	부정형	과거형
Can, (be) able to	가능, 능력	can't, be not able to	could could have + p.p
must	추측	may not, might not can't	must have + p.p
may, might	추측	may not, might not	may/might + have +p.p
have to, must	강한 의무	don't have to (필요가 없다) must not(금지)	had to
should	권고	shouldn't	should have + p.p
had better	권고(당연)	had better not	

PHRASES and STRUCTURES

* **heaved a gentle sigh** 부드러운 한숨을 쉬었다

* Language is closely associated with symbolism, **and so** with conceptual thought and creativity.
언어는 상징과 밀접히 연관되어 있으며 개념적인 생각과 창조성과도 밀접히 연관되어 있다.
= Language is closely associated with symbolism, **and** language is **also** closely associated with conceptual thought and creativity.

* These unique assets **make** us **by far the** most **adaptable** of all animals.
이러한 독특한 자산들은 우리로 하여금 단연 모든 동물들 중에서 가장 잘 적응하게 해 준다.
make + 목적어 + 형용사 목적어가 ~되게 하다
by far 최상급 강조(단연)

* Imagine what **it** would be like **to** live without language.
언어 없이 사는 것이 어떨까를 상상해 보아라.
it은 **to**이하를 받고 있음

* **Given the choice** 선택하라고 한다면

* The faculty of language is **so fundamental** to the human condition **that**, unlike the faculty of sight, we **take it** completely **for granted**.
언어능력은 인간의 조건에 너무나 기본적이어서 시력과는 달리 우리는 그것을 아주 당연하다고 여긴다.
so ~ that 구문 너무나 ~해서 ~하다
take it for granted 당연히 ~일거라고 여기다(믿다)

* **stand for** ~ ~을 나타내다(의미하다)

* **Taken at face value**, 그것을 그대로 믿는다면
= If we take that at face value(능동형)
= If that is taken at face value(수동형)

= ~~If that~~ (being) taken at face value(분사구문)
take something at face value ~을 액면가 그대로(곧이곧대로) 믿다

* **by some estimates** 대략의

* **no more than** 단지 …에 지나지 않다, …일 뿐(only)

* The English language has a word for children **who** have lost their parents.
영어는 그들의 부모를 잃은 아이들에 대한 단어가 있다.
= The English language has a word for children, **and they(children)** have lost their parents.
who = and + they(children)

* We often think about or remember things **that** cannot be put into words.
우리는 종종 말로 나타내어질 수 없는 것들을 생각하거나 기억한다.
= We often think about or remember things, **and they(things)** cannot be put into words.
= We often think about or remember things, and we cannot put them(things) into words. (능동형)
주격 관계대명사 that = and + they(things)
put into words 말로 나타내다, 말로 옮기다

* If language does not determine thought, how, **if at all**, does it interact with thought?
만일 언어가 생각을 결정하지 않는다면, 그리고 적어도 언어가 생각을 결정한다면 언어는 어떻게 생각과 상호작용을 하는가?
if at all 적어도 ~한다면, ~한다고 하더라도

* **in contrast to** ~ ~와는 대조적으로

* **in common with** ~ ~와 마찬가지로

* **leaving** Homer to speak of 'the wine-dark sea'
호머가 마음대로 'the wine-dark sea'를 말하도록 하게 했다
= **and it left** Homer to speak of 'the wine-dark sea'

leaving(분사구문) = ~~and it~~ left

leave + 목적어 + to + 동사원형 마음대로 ~하게하다, ~하게 내버려두다

* **including** philia, eros, storge, and agape, each one referring to a different type or concept of love

사랑에 대한 여러 개의 단어들은 philia, eros, storge, and agape를 포함하는데 각각은 사랑의 다른 유형이나 개념을 나타낸다

= **and they(words) include** philia, eros, storge, and agape, and each one refers to a different type or concept of love

including(분사구문) = ~~and they(words)~~ include

* **in the first place** 우선, 먼저

* Language is the scaffolding **by which** I arrive at my more subtle or syncretic thoughts.

언어는 발판인데 그 발판에 의해 나는 나의 더 미묘하고 혼합적인 생각들에 도달한다.

= Language is the scaffolding, **and by it(scaffolding)** I arrive at my more subtle or syncretic thoughts.

by which = and + by it(scaffolding)

* Much of the particularity of a language is extra-lexical, **built** into the syntax and grammar of the language.

언어의 많은 독특함은 어휘외적인데 그것은 언어의 문법과 통사론에 내재되어진다.

= Much of the particularity of a language is extra-lexical, **(and it(particularity) is) built** into the syntax and grammar of the language.

built(분사구문) = ~~and it(particularity) is~~(being) built

built into ~ ~에 들어가 있는

* **by extension** 더 나아가

* **attach blame** 책임을 가하다, 책임을 묻다

* Many languages forgo the explicit use of the personal pronoun, **which** is instead built into the verb.

많은 언어들은 인칭대명사의 명시적 사용을 하지 않는데 대신에 인칭대명사는 동사에 내재된다.
= Many languages forgo the explicit use of the personal pronoun, **and it(personal pronoun)** is instead built into the verb.
which = and + it(personal pronoun)

* This redoubling is **more** a feature of the spoken **than** the written word.
이러한 배가(중복)은 문어보다 구어에 더 많은 특징이다.
more A than B B보다 A가 더 많다
cf. **no more A than B**
A가 아닌 것은 B가 아닌 것과 같다, B가 아닌 것과 같이 A도 아니다
not A any more than B
B가 아닌 것처럼 A도 아니다

* **It stands to reason that** ~ ~은 당연한 이치이다, ~은 당연하다

* **as George Lakoff put it** 조지 레이코프의 표현대로

* Language, or at least grammar, serves to preserve the status quo, to crystallize the order and culture **that** it reflects.
언어는 다시 말해 적어도 문법은 현 상황을 보존하는데, 즉 언어가 반영하는 질서와 문화를 확고히 하는데 기여한다.
= Language, or at least grammar, serves to preserve the status quo, to crystallize the order and culture, **and** it(language) reflects **it(the order and culture)**.
목적격 관계대명사 that = and + it(the order and culture)

* **is also made up of** 또한 ~로 구성되어 있다

* **caught up with somebody** 결국 ~의 발목을 잡다

* **And guess what?** 그리고 무슨 일이 일어났는가?

* **all in all** 대체로

* **Thinking** differently about space, they seem to think differently about time as

well.
공간에 대해서 다르게 생각하듯이 그들은 시간에 대해서도 또한 다르게 생각하는 것처럼 보인다.
= **As they think** differently about space, they seem to think differently about time as well.
Thinking(분사구문) = ~~As they~~ think

* **to some extent** 어느 정도 까지, 다소

* Our language reflects and at the same time shapes our thoughts and, ultimately, our culture, **which in turn** shapes our thoughts and language.
우리의 언어는 우리의 생각을 반영하고 동시에 형성하고 궁극적으로 우리의 문화를 형성하는데 문화는 결국 우리의 생각과 언어를 형성한다.
= Our language reflects and at the same time shapes our thoughts and, ultimately, our culture, **and it (culture)** in turn shapes our thoughts and language.
which = and + it (culture)
in turn 결국(결과적으로)

* **a library burns to the ground** 하나의 도서관이 완전히 타버리다
to the ground 완전히

* **It is** a whole world **that** comes to an end.
죽는 것은 바로 온 세상이다.
it is ~ that 강조구문

Unit 12

Ten Different Views On The Meaning Of Life[1)]

WARMING UP

- **Theories** on just what the meaning of life actually is **range** from the optimistic to the mind-blowingly depressing
- **Named for** its originator, Mo Di, the movement is notable for~
- Originally born into a Christian belief system, **his ideas** about God and **the meaning** behind what he was studying **fluctuated** greatly throughout his career
- **It's up for debate just how** much of an effect Darwin thought the idea of a creator should have on how we live our lives
- The meaning of life is **nothing than** survival
- **Things** that we think we believe in **are** only true until something better comes along
- **Very similar** to Buddhism, Tibetan philosophy preaches one major goal in life
- That energy isn**'t so much** a deity **as** kind of like the Force

1) This article was written by Debra Kelly. The source is https://listverse.com/2014/08/16/10-different-views-on-the-meaning-of-life/

1. struggle
발버둥 치다
2. mind-blowingly
놀라울 정도로,
정말로
3. thought-provoking
시사하는 바가 많은
4. offshoot
파생물, 분파
5. innately
선천적으로,
본질적으로
6. unknowable
알 수 없는, 불가지의
7. utmost
최고의

It's a question that mankind has long *struggled[1] to answer. We've built philosophies and religions around it, *gone to war over it, and debated it for centuries. *Theories on just what the meaning of life actually is range from the optimistic to the *mind-blowingly[2] depressing, but they're all pretty *thought-provoking[3].

10 The *Cyrenaics[2)]

The Cyrenaics were an *offshoot[4] of the teachings of Socrates. The group was founded somewhere around 400 B.C. by one of Socrates's students, a North African man named *Aristippus[3)]. According to their beliefs, *everyone's knowledge and experience is subjective, based only on what has happened to them. They believed that truth is an *innately[5] personal thing, and no one can experience the world quite like another person does. They also believed that we can't know anything *for certain about the things and people around us, there is only what we feel for ourselves.

They taught that the only real goal in life should be pleasure *in the present, that people should do what makes them happiest in the moment instead of planning for a future that, *in the end, is always *unknowable[6] and uncertain. Physical pleasures were of the *utmost[7] importance, and *all measures should be taken to maximize the amount of pleasure a person takes in the moment. The view was a very self-centered one, stating that a person's own pleasure should

2) Cyrenaics[sìrənéiiks] 키레네학파의(기원전 4세기경 Aristippus가 창시한 쾌락주의의).
3) Aristippus 아리스티포스(B.C. 435?~B.C. 356?) 그리스의 철학자, 키레네 학파의 창시자.

*take priority over the pleasure and overall goodness of the community, city, or *populace[8].

There is a *blatant[9] *disregard[10] for not only the well-being of others in their philosophy but also for traditions and social *norms[11]. Aristippus taught that there was nothing *inherently[12] wrong with *taboos[13] like *incest[14], *it was only social convention that made it wrong. The true meaning of life is to ignore the restraints of social convention and do what is most pleasurable to yourself, in the moment.

9 *Mohism[4)]

Mohism developed in China at about the same time the Cyrenaics were establishing themselves in Greece. *Named for its originator, Mo Di, the movement is notable for being one of the first organized philosophical groups in China who debated and argued ideas like the meaning of life. Their *resulting[15] texts *outline[16] *10 doctrines that they said people should strive to follow in their everyday lives, most of which *espouse[17] *impartiality[18].

According to the doctrines, the meaning of life can only be achieved when every individual person shows the same amount of care and attention to every other person, putting no one's needs above anyone else's. That meant *getting rid of wasteful luxury, entertainment for its own sake, and wealth. They wanted people to strive for *equality[19], *making sure that everyone had the same

8. populace 대중
9. blatant 노골적인
10. disregard 무시
11. norm 규범
12. inherently 선천적으로, 본질적으로
13. taboo 금기
14. incest 근친상간
15. resulting 결과로 발생한
16. outline 윤곽을 보여주다
17. espouse 옹호하다
18. impartiality 공명정대
19. equality 평등

4) Mohism (고대 중국의) 묵자(墨子)의 사상(가르침).

20. compatible 양립할 수 있는, 화합할 수 있는
21. questionable 의심스러운
22. hypocrisy 위선
23. virtuous 도덕적인
24. deride 조롱하다
25. parrhesia 솔직하게 숨김없이 진실 말하기
26. tenet 교리
27. self-sufficiency 자급자족
28. companionship 동료애
29. tie down 얽매다, 구속하다

degree of happiness and comfort while honoring the wishes of the divine and helping everyone achieve the final goal in life: rewards in the afterlife.

8 The *Cynics[5)]

The Cynics are another group that descended from the teachings of Socrates, and according to them, the meaning of life was to live a moral existence that was more *compatible[20] with the natural order of things than with what they saw as the *questionable[21] ethics and social traditions of popular society. The Cynics recognized that many things that had become accepted tradition in their society, such as the *hypocrisy[22] and wealth they saw in temples, *had little or nothing to do with helping people to live *virtuous[23] lives.

While they didn't *deride[24] social convention completely, they said that each person should form their own thoughts about right and wrong, and follow the path of virtue even when it went against social norms. From this came the idea of *parrhesia[25], or speaking the truth. Another important *tenet[26] of this philosophy was *self-sufficiency[27], which meant being able to survive not just without the *companionship[28] of other people but without basic comforts or the need for possessions. *It was only when someone turned their back on the need to be *tied down[29] by people or things that they were truly free, and freedom was the meaning of life.

5) Cynics 명예와 부를 멀리 하고 자연과 일체 된 삶을 강조했던 고대 그리스의 금욕주의 학파다. 키니코스(Κυνικοί)는 그리스어로 '개(Κύνος)'라는 단어에서 유래한 까닭에 한국에서는 견유학파(犬儒學派)로 불리기도 함.

7 Albert Einstein

*Albert Einstein[6] will undoubtedly always have a place among the *pantheon[30] of mankind's most brilliant minds. In 1951, a young woman wrote him a letter asking about his belief on the meaning of life, and his reply was short and *poignant[31]. "To create satisfaction for ourselves and for other people," he wrote.

But letters between Einstein and his son, Eduard, show a deeper answer than that. In response to one letter, Einstein told his son that he believed in the "highest stage of consciousness as the highest ideal" and that *mankind's ability to think and create something from nothing is the greatest thing that we can do. He suggests that it's this creation that will allow us to experience true happiness. He also *stresses[32] that *it's necessary to create not out of a desire to be remembered but for the love of the thing you are bringing into the world.

6 *Darwinism[7]

*Charles Darwin[8] had something of a complicated relationship with religion and religious ideas about the meaning of life. *Originally born into a Christian belief system, his ideas about God and the meaning behind what he was studying *fluctuated[33] greatly

30. pantheon 유명인들
31. poignant 가슴 아픈
32. stress 강조하다
33. fluctuate 변동을 거듭하다

6) Albert Einstein(1879~1955)아인슈타인 독일 태생 미국의 이론물리학자. 1916년 일반상대성이론(Theory of general relativity)을 발표하였음.

7) Darwinism 다윈설(자연선택에 의한 생물의 진화를 주장한 이론).

8) Charles Darwin(1809~1882) 생물진화론을 정하여 뜻을 세운 영국의 생물학자. 그는 1859년 〈종의 기원〉(On the Origin of Species (or, more completely, On the Origin of Species by Means of Natural Selection, or the Preservation of Favoured Races in the Struggle for Life)을 발표해 진화론을 공표했음.

throughout his career.

*It's up for debate just how much of an effect Darwin thought the idea of a creator should have on how we live our lives - some texts imply that evolution itself is a *deity-like[34] idea, while others state that *evolution created a human state that was designed to need some sort of supernatural creator to worship. But *random[35] chance and environmental pressures are all that is required for evolution to work, *so what does that indicate for a higher meaning of life?

Darwin's *opponents[36] insist that evolution and Darwinism suggests that the meaning of life *is nothing than survival, but there are more complicated interpretations of his theories *with regards to the meaning of life. One suggests that the meaning of life is different for everyone and every species - the *point[37] of the existence of a plant is very different from the point of the existence of a fish. *One thing that many interpretations of Darwinism agree upon is that part of the meaning of life for any living organism is to pass their DNA on to the next generation.

5 *Nihilism[9]

*Perhaps the most common context in which we hear the term "nihilism" is from the Russian *revolutionaries[38] who denied the power of all traditionally accepted *authoritarian bodies[39], such as the government and religion. While the ideas of nihilism are more complicated than that, the movement took its name *with good

34. deity-like
신 같은

35. random
무작위의, 임의의

36. opponent
반대자

37. point
의미, 이유

38. revolutionary
혁명가

39. authoritarian body
권위주의 단체

9) Nihilism 허무주의(일체의 사물이나 현상이 실제 존재하지 않으며, 또한 아무런 가치도 지니지 않는다고 보는 사상).

reason.

A true nihilist believes that there is no such thing as value or knowledge, and there is no point *whatsoever[40] to a person's existence. *Friedrich Nietzsche[10)] argued that nihilistic beliefs would ultimately lead to the *downfall[41] of everything, because people would simply cease to *care about[42] anything. There is certainly no truth, and *things that we think we believe in are only true until something better comes along. *A quick look at the *overwhelming[43] number of scientific beliefs that have been *debunked[44] over the centuries seems to lend credence to this theory. Originally, the only thing that was believed to have a purpose of any sort was destruction, but later attempts to soften the image of the nihilist philosophy suggested a *route[45] of *indifference[46] instead.

The idea has *captivated[47] philosophers for centuries. According to Nietzsche, *everything we see around us is an artificial construct that won't last with the indifference of nihilism, a theory that's supported by *Oswald Spengler[11)]'s analysis of the attitudes that *beckon[48] the *collapse[49] of a society or civilization. Perhaps one of the most *depressing[50] theories on the meaning of life, nihilism says that there is no meaning, but that's almost all right, because *there's really not much of anything.

40. whatsoever = whatever 무엇이든
41. downfall 몰락
42. care about ~에 관심을 가지다
43. overwhelming 압도적인
44. debunk (생각·믿음 등이) 틀렸음을 드러내다(밝히다)
45. route 길, 노선
46. indifference 무관심
47. captivate ~의 마음을 사로잡다
48. beckon 손짓하다
49. collapse 붕괴
50. depressing 우울하게 만드는

10) Friedrich Nietzsche(1844~1900) 독일의 철학자, 시인.

11) Oswald Spengler(1880~1936) 독일의 역사가, 철학자.

51. preach
설파하다, 전하다

52. instruction
가르침

53. tiny
아주 작은

54. particle
입자

4 Tibetan Philosophy

Tibetan philosophy is a school of thought that developed in Tibet and other areas of the Himalayan Mountains. *Very similar to Buddhism, Tibetan philosophy *preaches[51] one major goal in life: to end the world's suffering. In order to do that, the first thing that you have to do is gain an understanding of the world and how it works. Through understanding, *you will eventually come to the knowledge required to end suffering.

The philosophy also provides a path by which you can measure your personal milestones, from being a "Person of Small Ability" who is most concerned with themselves to being a "Person of Great Ability" who takes suffering away from others by suffering themselves. It's one thing to believe a certain way, but *the true meaning of life is found by those who practice what they believe and act in such a way that benefits others above themselves. Tibetan philosophy is also unique in that *whatever point in the path a follower is on, they have a clear set of *instructions[52] for getting closer to the true meaning of life.

3 The *Epicureans[12)]

The Epicurean philosophy is often oversimplified. According to the teachings of *Epicurus[13)], everything is made up of *tiny[53] *particles[54], including the human body, which is made up of soul

12) Epicurean (쾌락주의자) 원래는 그리스의 철학자 에피쿠로스의 사상을 신봉하는 정신적 쾌락주의자를 가리키는 말이었으나, 오늘날에 와서는 원뜻을 떠나, 널리 관능적, 찰나적인 쾌락을 추구하는 사람을 말함.

13) Epicurus 에피쿠로스(B.C.342? ~ B.C.270) 고대 그리스의 철학자.

particles. Without these particles, the body is dead, and without a living body, the soul particles are incapable of feeling anything. Because of this dual existence, no part of the human can survive after death. There is no eternal rest or *torment[55], no great reward to work toward, and no great punishment to avoid. That means that all you have is what you have on Earth, so while you're here, you need to *make the most of it.

Soul particles are what allow us to feel pain and pleasure, and that's where the Epicurean's meaning of life comes from: maximize pleasure, minimize pain. This isn't as easy as it sounds, *because one of our main sources of pain and anxiety comes from either abstract concepts that we can't see or control or desires that we have no way of fulfilling. For example, the idea of death is one we often look upon with fear and *dread[56]. The Epicurean ideal says that *it's something we need to come to terms with not being able to control.

That doesn't mean, however, that we should go out and do whatever we want. If we think that robbing a bank might lead to some pleasurable consequences, we can't use Epicurean philosophy as a reason to do it. Epicurus says that behaving in a good, just manner is *vital[57] to the pleasure principle, because the guilt and anxiety of getting caught can *eat away at us and eventually cause pain. One of the most important aspects of the Epicurean meaning of life is the *cultivation[58] of friendships, *as friendship is one of the most pleasant, *secure[59], safe, and *everlasting[60] feelings to which *mortal[61] man can aspire.

55. torment
고통

56. dread
두려움

57. vital
필수적인

58. cultivation
구축

59. secure
확실한

60. everlasting
영원한, 변치 않는

61. mortal
영원히 살 수 없는,
언젠가는 반드시 죽는

62. polar opposite 완전히 반대인 것
63. precarious 불안정한
64. utmost 최고의, 극도의
65. earthly 세속적인
66. ensure 보장하다

2 Aztec Philosophy

According to the *Aztecs[14], the ultimate meaning of life was to live in balance with nature and allow the continuation of the energy that *gives rise to each generation. *That energy, called teotl, isn't so much a deity as kind of like the Force. It's an energy that surrounds all living things, joining everything we know and everything that's beyond our knowledge. Because teotl is always moving and changing, so is the universe, and *it's up to mankind to make sure they live in harmony with that.

Teotl is even more than that, though, *as it exists in the form of *polar opposites[62] whose struggle against each other maintains the end balance of the universe. Because of these opposing natures, life and death aren't thought of as good and bad but simply part of the cycle. The Aztecs believed that they were on a *precarious[63] point between the two, and *it was of the *utmost[64] importance to stay in the middle, maintaining balance and not enjoying wealth or excess but living wisely and goodly.

The goals outlined in Aztec wisdom are to live in such a manner that future generations may enjoy the same good life that you did, make sure your actions keep the cycle of life going, and *honor the mysterious sacred force that makes life possible. In many texts, *earthly[65] life is described as being filled with pain and sadness, and the only thing that can give the world meaning is taking small joy in the simple pleasures of life while *ensuring[66] the survival of the cycle.

14) Aztec (아즈텍족) 멕시코 원주민, 1519년 Cortes에게 정복당함.

1 *Stephen Fry[15] And The *Humanists[16]

Stephen Fry's narration of the humanist video *puts the question of the meaning of life in a perspective that relates to anyone, no matter what their belief system, age, race, or gender. According to Fry - and the humanists - there is no specific meaning of life. Everyone has their own meaning or meanings. Instead of *looking to the universe for meaning, people should look inside themselves to discover what makes them happy and gives their own life meaning. The only meaning is that we give to our actions, connections, desires, and *the legacy we leave for future generations.

Because everyone is different, the meaning of life is different for all of us. *For some, it might be creating a great work of art. For others, it might be *establishing a scholarship. It could even be as simple as creating a garden, adopting a child, or adopting an animal *in need. There's no right or wrong meaning of life or any mysterious answer out there - rather, it is a mysterious answer within ourselves.

Most important to this theory is the answer to how to be happy. It's a *deceptively[67] simple answer, and one that many other schools of thought and philosophy *overlook[68]: simply living life as completely and fully as possible.

67. deceptively
믿을 수 없게

68. overlook
간과하다, 못 보고 넘어가다

15) Stephen Fry(1957 ~) 영국 출신의 배우.

16) Humanist 인문주의자로 특히 서양의 문예부흥기의 고전문학 연구자를 가리킴. 이탈리아 르네상스기의 인문주의자들은 그리스 로마의 고전으로 돌아가 중세의 신(神) 중심의 세계관에서 탈피하여 인간 중심의 세계관을 가지게 됨.

GRAMMAR

대명사(Pronoun)

1. 대명사의 종류

일반적으로 명사를 대신하는 것을 대명사라고 하는데 다음과 같이 다섯 가지 종류로 나누어 볼 수 있다

1) 인칭(personal) 대명사: I, you, he, she, we, they, it

2) 지시(demonstrative) 대명사: this, that, these, those

3) 부정(indefinite) 대명사: some, any, both, all, one, another, each, every

4) 의문(interrogative) 대명사: who, what, which

5) 관계(relative) 대명사: who, whose, whom, which, that, what

이와 같은 대명사의 정의와 분류에 대해서는 여러 가지 견해가 있을 수 있지만 편의상 위와 같이 정의하고 분류하였다. 이러한 유형 외에도 소유(possessive)대명사, 재귀(reflexive)대명사, 상호(reciprocal)대명사도 있는데 이들 대명사는 인칭대명사와 관련이 있다

대명사는 단독으로 사용될 때 칭하여지는 용어이며, 위의 대명사 중에서 지시대명사가 this book과 같이 명사 앞에서 명사를 수식할 때는 지시형용사 혹은 한정사로 사용된다. 이와 같이 인칭대명사의 소유격(my, your, his, her, our, their), 지시대명사, 부정대명사가 명사 앞에 사용될 때는 관사, 수사와 함께 한정사(determiner)로 간주된다

2. 의문대명사

의문을 나타내는 말을 의문사라 하는데 의문사에는 의문대명사, 의문형용사, 의문부사가 있다

의문대명사	WHO(WHOSE, WHOM), WHAT, WHICH
의문형용사	WHAT, WHICH, WHOSE (주로 명사를 수식한다) What part of Ireland do you come from? Which book do you like best? (일정 수 가운데 어느 누구나 어느 것) What book do like best? (부정 수 가운데 어느 누구나 어느 것)
의문부사	WHEN, WHERE, WHY, HOW

PHRASES and STRUCTURES

* **gone to war over it** 그것을 두고 전쟁을 벌이다

* **Theories** on just **what** the meaning of life actually is **range from** the optimistic **to** the mind-blowingly depressing.
삶의 의미가 정말로 정확히 무엇인지에 관한 이론들은 낙관적인 것에서부터 정말로 우울한 것까지 다양하다.
what 의문대명사(무엇)
주어는 theories, 본동사는 range
range from A to B A에서 B까지 다양하다, 범위가 A에서 B에 이르다

* Everyone's knowledge and experience is subjective, **based** only on what has happened to them.
모든 사람의 경험과 지식은 주관적인데 그 경험과 지식은 오로지 그들에게 일어난 것에 기반을 두고 있다.
= Everyone's knowledge and experience is subjective, **(and it(knowledge and experience) is) based** only on what has happened to them.
based(분사구문) = ~~and it(knowledge and experience) is~~(being) based

* **for certain** 확실히

* **in the present** 현재의

* **in the end** 결국

* All measures should **be taken** to maximize the amount of pleasure a person takes in the moment.
사람이 그 순간에 취하는 쾌락의 양을 최대화 하도록 모든 조처를 취해야 한다.
= We should **take** all measures to maximize the amount of pleasure a person takes in the moment.(능동형)
= We should **take** all measures to maximize the amount of pleasure **(which)** a

person takes in the moment.

= We should **take** all measures to maximize the amount of pleasure, **and** a person takes **it(pleasure)** in the moment.

목적격 관계대명사 which 생략 = and + it(pleasure)

take measures 조처를 취하다

* **take priority over ~** ~에 대해 우선권을 갖다, ~에 우선하다

* **It was** only social convention **that** made it wrong.

그것이 잘못되게 한 것은 바로 오로지 사회적 관습이었다.

it is ~ that 강조 구문

* **Named** for its originator, Mo Di, the movement is notable for ~.

창시자 모디의 이름을 본 따 명명된 그 운동은 ~로 유명하다.

= **The movement was named** for its originator, Mo Di, and it(the movement) is notable for ~.

Named(분사구문) = ~~The movement was~~(being) named

name for ~ ~의 이름을 따서 명명하다

is notable for ~ ~로 유명하다

* 10 doctrines **that** they said people should strive to follow in their everyday lives, **most of which** espouse impartiality.

그들이 말했던 10개의 신조들은 사람들이 그들의 일상생활에서 따르려고(지키려고) 노력해야 하는 것들이었는데, 그 중의 대부분은 공명정대를 옹호한다.

= 10 doctrines, **and** (they said) people should strive to follow **them(10 doctrines)** in their everyday lives, **and most of them(doctrines)** espouse impartiality.

목적격 관계대명사 that = and + them(10 doctrines)

most of which = and + most of them(doctrines)

they said는 삽입절

* **get rid of ~** ~을 제거하다, 없애다

* **make sure that** 반드시 (~하도록) 하다, (~을) 확실히 하다

* The meaning of life was to live a moral existence **that** was more compatible with the natural order of things than with what they saw as the questionable ethics and social traditions of popular society.

삶의 의미는 도덕적인 생활을 하는 것이었는데, 도덕적인 생활은 그들이 의심스러운 윤리와 대중사회의 사회적 전통으로 간주했던 것 보다 사물의 자연적 질서와 더 화합할 수 있는 것이었다.

= The meaning of life was to live a moral existence, **and it(moral existence)** was more compatible with the natural order of things than with, **what** they **saw as** the questionable ethics and social traditions of popular society.

주격 관계대명사 that = and + it(moral existence)

what은 선행사를 포함하는 관계대명사

see A as B A를 B로 간주하다

* **had little or nothing to do with ~** ~와 거의 혹은 전혀 관계가 없었다

* **It was** only when someone **turned their back on** the need to be tied down by people or things **that** they were truly free.

그들이 진정으로 자유로운 때는 바로 누군가가 사람이나 사물에 의해 얽매어질 필요성을 외면할 때뿐이다.

It is ~ that 강조 구문

turn one's back on ~ ~에 등을 돌리다, 외면하다

* Mankind's ability to think and create something from nothing is the greatest thing **that** we can do.

무로부터 어떤 것을 생각하고 창조할 수 있는 인간의 능력이 우리가 할 수 있는 가장 위대한 것이다.

= Mankind's ability to think and create something from nothing is the greatest thing, **and** we can do **it(thing)**

목적격 관계대명사 that = and + it(doing)

* **It's** necessary **to** create **not** out of a desire to be remembered **but** for the love of the thing **(which)** you are bringing into the world.

기억되어지려는 바람에서가 아니라 당신이 세상에 가져올 것에 대한 사랑을 위해 창조하는 것이 필요하다.

= It's necessary to create not out of a desire to be remembered but for the love of the thing, **and** you are bringing **it(thing)** into the world.

it은 **to** 이하를 받음

목적격 관계대명사 **which = and + it(thing)**

not A but B A가 아니라 B다

* **Originally born** into a Christian belief system, **his ideas** about God and **the meaning** behind what he was studying **fluctuated** greatly throughout his career.

원래 기독교 신앙체계에서 태어난 신에 대한 그의 생각과 그가 연구하고 있었던 것 뒤에서의 의미는 그의 전 생애에 걸쳐서 변동을 거듭했다 .

= **Originally his ideas about God were born** into a Christian belief system, **and** his ideas about God and the meaning behind what he was studying fluctuated greatly throughout his career.

Originally born(분사구문) = Originally ~~his ideas about God were~~(being) born

주어는 **his ideas and the meaning,** 본동사 **fluctuate**

* **It's up for debate** just **how** much of an effect Darwin thought the idea of a creator should have on how we live our lives.

다윈이 생각했던 창조자라는 개념이 우리가 삶을 어떻게 사는지에 정확히 얼마나 많은 영향을 미치는지 논란의 여지가 있다.

= It's up for debate just how **(Darwin thought)** the idea of a creator should have much of an effect on how we live our lives.

Darwin thought는 삽입절

have an effect on ~ ~에 영향을 미치다

It's up for debate how ~ how 이하는 논란의 여지가 있다

* Evolution created a human state **that** was designed to need some sort of supernatural creator to worship.

진화가 인간의 상태를 만들어냈는데, 그 인간의 상태는 숭배할 어느 정도의 초자연적인 창조자를 필요로 하도록 고안되어졌다.

= Evolution created a human state, **and it(human state)** was designed to need some sort of supernatural creator to worship.

주격 관계대명사 that = and + it(human state)

* So what does that indicate for a higher meaning of life?
그렇다면 그것이 더 높은 삶의 의미에 대해 말하고 있는 것은 무엇인가?

* **is nothing than** ~ ~에 지나지 않다

* **with regards to** ~ ~에 관해서

* One thing **that** many interpretations of Darwinism agree upon
다윈설의 많은 해석들이 의견을 일치하는 한 가지는
= One thing, **and** many interpretations of Darwinism agree upon **it(thing)**
목적격 관계대명사 that = and + it(thing)
agree upon ~ ~에 대해 의견이 일치하다

* Perhaps the most common context **in which** we hear the term "nihilism" is from the Russian revolutionaries **who** denied the power of all traditionally accepted authoritarian bodies, such as the government and religion.
우리가 '허무주의'라는 용어를 듣게 되는 아마도 가장 일반적인 상황은 러시아 혁명가들로부터 온 것인데 그들은 전통적으로 받아들여졌던 모든 권위주의적인 단체들, 가령 정부와 종교 같은 것의 힘을 부정했다.
Perhaps the most common context, **and in it(context)** we hear the term "nihilism" is from the Russian revolutionaries, **and they** denied the power of all traditionally accepted authoritarian bodies, such as the government and religion.
in which = and + in it(context)
who = and + they(the Russian revolutionaries)

* **with good reason** 그럴만한 이유가 있어서

* <u>**Things**</u> **that** we think we believe in <u>**are**</u> only true until something better comes along.
우리가 생각하기로 우리가 믿는 것들은 더 좋은 어떤 것이 함께 올 때에야 비로소 사실이다.
= Things, **and** (we think) we believe in **them(things)** are only true until something better comes along.
목적격 관계대명사 that = and + them(things)
we think는 삽입절

주어는 Things, 동사는 are

* A quick **look** at the overwhelming number of scientific beliefs **that** have been debunked over the centuries **seems** to **lend credence to** this theory.
압도적인 수의 과학적 믿음을 재빨리 쳐다보는 것은, 그런데 그 믿음들은 수세기에 걸쳐 틀렸음이 드러났는데, 이 이론에 신빙성을 부여하는 것처럼 보인다.
= A quick look at the overwhelming number of scientific beliefs, **and they(beliefs)** have been debunked over the centuries seems to lend credence to this theory.
that = and + they(beliefs)
lend credence to ~ ~에 신빙성을 부여하다
주어는 look, 동사는 seems

* Everything we see around us is an artificial construct that won't last with the indifference of nihilism.
우리 주위에서 우리가 보는 모든 것은 인공적인 구조물인데 그 구성물은 허무주의의 무관심 때문에 지속되지 않을 것이다.
= Everything **(that)** we see around us is an artificial construct **that** won't last with the indifference of nihilism.
= Everything, **and** we see **it(everything)** around us is an artificial construct, **and it(construct)** won't last with the indifference of nihilism.
목적격 관계대명사 that = and + it(everything)
주격 관계대명사 that = and + it(construct)

* **There's really not much of anything.** 정말 아무 것도 없다.

* **Very similar** to Buddhism, Tibetan philosophy preaches one major goal in life.
불교와 아주 유사한 티베트 철학은 삶에서 한 가지 중요한 목적을 설파한다.
= **(Tibetan philosophy is) very similar** to Buddhism, **and it**(Tibetan philosophy) preaches one major goal in life.
Very similar = ~~Tibetan philosophy is~~(being) very similar

* You will eventually come to the knowledge **required** to end suffering.
여러분은 결국 고통을 끝내기 위해 요구되는 지식에 이르게 될 것이다.
= You will eventually come to the knowledge **(which is) required** to end suffering.

과거분사(required) 앞에서 관계대명사(which)의 주격과 be동사 생략

* The true meaning of life is found by those **who** practice what they believe and act in such a way **that** benefits others above themselves.
삶의 진정한 의미는 그들이 믿는 것을 실행하고 그들 자신보다 다른 사람들에게 이익이 되는 그런 식으로 행동하는 사람들의 해 발견된다.
= The true meaning of life is found by those, **and they** practice what they believe and act in such a way, **and it(way)** benefits others above themselves.
who = and + they
주격 관계대명사 that = and + it(way)

* **whatever point in the path a follower is on**
신봉자가 길 위의 어떤 지점에 있든지

* **make the most of ~** ~을 최대한 이용하다

* because one of our main sources of pain and anxiety comes from either abstract concepts **that** we can't see or control or desires **that** we have no way of fulfilling
우리의 고통과 걱정의 근원들 중의 하나는 우리가 볼 수 없거나 통제할 수 없는 추상적인 개념들에서 생겨나거나 실현시킬 방법이 없는 욕망에서 생겨나기 때문에
= because one of our main sources of pain and anxiety comes from either abstract concepts, **and** we can't see or control **them(concepts)** or desires, **and** we have no way of fulfilling **them(desires)**
목적격 관계대명사 that = and + them(concepts)
목적격 관계대명사 that = and + them(desires)

* It's something we need to **come to terms with** not being able to control.
그것은 우리가 통제할 수 없는 것과 타협하기 위해 필요한 어떤 것이다.
come to terms with ~ ~와 합의를 보다, ~와 타협하다

* **eat away at ~** ~을 조금씩 갉아먹다, ~을 계속 괴롭히다

* as friendship is one of the most pleasant, secure, safe, and everlasting feelings **to which** mortal man can aspire.

우정이 가장 확실하고, 안전하고, 영원한 느낌들 중의 하나이기 때문인데, 그 느낌은 언젠가는 죽는 인간이 갈망할 수 있는 것이다.

= as friendship is one of the most pleasant, secure, safe, and everlasting feelings, **and** mortal man can aspire **to them(feelings)**.

to which = and + to them(feelings)

aspire to ~ ~을 갈망하다

* **gives rise to** 낳다, ~이 생기게 하다

* That energy, called teotl, isn**'t so much** a deity **as** kind of like the Force.

티틀이라 불리는 그러한 에너지는 신이라기보다는 일종의 힘과 같다.

not so much A as B A라기보다는 차라리 B다

* **It**'s up to mankind **to make** sure they live in harmony with that.

그들이 그것(티틀)과 반드시(확실히) 조화롭게 사는 것은 인간에 달려있다.

= It's up to mankind to make sure **(that)** they live in harmony with that.

It은 to이하를 받음

make sure 반드시 (~하도록) 하다

* as it exists in the form of polar opposites **whose** struggle against each other maintains the end balance of the universe

그것이 극과 극의 형태로 존재하기 때문인데, 서로서로에 대한 그 극과 극의 싸움이 우주의 최종 균형을 유지한다

= as it exists in the form of polar opposites, **and their** struggle against each other maintains the end balance of the universe

whose = and + their

* **It was of** the utmost **importance to** stay in the middle, maintaining balance and not enjoying wealth or excess but living wisely and goodly.

중간에 머물고 균형을 유지하고 부나 과도함을 즐기지 않고 현명하게 그리고 선하게 사는 것이 아주 중요하다.

it ~ to + 동사원형 it은 가주어 to 이하는 진주어

be of importance 중요하다

* honor the mysterious sacred force **that** makes life possible
신비스러운 신성한 힘을 존경하는데 그 힘은 삶이 가능하게 한다
= honor the mysterious sacred force, **and it(force)** makes life possible
주격 관계대명사 that = and + it(force)
make + 목적어 + 형용사 목적어가 ~하게 하다

* **puts the question of ~** ~의 문제를 제기하다

* **looking to ~** ~에 기대를 걸다, ~에 의지하다

* the legacy we leave for future generations
우리가 미래 세대를 위해 남긴 유산
= the legacy **(which)** we leave for future generations
= the legacy, **and** we leave **it(the legacy)** for future generations
목적격 관계대명사 which 생략 = and + it(the legacy)

* For some, **it** might be creating a great work of art.
몇몇 사람들에게 삶의 의미는 위대한 예술작품을 창조하는 것일 수 있다.
it = the meaning of life

* **establishing a scholarship** 장학회를 만드는 것

* **in need** 어려움에 처한

Unit 13

Relation of Literature to Life[1)]

WARMING UP

- Life provides the raw material **on which** literature imposes an artistic form
- True reality consists in the ideas of things, **of which** individual objects are but reflections or imitations
- We are **comparing** the dog which we actually see **with** the ideal dog
- **Being** too much of a philosopher and moralist, he could not see clearly the relation between literature and life
- **Presenting as it must do** individual men or women in the trappings and circumstances of life, it does not leave them there, but pierces to what is significant in action and character
- The truth **with which** he deals is **not that** which the anatomist may lay bare on the dissecting-table, **but that** which a poet divines and translates
- We conclude that **the notion that** literature is not concerned with real life is wrong
- because he knows **more** about life **than** anyone can know without regarding life with his eyes

1) This article was written by Professor NAEEM, The source is https://neoenglish.wordpress.com/2010/12/16/relation-of-literature-to-life/

1. intimate
밀접한

2. raw material
소재

3. contradictory
모순되는

4. refer to
언급하다

5. condemn
비난하다

6. lame
절뚝거리는

There is an *intimate[1] connection between literature and life. *It is, in fact, life which is the subject matter of literature. *Life provides the *raw material[2] on which literature imposes an artistic form. Literature, as we defined in the previous section, is the communication of the writer's experience of life. But this connection between literature and life is not so simple as it seems. This problem has been discussed by some of the greatest literary critics of the world, and their conclusions have been sometimes *contradictory[3].

Plato, the great Greek philosopher, was the first to give a serious thought to this problem - the relation of literature to life. In his discussions he *referred mainly to[4] poetry, but what he said about poetry can be equally applied to literature as a whole. He regarded poetry as a mere 'imitation' of life, and thus he *condemned[5] the poets. His opposition to poetry was based on his theory of knowledge. According to him, *true reality consists in the ideas of things, of which individual objects are but reflections or imitations. For example, when we say a black dog, a good dog, a *lame[6] dog etc., *we are comparing the dog which we actually see with the ideal dog, our idea of the dog, which is the true, unchanging reality, while the dogs which we name as black, good, lame etc. are mere reflections and imitations of that reality. *Thus the poet, who imitates those objects which are themselves imitations of reality, is obviously producing something, which is still further removed from ultimate reality. Plato developed this argument first *with reference to the painter. Painting is an imitation of a specific object or group of objects, and if it is *nothing but that, if reality lies not in *apprehending[7] reality, the painter is not doing anything particularly valuable. Just as the painter only imitates what he sees and does not know how to make or to use what he sees (he could paint a bed, but not make it), so the poet imitates reality without necessarily understanding it. Poetry or literature as a whole is an imitation of imitation and thus twice removed from truth.

There is an obvious error in Plato's *reasoning[8]. *Being too much of a philosopher and *moralist[9], he could not see clearly the relation between literature and life. He is right when he says that *the poet produces something which is less than reality it *purports[10] to represent, but he does not perceive that he also creates something more than reality. This error was corrected by Plato's pupil, Aristotle. In *Poetics[2)] he *undertook[11] to examine the nature and qualities of imaginative literature with a view to demonstrating that it is true, and not false as Plato had shown it. He agreed with Plato that poetry is an imitation of reality, but according to him, this imitation is the objective representation of life in literature or, in other words, the imaginative reconstruction of life. Poetry is thus not connected with the outside world *in the simple and direct

7. apprehend 이해하다
8. reasoning 추론
9. moralist 도덕주의자
10. purport 의도하다, 칭하다
11. undertake 착수하다

2) Poetics 고대 그리스의 철학자 아리스토텔레스의 저서. 원제는 'peri poiētikēs'인데, '시작(詩作)에 관하여'라는 뜻으로 그는 시를 '모방의 기술'로 설명하고 있음.

12. derive
끌어내다

13. inspiration
영감

14. impulse
충동

15. actuality
실제

16. resultant
그 결과로 생긴

17. slavish
맹종하는

18. pierces to
~을 꿰뚫다

fashion supposed by Plato. The poet first *derives[12] an *inspiration[13] from the world by the power of his imagination; the art of poetry then imitates this imaginative inspiration in language. The art of poetry or literature as a whole exists to give shape and substance to a certain kind of imaginative *impulse[14]; the existence of the art implies the existence of the impulse. Now it is just possible to imagine life exactly *as it is; but the exciting thing is to imagine life *as it might be, and it is then that imagination becomes an impulse capable of inspiring poetry. This is true even in the case of what we call *realism[3)] in literature; it is true even when the life imagined was originally an *actuality[15] of some highly exciting nature in itself. Imagination may *no more than concentrate the actuality, by dropping out all its insignificant passages. But that will be enough to make the *resultant[16] poetry, or literature, *something different from the copy of the world which Plato's condemnation assumed it to be. This was Aristotle's reply to Plato. Art or literature is not a *slavish[17] imitation of reality twice removed from truth. *Presenting as it must do individual men or women in the trappings and circumstances of life, it does not leave them there, but *pierces to[18] what is significant in action and character, expressing through their words and action that is true for all human nature - the poet's truth, the universal truth. The poet is concerned with truth - but not the

3) realism 객관적 사물을 있는 그대로 정확하게 재현하려는 태도.

truth of the *annalist[19], the historian, or the photographer. The poet's business is not to write of events that have happened, but of what may happen, of things that are possible *in the light of probability or necessity. For this reason poetry is a more philosophical, a more serious thing than history. For whilst history deals with *the particular only - this event or that event - poetry deals with the universal. The poet selects from life according to the principle of poetic unity and poetic truth. He seeks to draw out what is relevant and representative, and to present it harmoniously, in a *self-contained[20] situation. *The truth with which he deals is not that which the *anatomist[21] may lay bare on the *dissecting-table[22], but that which a poet divines and translates.

Aristotle, thus, met Plato's *charge[23] that poetry is imitation of an imitation by showing that the poet, by *concerning himself with fundamental probabilities rather with *casual actualities[24], reaches more deeply into reality than the annalist or historian. *Sir Philip Sidney[4)], who next took up the question of the relation of literature to life also *refuted[25] *Plato's contention that literature is a mere imitation of an imitation. According to him, the poet does not imitate, but creates; *it is the reader who imitates what the poet creates. Taking his material from the actual world, the poet creates an ideal world *by means of his imagination. For Sidney *the ideal world of

19. annalist
연대기 편찬자

20. self-contained
독립적인

21. anatomist
해부학자

22. dissecting-table
해부용 탁자

23. charge
비난

24. casual actuality
우발적인 실제

25. refute
반박하다

4) Sir Philip Sidney(1554~1586) 영국의 시인.

26. illuminator
빛을 주는 것, 조명기

27. species
종(種: 생물 분류의 기초 단위)

28. exhibit
(감정특질 등을) 보이다[드러내다]

29. portrait
(상세한) 묘사

30. prominent
두드러진

31. striking
눈에 띄는, 두드러진

32. recall
생각나게 하다

33. minute
대단히 상세한, 미세한

34. discrimination
차이

35. remark
언급하다

36. vigilance
경계, 조심

the poet is of value because it is a better world than the real world and it is presented in such a way that the reader is stimulated to try and imitate it *in his own practice.

The problem of literature's relation to life was next taken up by *Dryden[5] who pointed out that imaginative literature gives us a 'just and lively' image of human nature by representing its 'passions and humors'. This point was further developed by *Dr. Johnson[6] who expressed the view that the poet '*holds up a mirror to nature". According to him, "*Nothing can please many, and please long, but just representation of general nature." The way to please the greatest number over the longest period of time, which is the duty of imaginative literature, is to provide accurate pictures of nature. Explaining his view that the poet is the *illuminator[26] of human nature Dr. Johnson wrote:

"The business of the poet is to examine, not the individual, but the *species[27]... *He must *exhibit[28] in his *portraits[29] of nature such *prominent[30] and *striking[31] features as *recall[32] the original to every mind, and must neglect the *minute[33] *discriminations[34], which one may have *remarked[35] and another have neglected, for those characteristics which are alike obvious to *vigilance[36] and carelessness.

"But the knowledge of nature is *only half the task of a poet;

5) Dryden, John(1631~1700) 영국의 시인·극작가·평론가.

6) Samuel Johnson (1709~1784) 종종 Dr Johnson으로 일컬어짐. 영국의 작가, 사전편집자.

he must *be acquainted *likewise[37] with all the modes of life. His character requires that he estimates the happiness and *misery[38] of every condition, observe the power of all the passions in all their combinations, and trace the changes of the human mind, as they are modified by various *institutions[39] and accidental influences of climate or custom, from the *sprightliness[40] of fancy to the *despondence[41] of *decrepitude[42]. He must *divert himself of the *prejudices[43] of his age or country; he must consider right and wrong in their *abstracted[44] and variable state; he must regard present laws and their opinions and *rise[45] to general and *transcendental[46] truths, which will always, be the same. He must, therefore, *content himself with the slow progress of his name, condemn the *applause[47] of his own time, and *commit his claims to the justice of *posterity[48]. He must write as the *interpretator[49] of nature and the legislator of mankind and consider himself as *presiding over[50] the thoughts and manners of future generations, as being superior to time and place."

According to Dr. Johnson, the poet must know the manners and customs of men of all times and conditions, *not because it is his duty to make vivid to the reader the different ways in which men hove lived and behaved, but so that he is not taken in by surface differences and is able to *penetrate[51] to the common humanity underlying there.

37. likewise
또한

38. misery
고통

39. institution
제도, 관습

40. sprightliness
활기

41. despondence
낙담

42. decrepitude
노쇠

43. prejudice
편견

44. abstracted
정신이 딴 데 팔린

45. rise
올라가다

46. transcendental
초월적인

47. applause
박수

48. posterity
후세, 후대

49. interpretator
해석자

50. preside over
~의 사회를 보다

51. penetrate
뚫고 들어가다

52. presentment
표현, 묘사

53. literary artist
문예가

54. reconstruct
재현하다

55. clutch at
~을 꽉 잡다

56. permanence
영구성

57. fleeting
순식간의, 순식간에 지나가는

*Walter Pater[7], a critic of the later nineteenth century, who discussed the relation of literature and life *in detail, remarked in his essay on "Style": "*Just as in proportion as the writer's aim, consciously or unconsciously, comes to be the transcribing, not of the world, not of mere fact, but his sense of it, he becomes an artist, his work fine art; and good art *in proportion to the truth of his *presentment[52] of that sense."

Thus, according to Pater, the *literary artist[53] does not give us a photographic 'imitation' of reality, but a transcription of his vision of it. *It is from reality or life from which the artist starts, but he tries to *reconstruct[54] it when he would '*see it steadily and see it whole'.

*Taking into consideration the views of Plato, Aristotle, Sidney, Dryden, Johnson and Pater, *we conclude that the notion that literature is not concerned with real life is wrong. All great pieces of literature are 'true to life'. But the literary artist is not content to '*hold the mirror up to nature', because his business, as Matthew Arnold has pointed out, is a 'criticism, of life'. *He concentrates on those characteristics and aspects of life which are permanent, but which might easily pass unobserved. He *clutches at[55] anything which promises some *permanence[56] among what is always *fleeting[57]. That is why he gives us a picture of reality which is more characteristic of life than anything which we discover by our own day-to-day

7) Walter Pater(1839~1894) 영국의 평론가.

observation. The images which we are creating by our own observation of life at every moment of our working experience are *hazy[58], half-finished and unrelated. It is the literary artist who finishes them, makes them clear and puts them in their wider setting, and *to that extent makes life less *obscure[59], *because he knows more about life than anyone can know without regarding life with his eyes.

58. hazy
흐릿한

59. obscure
모호한

GRAMMAR

유사관계대명사

격에 따라 형태가 바뀌는 일반적인 관계대명사(who, whose, whom, which, whose, which 등)와는 다른 고정된 형태(as, but, than)를 취하면서 본래의 뜻을 유지하는 관계대명사를 말한다.

1. As

> He is just such a teacher.
> We all admire such a teacher(him).
> 위의 두 문장을 일반적인 관계대명사로 연결해 보면
> He is just such a teacher that(whom) we all admire가 되는데,
> 여기서 앞에 such가 있어 이에 대응하는 단어로 바꾸면
> He is just such a teacher as we all admire가 된다.

이처럼 두 개의 절(문장)을 연결하는 점에서는 관계대명사와 같은데 고정된 형태를 취하는 것을 유사관계대명사라 한다.

다음 두 문장도 관계대명사로 연결하면 I have the same trouble as you had가 된다.

> I have the same trouble. You had the same trouble(it).

아래의 두 문장은 차이가 나는데 a)는 내가 잃어버린 시계와 유사한 시계이지만, b)는 내가 잃어버린 바로 그 시계가 된다.

> a) This is the same watch as I lost. b) This is the same watch that I lost.

또한 계속적 용법으로도 사용된다.

He was a foreigner, as I knew from his accent.
(그는 외국인이었는데, 그와 같은 것(그가 외국인이라는 것)을 그의 말투로 알았다)

이 문장은 다음의 두 문장에서 나온 것이다.

He was a foreigner.
I knew that he was a foreigner from his accent.

She was late, as is often the case with her.
She was late.
That she was late is often the case with her.

2. **But**(**=that(who)** – not)

But도 위의 경우와 같이 두 개의 문장을 연결한 것이다. 이 경우 but 앞에는 대개 부정어가 온다.

다음 두 문장을 관계대명사로 연결해 보자.

There is no rule. It(no rule) has some exceptions.

이것을 일반적인 형태의 관계대명사로 연결해 보면 다음과 같이 된다.

There is no rule that does not have some exceptions.

여기서 that - not을 한 단어로 바꾸면 but이 되어 위의 문장이 나오게 된다.

There is no rule but has some exceptions.
(몇 가지 예외가 없는 어떠한 규칙도 없다)

3. Than

다음 두 문장도 관계대명사로 연결해 보자.

There is more money. More money(it) is needed.

이것을 일반적인 관계대명사로 연결하면

There is more money that(which) is needed.

여기서 앞의 more와 대응해서 that을 than으로 바꾸면 다음과 같은 문장이 된다.

There is more money than is needed. (필요 되는 돈 보다 많은 돈이 있다)

Don't use more words than are necessary.
(필요한 것 보다 더 많은 단어들을 사용하지 마시오)

이것은 다음의 두 문장에서 나온 것이다.

Don't use more words. More words(they) are necessary

이것을 관계대명사로 연결하면

Don't use more words that are necessary.

다시 앞의 more와 대응해서 that을 than으로 바꾸면 위의 문장이 된다.

PHRASES and STRUCTURES

* **It is**, in fact, life **which** is the subject matter of literature.
사실 문학의 주제가 되는 것이 바로 삶이다.
It is ~ which 강조구문

* Life provides the raw material **on which** literature imposes an artistic form.
삶은 소재를 제공하는데 그 소재에 예술적 형태를 도입한다.
= Life provides the raw material, **and** literature imposes an artistic form **on it(the raw material).**
which = and + on it(the raw material)

* True reality consists in the ideas of things, **of which** individual objects are but reflections or imitations.
진짜의 실체는 사물이라는 생각에 있는데 그 중에서 개개의 물체는 단지 상이거나 모조품이다.
= True reality consists in the ideas of things, **and of them(the ideas)** individual objects are but reflections or imitations.
of which = and + of them(the ideas)
consist in ~ ~에 있다
but 단지, 그저 ~일 뿐(only)

* We are **comparing** the dog **which** we actually see **with** the ideal dog, our idea of the dog, **which** is the true, unchanging reality, while the dogs **which** we **name as** black, good, lame etc. are mere reflections and imitations of that reality.
우리는 우리가 실제로 보는 그 개를 이상적인 개와, 즉 개라는 우리의 생각, 그것은 실제의 변하지 않는 실체인데, 비교하고 있지만 우리가 검고, 좋고, 절뚝거리는 것으로 명명한 바로 그 개들은 그러한 실체의 단순한 상들이고 모조품들이다.
= We are comparing the dog, **and** we actually see **it(the dog)** with the ideal dog, our idea of the dog, **and it(idea of the dog)** is the true, unchanging reality, while the dogs, **and** we name **them(the dogs)** as black, good, lame etc. are mere reflections and imitations of that reality.
compare A with B A와 B를 비교하다
the ideal dog, our idea of the dog에서 **,는 동격을 나타냄**

목적격 관계대명사 which = and + it(the dog)
주격 관계대명사 which = and + it(idea of the dog)
목적격 관계대명사 which = and + them(the dogs)
name A as B A를 B로 명명하다

* Thus the poet, **who** imitates those objects **which** are themselves imitations of reality, is obviously producing something, **which** is still further removed from ultimate reality.
따라서 시인은, 그런데 시인은 그러한 물체들을 모방하는데 그 물체들은 그 자체가 실체의 모조품들이고, 분명히 어떤 것을 만들어내고 있는데 그것은 여전히 궁극적인 실체와는 크게 동떨어져 있다.
= Thus the poet, **and he(the poet)** imitates those objects, **and they(objects)** are themselves imitations of reality, is obviously producing something, **and it(something)** is still further removed from ultimate reality.
who = and + he(the poet)
which = and + they(objects)
which = and + it(something)
be further removed from something ~와는 크게 동떨어져 있다(관련이 없다)

* **with reference to ~** ~와 관련하여

* **nothing but ~** 단지 ~일 뿐인

* **Being** too much of a philosopher and moralist,
그는 지나치게 철학자이면서 도덕주의자 이었기 때문에
= **As he was** too much of a philosopher and moralist,
be too much of 과분하다(지나치다)

* The poet produces something **which** is less than reality it purports to represent.
시인은 어떤 것을 만들어내는데 그것은 그 어떤 것이 나타내려고 의도하는 실체보다 적은 것이다.
= The poet produces something, **and it(something)** is less than reality **(which)** it(=something) purports to represent.
= The poet produces something, **and it(something)** is less than reality, **and** it(=something) purports to represent **it(reality)**.

which = and + it(something)
목적격 관계대명사 which 생략 = and + it(reality)

* **in the simple and direct fashion** 단순하고 직접적인 방식으로

* **as it is** 있는 그대로

* **as it might be** 있을지도 모르는 대로

* **no more than ~** 단지 ~일뿐

* something different from the copy of the world **which** Plato's condemnation assumed it to be
세계의 복사와는 다른 어떤 것, 그런데 플라톤의 비난은 그것(시나 문학)을 세계의 복사라고 추정했다
= something different from the copy of the world, **and** Plato's condemnation assumed it(poetry or literature) to be **it(the copy of the world)**
목적격 관계대명사 which = and + it(the copy of the world)

* **Presenting as it must do** individual men or women in the trappings and circumstances of life, it does **not** leave them there, **but** pierces to what is significant in action and character, **expressing** through their words and action **that** is true for all human nature.
문학이나 예술이 삶의 함정과 환경에 빠져있는 개개의 남자나 여자를 나타내야 한다 하더라도 문학이나 예술은 그들을 그곳에 내버려두는 것이 아니라 행동과 성격에서 중요한 것을 꿰뚫고 그렇게 해서 인간의 본성에 사실인 그들의 말과 행동을 통해 표현한다.
= **Presenting as it(art or literature) must do** individual men or women in the trappings and circumstances of life, it(art or literature) does **not** leave them(=individual men or women) there, **but** pierces to what is significant in action and character, **and it expresses** through their words and action, **and it(their words and action)** is true for all human nature.
형용사 + as + 주어 + be 비록 ~이(하)지만
Rich as she is, she is not happy 부유하지만 그녀는 행복하지 않다
not A, but B A가 아니라 B다
expressing(분사구문) = ~~and it~~~~(what is significant in action and character)~~

expresses
주격 관계대명사 that = and + it(their words and action)

* **in the light of ~** ~을 고려하여(감안하여)

* **the particular only** 특별히 유일한 것

* The truth with **which** he deals is not that **which** the anatomist may lay bare on the dissecting-table, but that **which** a poet divines and translates.
그가 다루는 진리는 해부학자가 벌거벗은 채로 해부용 테이블위에 그것을 둘 수도 있는 것(그 진실을 들추어 낼 수 있는 것)이 아니라 시인이 예측하고 번역하는 것이다.
= The truth, **and** he deals with **it(the truth)**, is not that, **and** the anatomist may lay **it(the truth)** bare on the dissecting-table, but that, **and** a poet divines and translates **it(the truth)**.
목적격 관계대명사 which = and + it(the truth)
목적격 관계대명사 which = and + it(the truth)
목적격 관계대명사 which = and + it(the truth)
lay it bare = uncover(=reveal) it 그것을 노출시키다, 폭로(누설)하다

* **concern himself with ~** ~에 관여하다

* Plato's **contention that** literature is a mere imitation of an imitation
문학은 단순한 모방의 모방이라는 플라톤의 주장
contention과 that절은 동격

* **It is** the reader **who** imitates **what** the poet creates.
시인이 창작한 것을 모방하는 사람은 바로 독자이다.
= **It is** the reader **who** imitates **the thing which** the poet creates.
= **It is** the reader **who** imitates the thing, **and** the poet creates **it(the thing)**.
it is ~ that(who) 강조구문
what = the thing which = and + it(the thing)

* **by means of ~** ~에 의하여, ~의 도움으로

* The ideal world of the poet is **of value**.

시인의 이상적인 세계는 가치가 있다.

* **in his own practice** 그 자신의 실천으로

* **holds up a mirror to nature** 자연을 거울에 비추다, 있는 그대로 그리다(묘사하다)

* Nothing can please many, and please long, but just representation of general nature.
어떤 것도 많은 사람들을, 그리고 오래도록 기쁘게 할 수 없지만 단지 일반적인 자연의 표현은 그렇게 할 수 있다.

* He must exhibit in his portraits of nature **such** prominent and striking features **as** recall the original to every mind, and must neglect the minute discriminations, **which** one may have remarked and another have neglected, for those characteristics **which** are alike obvious to vigilance and carelessness.
그는 자연에 대한 묘사에서 두드러지고 눈에 띄는 특징들을 드러내야하는데 그런 특징들은 모든 사람에게서 원본을 생각나게 하는 것들이다. 그리고 그는 그런 특성들에 대한 상세한 차이들을 소홀히 해야 하는데, 어떤 사람은 그 상세한 차이들을 언급을 했을지도 모르고 또 다른 사람은 소홀히 했을지도 모르는데, 그런 특성들은 주의와 부주의에 똑같이 분명하다.
= He must exhibit (in his portraits of nature) **such** prominent and striking features, **and they(features)** recall the original to every mind, and must neglect the minute discriminations, **and** one may have remarked and another have neglected **them(minute discriminations)**, for those characteristics, **and they(characteristics)** are alike obvious to vigilance and carelessness.
such ~ as 여기서 **as**는 유사 관계대명사로 사용됨
as = and + they(features)
the minute discriminations는 , , 다음의 for those characteristics로 연결됨
목적격 관계대명사 which = and + them(discriminations)
which = and + they(characteristics)
one ~, another ~ 어떤 사람은 ~, 또 다른 사람은
another는 '그 밖에도 몇 개(사람) 있다'라고 예상했을 때의 '또 하나'를 가리킴
예를 들어 둘 이상의 것 중 하나를 취하고 그 다음에 '또 다른 하나(사람)'라는 뜻으로 another를 씀
another는 an+other에서 온 것으로 the, this, that, my 등이 앞에 오지 않음
the other door 또 하나의 문
my other son 나의 또 하나의 아들

* **only half the task of a poet** 시인의 일의 절반 밖에 되지 않는 일

* **be acquainted with ~** ~을(사실 따위를) 알다(알게 되다)

* **divert himself of ~** ~에서 벗어나다

* **content himself with ~** ~에 만족하다

* **commit his claims** 그의 주장을 관철하다

* not because **it** is his duty **to** make vivid to the reader the different ways **in which** men have lived and behaved, but **so that** he is not taken in by surface differences and is able to penetrate to the common humanity underlying there
  인간이 살고 행동해 온 여러 가지 방식들을 독자에게 생생하게 해주는 것이 그의 임무이기 때문이 아니라 그가 표면적인 차이 때문에 받아들여지지 않고 그 밑에 있는 공통된 인간성까지 뚫고 들어갈 수 있도록
  = not because it is his duty to make vivid to the reader the different ways, **and in them(ways)** men have lived and behaved, but **so that** he is not taken in by surface differences and is able to penetrate to the common humanity underlying there
  it ~ to + 동사원형
  it는 가주어 to이하는 진주어
  in which = and + them(ways)
  so that ~ ~하도록

* **in detail** 상세하게

* **Just as in proportion as** the writer's aim, consciously or unconsciously, comes to be the transcribing, not of the world, not of mere fact, but his sense of it, he becomes an artist, his work fine art.
  작가의 목적이 의식적이든 무의식적이든 세계가 아니고 단순한 사실이 아닌 세계에 대한 그의 느낌을 기록하는 것이 되는 것과 꼭 비례해서 그는 화가가 되고 그의 작품은 미술이 된다.
  = Just as in proportion as the writer's aim, consciously or unconsciously, comes to be the transcribing, not of the world, not of mere fact, but his sense of it, he becomes an artist, his work **(becomes)** fine art.
  Just as in proportion as ~ ~만큼 꼭 비례해서

in proportion to ~ ~에 비례하여

* **It is** from reality or life from **which** the artist starts.
예술가가 시작하는 곳은 바로 실체와 삶이다.
It is ~ which 강조 구문

* **see life (steadily and see it) whole** 분별 있는(균형 잡힌) 태도를 가지다

* **Taking into consideration ~** ~을 고려해 볼 때

* We conclude that **the notion that** literature is not concerned with real life **is** wrong.
우리는 문학이 실제 삶과 관계가 없다라는 개념이 잘못된 것이라고 결론짓는다.
the notion은 that 이하와 동격
That절 속에서 주어는 the notion, 동사는 is

* He concentrates on those characteristics and aspects of life **which** are permanent, but **which** might easily pass unobserved.
그는 삶의 그러한 특성과 양상에 집중을 하는데 그러한 것들은 영구적이지만 쉽게 간과될 수 있는 것들이다.
= He concentrates on those characteristics and aspects of life, **and they(characteristics and aspects)** are permanent, but **which** might easily pass unobserved.
which = and + they(characteristics and aspects)
pass unobserved 간과되다

* **to that extent** 그 정도로, 그만큼

* because he knows **more** about life **than** anyone can know without regarding life with his eyes
왜냐하면 그는 그의 눈으로 삶을 보지 않고서도 누구나 알 수 있는 것 보다 삶에 관해 더 많이 알기 때문이다
= because he knows more about life, **and** anyone can know **it(life)** without regarding life with his eyes
than = and it(life)
than 유사관계대명사

Unit 14

Feminism's Long History[1)]

WARMING UP

- We will not hold ourselves bound by any Laws **in which** we have no voice
- We **hold** these truths **to be** self-evident
- The feminists demanded "their sacred right to the elective franchise," **or** the right to vote
- **With** these rights **secured**, feminists embarked on **what** some scholars refer to as the "second wave" of feminism
- Many women found work in industries previously reserved for men, **making** Rosie the Riveter a **feminist icon**
- It was a massive protest **aimed** at the new administration and the perceived threat it represented to reproductive, civil and human rights

1) The source of this article is https://www.history.com/topics/womens-history/feminism-womens-history

Feminism, a belief in the political, economic and cultural *equality[1] of women, has roots in the earliest eras of *human civilization[2]. It is typically separated into three waves: first wave feminism, dealing with *property rights[3] and the right to vote; second wave feminism, focusing on equality and *anti-discrimination[4], and third wave feminism, which started in the 1990s as a *backlash[5] to the second wave's *perceived[6] *privileging[7] of white, *straight[8] women. From Ancient Greece to the fight for women's *suffrage[9] to women's marches and the *#MeToo movement[2)], the history of feminism is as long as it is *fascinating[10]. *Here is everything you need to know about the fight for gender equality.

Early Feminists

In his classic *Republic*, Plato advocated that women possess "*natural capacities[11]" equal to men for governing and defending ancient Greece. Not everyone agreed with Plato; when the women of ancient Rome *staged[12] a *massive protest[13] over the *Oppian Law[3)], which restricted women's access to gold and other goods, Roman *consul[14] *Marcus Porcius Cato[4)] argued, "As soon as they begin to be your equals, they will have become your superiors!" (Despite Cato's fears, the law was *repealed[15].)

1. equality 평등
2. human civilization 인류문명
3. property right 재산권
4. anti-discrimination 차별금지
5. backlash 반발
6. perceived 인지하고 있는
7. privileging 특권화
8. straight 동성애자가 아닌
9. suffrage 투표권, 참정권
10. fascinating 대단히 흥미로운
11. natural capacity 천부적 능력
12. stage ~을 벌이다, 개최하다
13. massive protest 대규모 시위
14. consul 로마의 집정관
15. repeal 폐지하다

2) #MeToo movement 온라인에서 성희롱이나 성폭행 등을 고발하는 운동으로 자신도 피해자임을 밝히고 또 다른 피해자의 참여를 독려하는 데에서 붙여진 이름.

3) Oppian Law(Lex Oppia) B.C. 215년 고대 로마에서 제정된 법률로 B.C. 195년에 폐지됨. 첫 번째 일련의 사치금지법으로 여성의 부뿐만 아니라 부의 과시를 제한했음. 특히 모든 여성이 반 온스 이상의 금을 소유하지 못하게 했으며 여러 가지 색깔의 옷을 입지 못하게 했으며 공식적인 종교적 행사를 제외하고는 도시나 읍에서 동물이 끄는 마차를 타지 못하도록 했음.

4) Marcus Porcius Cato(B.C.234~B.C.149) 로마의 장군, 정치가.

16. misogyny 여성혐오
17. vigorously 활발하게
18. ballot 투표용지
19. foment 조장하다, 선동하다
20. rebellion 반란
21. abolitionist 폐지론자
22. unsettling 불안하게 하는

In *The Book of the City of Ladies*, 15th-century writer *Christine de Pizan[5)] protested *misogyny[16] and the role of women in the Middle Ages. Years later, during the Enlightenment, writers and philosophers like Margaret Cavendish, the Duchess of Newcastle-upon-Tyne, and Mary Wollstonecraft, author of *A Vindication of the Rights of Woman*, argued *vigorously[17] for greater equality for women.

Abigail Adams, first lady to *President John Adams[6)], specifically saw access to education, property and the *ballot[18] as critical to women's equality. In letters to her husband John Adams, Abigail Adams warned, "If particular care and attention is not paid to the Ladies we *are determined to *foment[19] a *Rebellion[20], and *will not hold ourselves bound by any Laws in which we have no voice."

The "Rebellion" that Adams threatened began in the 19th century, *as calls for greater freedom for women joined with voices demanding the end of slavery. Indeed, *many women leaders of the *abolitionist[21] movement found an *unsettling[22] irony in advocating for African Americans rights that they themselves could not enjoy.

First Wave Feminism: Women's Suffrage and The Seneca Falls Convention

At the 1848 *Seneca Falls Convention[7)], abolitionists like Elizabeth

5) Christine de Pizan 유럽 최초의 여성 작가로, 그의 저작은 15세기 영국문학계에 큰 영향을 미쳤으며 여성의 사회적 지위에 대한 논쟁을 불러 일으켰음.

6) President John Adams(1735~1826) 미국의 제2대 대통령(1797~1801).

7) Seneca Falls Convention 1848년 7월 19~20일 양일간에 뉴욕 세네카 폴스의 웨슬리교파의 한 교회에서 개최되었던 첫 번째 여성 권리 대회로 사회적, 민간의, 종교적 상황과 여성 권리를 논의하기 위해 개최됨.

Cady Stanton and Lucretia Mott *boldly[23] *proclaimed[24] in their now-famous *Declaration of Sentiments[8)] that "*We hold these truths to be self-evident; that all men and women are created equal." *Controversially[25], the feminists demanded "their *sacred[26] right to *the *elective franchise[27]," or the right to vote.

Many *attendees[28] thought *voting rights[29] for women were *beyond the pale, but were *swayed[30] when *Frederick Douglass[9)] argued that he could not accept the right to vote as a black man if women could not also claim that right. When the *resolution[31] passed, the women's suffrage movement began *in earnest, and dominated much of feminism for several decades.

The 19th Amendment: Women's Right to Vote

Slowly, *suffragettes[32] began to claim some successes: In 1893, *New Zealand became the first *sovereign state[33] giving women the right to vote, followed by Australia in 1902 and Finland in 1906. In a limited victory, the United Kingdom *granted[34] suffrage to women over 30 in 1918.

In the United States, women's participation in World War I proved to many that they were deserving of equal *representation[35]. In 1920, thanks largely to the work of *suffragists[36] like *Susan B. Anthony[10)]

23. boldly 대담하게
24. proclaim 선언(선포)하다
25. controversially 논란의 여지가 있지만
26. sacred 신성한
27. elective franchise 선거권
28. attendee 참석자
29. voting right 선거권
30. sway 흔들다(동요시키다)
31. resolution 결의안
32. suffragette (20세기 초 영국과 미국의) 여성 참정권 운동가
33. sovereign state 주권국, 독립국
34. grant 인정하다
35. representation 대의권
36. suffragist 여성 참정권론자

8) Declaration of Sentiments (감성선언서) 19세기 미국 여성의 인권 신장에 기여한 가장 중요한 문서로, 미국 여성 운동의 시초라 간주됨.

9) Frederick Douglass(1817~1895) 미국의 노예제 폐지론자, 웅변가. 메릴랜드에서 흑인 노예로 출생해 21세에 매사추세츠 주(州)에 도망갔으며 노예 제도 반대 웅변으로 인기를 끌어 그 주의 반(反) 노예 제도 협회원이 되었음.

10) Susan B. Anthony(1820~1906) 미국의 여성 참정권·노예제도 폐지 운동가.

37. earn
얻다

38. breadwinner
생계비를 버는 사람, 가장

39. military
군대

40. reserve
따로 남겨두다

41. civil right
시민의 평등권

42. forefront
선두

43. confront
맞서다

and *Carrie Chapman Catt[11], the *19th Amendment[12] passed. American women finally *earned[37] the right to vote. *With these rights secured, feminists embarked on what some scholars refer to as the "second wave" of feminism.

Women And Work

Women began to enter the workplace *in greater numbers following the *Great Depression[13], *when many male *breadwinners[38] lost their jobs, forcing women to find "women's work" in lower paying but more stable careers like housework, teaching and secretarial roles.

During World War II, many women actively participated in the *military[39] or *found work in industries previously *reserved[40] for men, making *Rosie the Riveter[14] a feminist icon. Following the *civil rights[41] movement, women sought greater participation in the workplace, with equal pay at the *forefront[42] of their efforts. The *Equal Pay Act[15] of 1963 was among the first efforts to *confront[43] this still-relevant issue.

11) Carrie Chapman Catt(1859~1947) 미국의 여성 참정권 운동가.

12) 19th Amendment 미국의 헌법 수정 제 19조(920년의 여성 참정권 수정 조항).

13) Great Depression 1929년의 대공황 또는 1929년의 슬럼프라고도 함. 1929년 10월 24일 뉴욕 월가(街)의 '뉴욕주식거래소'에서 주가가 대폭락한 데서 발단된 공황은 1933년 말까지 거의 모든 자본주의 국가들이 여기에 말려들었으며, 여파는 1939년까지 이어졌음.

14) Rosie the Riveter 제2차 세계대전으로 야기된 여성의 경제 참여를 나타내는 것으로 '리벳공 로지'는 방위산업체에 종사하는 여성을 상징하는 이미지로 사용됨. 제2차 세계대전은 미국 여성사에 전환점을 제공해 준 획기적인 사건으로 간주되는데 수많은 미국 여성들이 집을 벗어나 직업을 가질 수 있도록 길을 열어 주었을 뿐만 아니라 제2기 여성해방 운동의 등장에도 큰 기여를 했다고 여겨짐.

15) Equal Pay Act of 1963 (동일임금법) 미국의 노동법으로 성(sex)에 따른 임금 불일치를 철폐하는 것을 목표로 1963년 케네디 대통령에 의해 1963년에 서명됨.

Second Wave Feminism

But cultural obstacles remained, and with the 1963 publication of *The Feminine Mystique*, *Betty Friedan[16) - who later co-founded the National Organization for Women - argued that women were still *relegated[44] to *unfulfilling[45] roles in *homemaking[46] and child care. *By this time, many people had started referring to feminism as "women's liberation." In 1971, feminist *Gloria Steinem[17) joined Betty Friedan and *Bella Abzug[18) in founding the National Women's Political Caucus. Steinem's *Ms. Magazine* became the first magazine to *feature[47] feminism as a subject on its cover in 1976.

The *Equal Rights Amendment[19), which sought legal equality for women and banned *discrimination[48] on the basis of sex, was passed by Congress in 1972 (but, following a conservative *backlash[49], was never *ratified[50] by enough states to become law). One year later, *feminists celebrated the *Supreme Court[51] decision in*Roe v. Wade[20), the landmark *ruling[52] that guaranteed a woman's right to choose an abortion.

Third Wave Feminism: Who Benefits From the Feminist Movement?

Critics have argued that the *benefits[53] of the feminist movement,

44. relegate 격하시키다
45. unfulfilling 성취감을 주지 못하는
46. homemaking 가사
47. feature 크게 다루다
48. discrimination 차별
49. backlash 반발
50. ratify 비준하다
51. Supreme Court 대법원
52. ruling 판결
53. benefit 혜택, 이득

16) Betty Friedan(1921~2006) 미국의 여권 운동가, 전미 여성 기구(NOW) 창립.
17) Gloria Steinem(1934~) 미국의 여권 운동가, 작가.
18) Bella Abzug(1920~1998) 미국의 법률인·정치인. 미국 여성운동의 선구자로 미국 여성해방운동의 기수 베티 프리단, 글로리아 스타이넘과 함께 공격적인 여권운동을 전개했으며 또한 베트남전쟁 반전운동에도 앞장섰음.
19) Equal Rights Amendment 미국 헌법 수정안으로 모든 미국 시민들에게 성(sex)에 상관없이 동등한 권리를 부여하기 위해 제안된 법안으로 이혼, 재산, 취업 등의 문제에서 남자와 여자의 법적인 차별을 없애고자 하는 것임.
20) Roe v. Wade 미국에서 낙태를 헌법에 의해 인정한 최고 재판소의 1973년 판례.

54. address
(문제)다루다

55. concern
우려

56. lesbian
여성동성애자

57. minority
소수

58. lament
통탄하다

59. stirring
마음을 뒤흔드는

60. plough
쟁기로 갈다

61. barn
곳간

62. head
~을 이끌다

63. bear
참다, 견디다

64. lash
채찍질

65. point to
가리키다

66. sexual assault
성폭행

67. emblematic
상징하는

68. combat
(방지하기 위해)
싸우다

69. ensure
보장하다

70. prominence
명성

especially the second wave, are largely limited to white, college-educated women, and that feminism has failed to *address[54] the *concerns[55] of women of color, *lesbians[56], immigrants and religious *minorities[57]. Even in the 19th century, *Sojourner Truth[21)] *lamented[58] racial distinctions in women's status by demanding "Ain't I a Woman?" in her *stirring[59] speech before the 1851 Ohio Women's Rights Convention:

"And ain't I a woman? Look at me! Look at my arm! I have *ploughed[60] and planted, and gathered into *barns[61], and no man could *head[62] me! And ain't I a woman? I could work as much and eat as much as a man - when I could get it - and *bear[63] the *lash[64] as well! And ain't I a woman? *I have borne 13 children, and seen most all sold off to slavery, and when I cried out with my mother's grief, *none but Jesus heard me! And ain't I a woman?"

#MeToo and Women's Marches

More recently, feminists have *pointed to[65] prominent cases of *sexual assault[66] and "rape culture" as *emblematic[67] of the work still to be done *in *combating[68] misogyny and *ensuring[69] women have equal rights. The #MeToo movement gained new *prominence[70] in October 2017, *when the *New York Times*

21) Sojourner Truth(1797~1883) 노예 시절의 이름은 Isabella Van Wagener로 미국 흑인 해방운동가, 사회개혁가였으며 남북전쟁 당시 여성 선거권과 노예제도 폐지를 주창했던 흑인 여성.

published a *damning[71] investigation into *allegations[72] of *sexual harassment[73] made against influential film producer *Harvey Weinstein[22]. Many more women came forward with allegations against other powerful men - including President Donald Trump.

On January 21, 2017, the first full day of Donald Trump's *presidency[74], hundreds of thousands of people joined the Women's March on Washington in D.C., *a massive protest aimed at the new administration and the perceived threat it *represented[75] to reproductive, civil and human rights. It was not limited to Washington: Over 3 million people in cities around the world held simultaneous demonstrations, *providing feminists with a high-profile platforms for advocating on behalf of full rights for all women worldwide.

71. damning
유죄를
강력 시사하는

72. allegation
혐의

73. sexual harassment
성희롱

74. presidency
대통령임기

75. represent
(의견, 항의)
제기하다

22) Harvey Weinstein(1952~) 미국의 영화제작프로듀서, 영화감독.

GRAMMAR

부정대명사

1. Some and any

1) 일반적으로 some(다음에 body, one, thing이 오는 것도 포함해서)은 긍정문에서 사용되고, any(다음에 body 등이 오는 것을 포함)는 부정문, 의문문, 조건문에서 사용되는데 '약간'의 의미를 갖는다.

We bought some flowers(긍정문). We didn't buy any flowers(부정문).
There's somebody at the door(긍정문) There isn't anybody at the door(부정문)

* 다음 예들은 부정문이 아닌데도 any가 사용되는데 이것은 의미가 부정적이기 때문이다.
She went out without any money. (= She didn't take any money with her)
(그녀는 돈이 한 푼도 없이 외출했다)
He refused to eat anything. (= He didn't eat anything)
(그는 어떤 것도 먹기를 거절했다)
Hardly anybody passed the examination. (= almost nobody passed)
(그 시험에 거의 아무도 통과하지 못했다)

2) 대부분의 의문문에서는 any가 사용된다.
Do you have any luggage? (짐이 좀 있느냐?)
Has anyone seen my bag? (누가 나의 가방을 보았느냐?)

* 그러나 다음 경우에는 의문문에서도 some을 사용한다.
a) 질문에 대한 답이 'yes'로 기대될 때
What's wrong? Do you have something in your eye?
(너의 눈에 무언가 들어간 것처럼 보이고 그래서 네가 'yes'라고 답할 것으로 기대한다)

b) 제의나 어떤 것을 요청할 때

Would you like something to eat?(뭐 좀 드시겠습니까?)

Can I have some sugar, please?(설탕 좀 주세요)

3) if절 내에서 any를 사용한다.

If there are any letters for me, can you forward them to this address?

(만일 나에게 온 편지가 좀 있으면 이 주소로 그것들을 보내주시겠습니까?)

Let me know if you need anything.(어떤 것이 필요하다면 나에게 알려 주세요)

다음 예는 문장 속에 if의 의미가 포함되어 있다.

I'm sorry for any trouble I've caused.(= if I have caused any trouble)

(내가 문제를 일으켰다면 용서하세요)

Anyone who wants to take the exam should give me their name today.

(= if there is anyone)

(시험을 치고 싶은 사람이 있다면 오늘 그들의 이름을 나에게 제출해야 한다)

4) '어느 것이든지'를 의미할 때는 긍정문에서도 any를 사용한다.

You can catch any bus. They all go downtown.

(= it doesn't matter which bus you catch)

(너는 어떤 버스든 타도된다. 모든 버스가 시내로 간다)

"Sing a song." "Which song should I sing?" "Any song. I don't care."

(노래 한 곡 불러라. 어떤 노래를 불러야 하지? 아무 노래든 괜찮다. 상관 않는다)

다음의 something과 anything을 비교해 보자.

A: I'm hungry. I want something to eat.(배고프다. 먹을 어떤 것을 원한다)

B: What would you like?(뭐 먹고 싶니?)

A: I don't care. Anything.(= something, but it doesn't matter what)

(상관없어. 아무거나)

2. Much, many, little, few, a lot, plenty

1) much, little + 불가산명사
much time, much luck, little energy, little money
many, few + 가산명사(복수형)
many friends, many people, few cars, few countries

2) a lot of/ lots of/ plenty of + 불가산명사나 가산명사(복수형) 둘 다 가능
a lot of luck, lots of time, plenty of money
a lot of friends, lots of people, plenty of ideas
plenty = 충분한 것 이상(more than enough)
There's no need to hurry. We've got plenty of time.
(서두를 필요가 없다. 충분한 시간이 있다)

3) much는 긍정문에 사용되지 않는다.(특히 구어체 영어에서).
We didn't spend much money.(부정문)
Does he go out much?(의문문)
* We spent a lot of money.(*We spent much money)
He goes out a lot.(*He goes out much)

모든 종류의 문장에서 many, a lot (of), lots of를 사용한다.
Many people drives too fast. 혹은 A lot of/ Lots of people drive too fast.(긍정문)
Do you know many people? 혹은 Do you know a lot of / lots of people?(의문문)
He doesn't go out a lot. 혹은 He doesn't go out much.(부정문)

4) little과 few는 부정적인 개념이다(= not much/ not many)
We had to make a quick decision. There was little time to think.
(= not much time; not enough time)
(우리는 빠른 결정을 내려야 했다. 생각할 시간이 거의 없었다)

종종 very little, very few를 사용한다.
There was very little time to think.(생각할 시간이 아주 적었다)
Dave has very few friends at the company.(데이브는 회사에 친구들이 아주 적었다)

5) a little과 a few는 더 긍정적이다.
a little = some, or small amount
Let's go and get something to drink. We've got a little time before thc train leaves.
(a little time = some time; enough time to have a drink)
(가서 뭐 좀 마시자. 열차가 떠나기 전에 시간이 조금 있다)
"Do you speak English?" "A little." (so we can talk a bit)

a few = some, or a small number
I enjoy my life here. I have a few friends, and we get together pretty often.
(a few friends = not many, but enough to have a good time)
(나는 여기서의 생활을 즐긴다. 몇몇 친구들이 있고 아주 자주 만난다)
"When was the last time you saw Claire?" "A few days ago." (= some days ago)
(언제 클레어를 마지막으로 만났지? 며칠 전)

다음 문장을 비교해 보자.
She's lucky. She has few problems.(= not many problems)
(그녀는 운이 좋다. 그녀는 문제가 거의 없다)
Things are not going so well for her. She has a few problems.(= some problems)
(사태가 그녀에게 그렇게 좋아지지 않고 있다. 그녀는 몇몇 문제가 있다)

only a little과 only a few는 부정적인 의미를 갖는다.
We have to hurry. We only have a little time.
(서둘러야 한다. 시간이 겨우 조금밖에 없다)
The town was very small. There were only a few houses.
(그 읍은 아주 작다. 집들이 겨우 몇 채 밖에 없다)

PHRASES and STRUCTURES

* Here is everything you need to know about the fight for gender equality.
여기에 여러분이 성평등을 위한 싸움에 관해 알아야 하는 모든 것이 있다.
= Here is everything **(that)** you need to know about the fight for gender equality.
= Here is everything, **and** you need to know **it(everything)** about the fight for gender equality.
목적격 관계대명사 that 생략 = and + it(everything)

* **are determined to + 동사원형** ~하기로 결심하다

* will not hold ourselves bound by any Laws **in which** we have no voice
어떤 법률로도 우리자신이 속박되게 하지 않을 것인데, 그 법률에서 우리는 발언권이 없다
= will not hold ourselves bound by any Laws, **and** we have no voice **in them(laws)**
in which = and + in them(laws)
have no voice 발언권이 없다

* as calls for greater freedom for women **joined** with voices demanding the end of slavery
여성들의 더 많은 자유에 대한 요구로, 그런데 여성들은 노예제도의 종말을 요구하는 목소리와 함께 합류하게 되었다
= as calls for greater freedom for women **(who were) joined** with voices demanding the end of slavery
= as calls for greater freedom for women, **and they(women) were joined** with voices demanding the end of slavery
과거분사(joined) 앞에 관계대명사의 주격(who)과 be동사 생략
who = and + they(women)

* Many women leaders of the abolitionist movement found an unsettling irony in advocating for African Americans rights **that** they themselves could not enjoy.
철폐론 운동의 많은 여성 지도자들은 아프리카계 미국인들의 권리를 옹호하는데 불안하게 하는 역설을 발견했는데, 그들 스스로는 그 권리를 향유하지 못했다.

= Many women leaders of the abolitionist movement found an unsettling irony in advocating for African Americans rights, **and** they themselves could not enjoy **them(rights).**

목적격 관계대명사 that = and + them(rights)

* We **hold** these truths **to be** self-evident.

우리는 이러한 진리들이 자명하다고 생각한다.

hold + 목적어 + to + be ~ ~라고 생각하다

* the elective franchise, **or** the right to vote

선거권, 다시 말해 투표할 권리

, or = 즉, 다시 말해

* **beyond the pale** 도리를 벗어난

* **in earnest** 본격적으로

* New Zealand became the first sovereign state **giving** women the right to vote, **followed** by Australia in 1902.

뉴질랜드는 여성에게 투표권을 부여한 첫 독립국가가 되었으며 1902년 호주가 뒤를 이었다.

= New Zealand became the first sovereign state, **and it(New Zealand) gave** women the right to vote, **(and it(New Zealand) was) followed** by Australia in 1902.

giving(현재분사) = ~~and it(New Zealand)~~ gave

followed by Australia = ~~and it(New Zealand)~~ was(being) followed by Australia

능동형 → Australia followed New Zealand

* With these rights secured, feminists **embarked on what** some scholars **refer to as** the "second wave" of feminism.

이러한 권리가 확보되자 페미니스트들은 몇몇 학자들이 페미니즘의 제2의 물결로 일컫는 것을 착수했다.

= **With** these rights **secured**, feminists embarked on **the thing which** some scholars refer to as the "second wave" of feminism.

= **With** these rights **secured**, feminists embarked on the thing, **and** some scholars refer to **it(the thing)** as the "second wave" of feminism.

관계대명사 what = the thing which = and + it(the thing)

with + 명사 + 보어(형용사, 분사, 전치사구 등) ~한 채, ~한 상태로

He sits **with** his eyes **closed**

He stood **with** his back **against the wall**

He left the kitchen **with** the kettle **boiling**

embark on ~ ~에 착수하다

refer to A as B A를 B로 일컫다

* **in greater numbers** 더 많이

* **when** many male breadwinners lost their jobs, **forcing** women **to find** "women's work" in lower paying

그 때 많은 남자 가장들이 그들의 직장을 잃었으며 그것이 여자들로 하여금 낮은 임금을 받는 여성의 일을 찾도록 했다

= **and then** many male breadwinners lost their jobs, **and it(many male breadwinners lost their jobs) forced** women to find "women's work" in lower paying

when = and then

forcing(분사구문) **= ~~and it(many male breadwinners lost their jobs)~~ forced**

force + 목적어 + to + do 억지로 ~시키다, 강제로 ~시키다

We **forced** him **to sign** the paper. 우리는 그에게 강제로 그 서류에 서명하게 했다.

* found work in industries **previously reserved** for men, **making** Rosie the Riveter a feminist icon

= found work in industries **(which was) previously reserved** for men, **and it(found work in industries) made** Rosie the Riveter a feminist icon

= found work in industries, **(and it(work) was) previously reserved** for men, **and it(found work in industries) made** Rosie the Riveter a feminist icon

제조업에서 일을 찾았는데 그 일은 이전에는 남자들을 위해 남겨진 일이었는데, 그것이 리벳공 로지에게 페미니스트 아이콘이 되게 했다

과거분사(reserved) 앞에 관계대명사의 주격(which)과 be동사 생략
which was previously reserved = and + it(work) was previously reserved
making(분사구문) = ~~and it(found work in industries)~~ made
make + 목적어 + 보어(명사, 형용사) 목적어를 ~하게 하다
He **made** her **his wife**
Flowers **make** our room **cheerful**

* **by this time** 이때까지는

* Feminists celebrated the Supreme Court decision in Roe v. Wade, the landmark ruling **that** guaranteed a woman's right to choose an abortion.
페미니스트들은 로 대 웨이드 사건에서의 대법원 결정을 축하했는데 그 결정은 획기적인 판결로 낙태를 선택할 여성의 권리를 보장하는 것이었다.
= Feminists celebrated the Supreme Court decision in Roe v. Wade, **and it(decision) was** the landmark ruling, **and it(the ruling)** guaranteed a woman's right to choose an abortion.
, = ~~and it(decision) was~~(being) the landmark ruling 여기서 ,는 동격으로 사용됨
주격 관계대명사 that = and + it(the ruling)

* I have borne 13 children, and seen **most** all sold off to slavery.
나는 13명의 아이들을 낳았으며 거의 모두가 노예로 팔리는 것을 보았다.
= I have borne 13 children, and (I have) seen **almost** all sold off to slavery.

* **None but Jesus heard me!**
예수님을 제외하고는 어느 누구도 나의 말을 듣지 않았다!
but = except ~을 제외하고

* in combating misogyny and ensuring women have equal rights
여성혐오와 싸우고 여성들이 동등한 권리를 갖는다는 것을 보장할 때
= in combating misogyny and ensuring **(that)** women have equal rights
ensure의 목적절을 이끄는 that이 생략되어 있음

* **when** the New York Times published a damning investigation into allegations of sexual harassment **made** against influential film producer Harvey Weinstein

그 때 뉴욕 타임즈는 성희롱 혐의에 대한 유죄를 강력 시사하는 조사서를 출판했는데 그 혐의는 영향력 있는 영화제작자 하비 웨인스타인에게 불리하게 작용하였다

= **and then** the New York Times published a damning investigation into allegations of sexual harassment **(which were) made** against influential film producer Harvey Weinstein

= **and then** the New York Times published a damning investigation into allegations of sexual harassment, **and they(allegations) were made** against influential film producer Harvey Weinstein

과거분사(made) 앞에 관계대명사의 주격(which)과 be동사 생략

which = and + they(allegations)

make against ~ ~에게 불리하게 작용하다

* a massive protest **aimed** at the new administration and the perceived threat it represented to reproductive, civil and human rights

그것(여성 행진)은 새 행정부를 겨냥한 대규모 시위였으며 그 시위가 생식권, 시민권, 인권에 제기한 인지된 위협이었다

= (and it(the Women's March) was) a massive protest **(which was) aimed** at the new administration and the perceived threat **(which)** it(protest) represented to reproductive, civil and human rights

= (and it(the Women's March) was) a massive protest **(which was) aimed** at the new administration and the perceived threat, **and** it(protest) represented **it(threat)** to reproductive, civil and human rights

과거분사(aimed) 앞에 관계대명사의 주격(which)과 be동사 생략

목적격 관계대명사 which 생략 = and + it(threat)

* **providing** feminists **with** a high-profile platforms for advocating on behalf of full rights for all women worldwide

그 데모는 페미니스트에게 전 세계 모든 여성들의 완전한 권리를 옹호하기 위한 세간의 이목을 끄는 무대를 제공했다

= **and they(demonstrations) provided** feminists with a high-profile platforms for advocating on behalf of full rights for all women worldwide

providing(분사구문) = ~~and they(demonstrations)~~ provided

provide A with B A에게 B를 제공하다

on behalf of ~ ~을 위해

Unit 15

Religion and Morality in the Same-Sex Marriage Debate[1)]

WARMING UP

- **To say** these arguments for marriage are not religious in nature **is** not to disparage the important place of faith and morality in public life
- **Far from** disclaim**ing** religious support for same-sex marriage, professional gay-rights activists welcome and encourage it
- Everyone has a world view and everyone inevitably **brings** that world view **to bear on** issues of public policy, including marriage
- Marriage **has more to do with** the morals and civilization of a people **than** any other institution
- He sees in the movement for same-sex marriage an opportunity "to **make the case for**" the "normative moral equivalence" of "gay and heterosexual sex"
- Current advocates for gay rights are not really engaging their opponents **unless** they are engaged with the moral nature of 'their opponents' views and arguments

1) This article was written by Thomas Messner, who is an American legal scholar who specializes in issues of religious liberty. The source is https://www.heritage.org/marriage-and-family/report/religion-and-morality-the-same-sex-marriage-debate

1. development 전개
2. measure 조치
3. lawsuit 소송
4. challenge 이의를 제기하다
5. understanding (암묵적인) 합의
6. teaching 교리
7. faith (특정) 종교

*Developments[1] in the same-sex marriage debate have focused new attention on the place of religion and morality in shaping the legal definition of marriage. For example, after voters passed *Proposition 8[2)], the California marriage amendment, the *Church of Jesus Christ of Latter-day Saints[3)] *was subjected to heavy criticism and based on its support for the *measure[2]. Now, in a federal *lawsuit[3] *challenging[4] Proposition 8, *one issue is whether evidence of religious support for Proposition 8 somehow renders the measure suspect.

Three *understandings[5] should form the basis of any discussion about the place of religion and morality in the same-sex marriage debate. First, though some people who defend marriage are personally religious or have religious motivations, support for marriage as the union of husband and wife does not require belief in the religious *teachings[6] of any particular *faith[7]. Second, many people, including some professional gay-rights activists, enthusiastically mix religion with law and politics *in support of same-sex marriage. Third, *the question of how marriage should be defined in law raises inescapable moral considerations that should be confronted directly.

2) Proposition 8 법률개정안 8은 캘리포니아 투표 제안으로 2008년 11월 캘리포니아 주 선거에서 통과된 주 헌법 수정안임. 그 개정안은 캘리포니아 대법원의 2008년 5월 항소심 판결에 앞서 동성결혼 반대자들에 의해 발의됨. 법률개정안 8은 2010년 연방법원에 의해 위헌으로 결정 났으나 2013년 6월 26일에야 발효됨.

3) Church of Jesus Christ of Latter-day Saints 말일 성도 예수 그리스도 교회(Mormon Church의 정식 명칭).

Many Arguments for Marriage as the Union of Husband and Wife Are Not Religious *in Nature

Some proponents of same-sex marriage have suggested that religion is the primary obstacle to *redefining[8] marriage to include homosexual *unions[9]. "[R]eligion is the chief obstacle for gay and lesbian political progress," *testifies[10] one expert. Says one activist, "There's no road to success that doesn't go through religion-based *homophobia[11]." According to the American Civil Liberties Union, "The primary opposition to same-sex marriage appears to be *theologically[12] based - the claim that God doesn't like it."

It might be true, of course, that many people who defend marriage are personally religious or act in part from a religious motivation to *promote[13] the *common good[14]. But support for marriage does not require belief in the religious teachings of any particular faith.

*Many arguments for marriage focus on it as a natural, pre-political social *institution[15] *intrinsically[16] connected to the *vital[17] *public interest[18] in the *begetting[19] and raising of children. "Across history and cultures," reports marriage scholar *David Blankenhorn[4)], "marriage's single most fundamental idea is that every child needs a mother and a father. Changing marriage to *accommodate[20] same-sex couples," argues Blankenhorn, "would *nullify[21] this principle in culture and in law."

It is precisely the connection between marriage, on the one hand,

8. redefine 재정립하다
9. union 결혼
10. testify 증언(진술)하다
11. homophobia 동성애혐오증
12. theologically 신학 상으로
13. promote 증진시키다
14. common good 공익
15. institution 제도(관습)
16. intrinsically 본질적으로
17. vital 필수적인
18. public interest 공익
19. begetting 생식, 아이를 낳는 것
20. accommodate 수용하다
21. nullify 무효화하다

4) David Blankenhorn(1955~) 미국의 동성결혼 반대 운동에서 유명한 인물이었는데 입장을 바꿔 2012년 동성 결혼을 입법화하는데 지지의 목소리를 내었음.

22. procreation
생식, 자식을 낳음

23. prolonged
오래 계속되는

24. profound
엄청난

25. irreplaceable
그 무엇으로도 대체 할 수 없는

26. solidify
확고히 하다

27. encourage
권장하다

28. cornerstone
초석

29. building block
기본토대

30. disparage
폄하하다

31. higher law
도덕률

32. good will
선의

and the begetting and raising of children, on the other hand, that makes marriage, as the Supreme Court wrote in *Loving v. Virginia[5)], "fundamental to our very existence and survival." This connection is also why race is not relevant to marriage but gender is. With *procreation[22], *the most important public purpose of marriage remains uniting men and women in a "formal partnership" that will last through "the *prolonged[23] period of dependency of a human child."

The intergenerational and long-term benefits of marriage to society are *profound[24] and *irreplaceable[25]. The public has a strong interest in using law and policy to recognize, affirm, support, *solidify[26], *encourage[27], strengthen, and defend marriage as the *cornerstone[28] of the family and the *building block[29] of society.

*To say these arguments for marriage are not religious in nature is not to *disparage[30] the important place of faith and morality in public life or the *higher law[31] foundation of moral truth. *This nation was founded on truths said to be "self-evident, according to 'the Laws of Nature and Nature's God,'" and *concepts like inalienable rights have meaning only in reference to a higher law that binds even the state. The point is merely that, using the light of reason and evidence from the world around them, people of *good will[32] can support the traditional understanding of marriage without accepting the religious teachings of any particular faith.

5) Loving v. Virginia 1967년의 미국 대법원의 혁기적인 판결로 타인종간의 결혼을 금지하는 법률이 미국 헌법 수정 조항 14의 위반으로 위헌 판결함. 그 판결로 미국에서 많은 타인종간 결혼이 잇따랐고 매년 Loving Day로 기념됨.

*Religion *Harnessed[33] to Support Same-Sex Marriage

*If religion is viewed as the primary obstacle to making same-sex marriage a reality in law, it should be no surprise if some activists wish to exclude certain religious viewpoints from the same-sex marriage debate. One activist expressed this view quite *plainly[34] in explaining why he sponsored an advertisement *exploiting[35] anti-Mormon *bigotry[36]. "I'm not intending it to harm the religion," this activist said "I think they do wonderful things. . . . My single goal is to get them out of the same-sex marriage business and back to helping hurricane victims."

Evidence shows, however, that religion is often harnessed *in support of same-sex marriage. In California, for example, *a wide range of religious institutions supported same-sex marriage *legislation[37] that was *vetoed[38] by Governor *Schwarzenegger[6].

Similarly, *there was significant religiously based political opposition to Proposition 8, the marriage amendment California voters passed in 2008. Religious institutions and leaders that support same-sex marriage in California contributed money, resources, and support to *No on Prop 8 efforts and *urged citizens to oppose Proposition 8. In one event over a hundred "multi-faith leaders,"

including "*rabbis[39], *ministers[40], *pastors[41], *priests[42] and *priestesses[43]," stood on the steps of the San Francisco City Hall and "*proclaim[ed][44] their opposition to California's Proposition 8."

33. harness 이용(활용)하다
34. plainly 솔직하게
35. exploit 이용하다
36. bigotry 편협성
37. legislation 법률의 제정
38. veto 거부하다
39. rabbi (유대교) 지도자
40. minister (프로테스탄트 기독교의) 목사
41. pastor (비국교도 교회의) 목사
42. priest (가톨릭) 신부
43. priestess 여사제
44. proclaim 선언(선포)하다

6) Arnold Schwarzenegger(1947~) 오스트리아 출신의 미국 배우, 정치가로 2003년부터 2011년까지 미국 캘리포니아 주지사를 역임함.

45. favor
찬성하다

46. judicial process
재판절차

47. representative
대표자

48. interfaith
종교 간의, 종파를 초월한

49. association
협회

50. synagogue
유대교 회당

51. sangha
(불교에서 같은 가르침을 신봉하고 모인) 교단(教團)

52. constituent
주민(유권자)

53. exhaust
철저히 다루다

54. illustration
예

55. cause
대의

56. disclaim
부인하다

57. convene
소집하다

Many religious institutions and leaders *favoring[45] same-sex marriage also actively engage in *judicial processes[46]. In a state court lawsuit claiming a right to same-sex marriage under the California constitution, *representatives[47] from a wide range of religious and faith organizations supported an "**interfaith[48] 'friend of the court' brief" that was signed by hundreds of "religious *associations[49], churches, *synagogues[50], *sanghas[51], ministers, and rabbis across California and the nation." In a legal challenge against Proposition 8 "nearly one thousand faith communities and faith leaders with *constituents[52] in California" supported a brief favoring same-sex marriage.

These examples do not *exhaust[53] the possible *illustrations[54] of how religion has been mixed with law and politics to oppose measures like Proposition 8 and support the *cause[55] of same-sex marriage more generally. Many additional instances can be identified in California and elsewhere.

*Far from *disclaiming[56] religious support for same-sex marriage, professional gay-rights activists welcome and encourage it. *The National Religious Leadership Roundtable, which supported the multi-faith event on the steps of the San Francisco City Hall described above, is *convened[57] by the National Gay and Lesbian Task Force. On its website *Lambda Legal[7)] posts statements from "faith supporters" of same-sex marriage. Harry Knox, Director of the

7) Lambda Legal(Lambda Legal Defense and Education Fund) 동성애자, 양성애자, 성전환자 뿐만 아니라 에이즈 환자와 함께 사는 사람들에 관심을 두는 미국의 시민 권리 기구.

Human Rights Campaign's Religion and Faith Program and a member of President Obama's Advisory Council on Faith-based and Neighborhood Partnerships, has traveled to California to help "*mobilize[58] *clergy[59] and people of faith for marriage equality."

As a general principle, the *robust[60] participation of religious people and institutions in public life is good for this nation. President *George Washington[8)] described religion and morality as the "great *Pillars[61] of human happiness," the "firmest props of the duties of Men and citizens," and "indispensable supports" of "all the *dispositions[62] and habits which lead to political *prosperity[63]." *President Washington also had the insight to warn that Americans should indulge only with caution the supposition that "morality can be maintained without religion. Whatever may be *conceded[64] to the influence of *refined[65] education on minds of peculiar structure," he said, "*reason and experience both forbid us to expect that National morality can *prevail[66] in exclusion of religious principle."

More *pragmatically[67], *everyone has a world view and everyone *inevitably[68] brings that world view to bear on issues of public policy, including marriage. Therefore, as Barack Obama stated when he was still a U.S. *Senator[69], "*[S]ecularists[70] are wrong when they ask believers to leave their religion at the door before entering into the public square.... [T]o say that men and women should not *inject[71] their 'personal morality' into public policy debates is a practical *absurdity[72]. Our law is by definition a *codification[73] of

58. mobilize 동원하다
59. clergy 성직자
60. robust 왕성한
61. pillar 기둥, 대들보
62. disposition 성향
63. prosperity 번영
64. concede 인정하다
65. refined 세련된, 고상한
66. prevail 이기다
67. pragmatically 실용적으로
68. inevitably 불가피하게
69. Senator 상원 의원
70. secularist 세속주의자
71. inject 주입하다
72. absurdity 부조리, 불합리
73. codification 체계화, 성문화

8) George Washington(1732~1799) 미국의 초대 대통령.

74. reasoned 조리 정연한
75. frame 표현하다
76. neutrality 중립
77. chorus 이구동성
78. fruitful 유익한
79. normative 규범적인

morality . . . ."

Advocates on both sides of the marriage debate should respect the *reasoned[74] participation in that debate of people of all faiths and no faith at all.

Defining Marriage in Law Involves Moral Considerations

Some activists might prefer to *frame[75] arguments for same-sex marriage in terms of state *neutrality[76] and formal legal equality, but the question of how society recognizes marriage through its laws and policies raises inescapable moral considerations. In the words of President Obama, "Our law is by definition a codification of morality" and, as the U.S. Supreme Court asserted long ago, *marriage has "more to do with the morals and civilization of a people than any other institution."

A growing *chorus[77] of scholars who support same-sex marriage recognize that it is impossible to have a "*fruitful[78] discussion" of same-sex marriage "without engaging the *normative[79] questions." According to Yale Law Professor William Eskridge, for example, "Opponents and supporters of same-sex marriage both realize that the legal debate is strongly connected to the larger normative debate. *What is at stake is not just technical legal equality, but fundamental social norms and public values in the United States."

Georgetown Law Professor Chai Feldblum, who recently was appointed by President Obama to serve as a *Commissioner on the U.S. Equal Employment Opportunity Commission, sees in the movement for same-sex marriage an opportunity "to *make the case for" the "normative moral *equivalence[80]" of "gay and heterosexual sex" - *an argument, Professor Feldblum *observes[81], "that is hardly ever heard in political circles." Professor Feldblum has even created what she calls "The Moral Values Project" to promote this argument.

Rutgers Law Professor Carlos Ball believes that the struggle for "societal acceptance" of same-sex relationships *entails[82] a "*frontal attack[83]" on the "deeply held views of many Americans regarding the (im)morality of homosexuality." It is "impossible," Professor Ball writes, "to *grapple with[84] the complexities of the issue by simply asking for equality and state-neutrality and for protection against discrimination."

Recently, a group of professors favoring same-sex marriage published an entire book on the topic of morality, religion, and same-sex marriage. The authors, who include Professors Feldblum and Ball, believe that "*current *advocates[85] for gay rights are not really *engaging[86] their opponents unless they are engaged with the moral nature of their opponents' views and arguments." This book *self-consciously[87] engages "the moral questions" that often arise in connection with issues like same-sex marriage and argues that "the moral case" favors outcomes like the legalization of same-sex marriage.

*These law professors are not the only advocates prepared to advance moral arguments for same-sex marriage. When political activists assert that not allowing two people of the same sex to marry

80. equivalence 등가
81. observe (의견) 말하다
82. entail 수반하다
83. frontal attack 정면공격
84. grapple with ~을 해결하려고 노력하다
85. advocate 옹호자
86. engage 사로잡다, ~와 관계를 맺다
87. self-consciously 남의 이목을 의식하여

88. dimension
관점

89. charged
격론을 부를

90. capital punishment
사형제

91. party
당사자

92. argumentation
논증

93. contested
이론이 있는

94. alarming
걱정스러운

95. enlist
(협조, 참여) 얻다

96. figure
인물

97. suppress
금하다

is "wrong," *allude to the "long arc of justice," or invoke concepts of "human rights," they too make arguments of a moral nature.

At some level all legal and policy issues involve a moral *dimension[88], and activists and lawmakers who take liberal and progressive political positions often have no problem using morally *charged[89] language to support those political positions on issues as diverse as *capital punishment[90], environmentalism, and health care. Problems of fundamental fairness arise, however, when *parties[91] who use moral *argumentation[92] to support their own position suggest that opposing parties should not do the same thing.

Whether to recognize same-sex marriage in law involves inescapable moral considerations. Parties on both sides of the issue should be free to bring their moral viewpoints to bear on the issues involved.

Conclusion

Religion and morality occupy a vital place in the public life of this country and the question of marriage is one of the most important and *contested[93] public issues of the time. It is neither surprising nor *alarming[94] if parties on both sides of the marriage debate seek to use moral argumentation and *enlist[95] the support of religious *figures[96] and institutions. Attempts to *suppress[97] the open expression of a diversity of viewpoints on the issue of marriage should be strongly resisted.

GRAMMAR

형용사의 종류

1. 의미에 따른 분류

성상(qualifying) 형용사	a tall tree/ She is beautiful
수량(quantitative) 형용사	one, two, first, second ... some water, any book, many books, a few people, little space, much money...
대명(pronominal) 형용사	대명사가 명사 앞에서 한정을 하게 될 때
지시형용사	this book, that book, these, those
소유형용사	my, your, his, her...
의문형용사	Which girl do you like best?
부정(indefinite)형용사	all, each, every, both, no, other ...

2. 비교형과 최상형

비교를 위해 사용되는 여러 가지 문법적인 구조들이 있다.

1) 만일 사람이나 행위가 유사하다고 말하고 싶다면 as나 like를 사용할 수 있다.

Your sister looks just like you.(너의 누이는 너와 꼭 닮았다)

유사성에 관해 이야기하는 다른 방법들은 too, also, as well, so do I, so am I, neither/nor do I 등이 있다.

2) 사물이 어떤 면에서 동등하다고 말하고 싶다면 as - as 구조(형용사와 부사)나 as much/many - as 구조(명사와 동사)를 사용한다.

Drive as fast as you can.(할 수 있는 한 빨리 운전해라)

We've got as many packets as we need.

(우리는 필요한 것만큼 많은 소포를 가지고 있다)

Practise as much as you can.(할 수 있는 한 많이 연습을 하시오)

3) 사물들 사이의 차이에 관해 말하는 한 가지 방법은 형용사, 부사, 동사, 명사 등과 함께 more (-than) 이나 less (-than)을 사용하는 것이다.

His new book is much more interesting than his last.

(그의 새 책은 그의 지난 책 보다 훨씬 더 재미있다)

The car is running less smoothly than it used to.

(그 차는 과거보다 덜 부드럽게 달린다)

I like you more and more every day.

(나는 매일 점점 더 당신을 좋아한다)

They want us to do more work for less money.

(그들은 우리가 돈은 덜 주고 일은 더하기를 원했다)

또 다른 방법은 (the) most와 (the) least를 사용하는 것이다.

You're the most annoying person I've ever met.

(당신은 내가 만난 사람 중에서 가장 성가신 사람이다)

My ambition is to spend the least possible time working.

(나의 야망은 일하는데 가능한 한 가장 적게 시간을 보내는 것이다)

4) 비교형을 갖는 문장

(1) 비교형은 than이 뒤따른다.

The weather is warmer than last week.

(날씨가 지난 주 보다 더 따뜻하다)

(2) older than I 와 older than me

비격식체 영어에서 than 뒤에 종종 목적격 대명사(me, him, her, us, them)를 사용한다. 격식체에서는 주격 대명사(I, he, 등)가 더 올바른 표현이라 간주된다.

She's older than me.(informal)

She's older than I (am). (formal)

※ 대명사가 동사와 함께 사용될 때는 주격 대명사만이 가능하다.
Lucy found more mushrooms than I did. (*than me did)

(3) The + 비교형… , the + 비교형…

두 변화가 함께 일어난다고 말할 때 특별한 방식으로 the와 함께 비교형을 사용한다.

The older I get, the happier I am. (내가 나이가 더 들면 들수록 나는 더 행복하다)

(4) 지속적인 변화를 나타내기 위해 '이중비교형'을 사용한다.

I'm getting fatter and fatter. (나는 점점 더 뚱뚱해지고 있다)

5) 비교형과 함께 사용된 much와 far

비교형을 강조하기 위해 very를 사용할 수 없고 대신 much나 far를 사용한다.

My boy-friend is much older than me.

(나의 남자 친구는 나보다 훨씬 나이가 더 많다)

You're far more tolerant than I am.

(당신은 나보다 훨씬 더 관대하다)

비교형을 수식하기 위해 사용되는 다른 단어나 표현들:

very much, a lot, any, no, rather, a little, a bit

Things are no better than before. (일들이 이전 보다 아주 더 좋지 않다)

Is your mother any more relaxed? (당신의 어머니가 조금 더 편안한가?)

※ more가 복수 명사가 뒤따를 때 far나 many가 수식할 수는 있지만 much는 수식할 수 없다.

many more opportunities(혹은 far more opportunities) much more money(혹은 far more money)

6) 최상형을 갖는 문장

(1) 최상형 뒤에서 장소에 관해 이야기하고 있다는 것을 보이기 위해 전치사 in을 사용한다.

It's the most expensive car in the world.

※ of는 보통 사용되지 않지만 명사가 없는 최상급 뒤에서 가능하다.
She's the most sensible of the Smith girls.
(그녀는 스미스네 딸들 중에서 가장 지각이 있다)

(2) 최상형과 함께 정관사 the가 사용된다.

It's the best book ....

You're the fastest, but I'm the strongest.

(당신은 가장 빠르지만 나는 가장 강하다)

(3) 최상형 형용사는 명사 없이 사용될 수 있다.

This one is the fastest.(이것은 가장 빠르다)

I'm the greatest.(나는 가장 위대하다)

PHRASES and STRUCTURES

* **be subjected to ~** ~을 받다(당하다)

* One issue is whether evidence of religious support for Proposition 8 somehow **renders** the measure **suspect**.
  한 가지 문제는 개정안 8에 대한 종교적 지지의 증거가 어쨌든 그 조처에 의심을 품게 하는지 하는 것이다.
  render + 목적어 + 보어 목적어가 ~되게 하다

* **in support of ~** ~을 지지(옹호)하여

* **The question** of how marriage should be defined in law **raises** inescapable moral considerations **that** should be confronted directly.
  결혼이 법에서 어떻게 정의되어야 하는지 하는 문제는 피할 수 없는 도덕적 고려사항들을 제기하는데 그 고려사항들은 직접적으로 부딪쳐져야 하는 것들이다.
  = The question of how marriage should be defined in law raises inescapable moral considerations, **and they(considerations)** should be confronted directly.
  The question은 주어, 본동사는 **raise**
  주격 관계대명사 that = and + they(considerations)

* **in nature** 사실상

* Many arguments for marriage focus on it as a natural, pre-political social institution **intrinsically connected** to the vital public interest in the begetting and raising of children.
  결혼을 찬성하는 많은 주장들은 자연적이고, 정치이전의 사회적 관습으로서의 결혼에 집중하는데 그 관습은 본질적으로 아이를 낳고 기르는 것에서의 필수적인 공익과 연관이 된다.
  = Many arguments for marriage focus on it(marriage) as a natural, pre-political social institution **(which is) intrinsically connected** to the vital public interest in the begetting and raising of children.
  = Many arguments for marriage focus on it(marriage) as a natural, pre-political

social institution, **and it(institution)** is intrinsically connected to the vital public interest in the begetting and raising of children.

과거분사(concerned) 앞에서 관계대명사의 주격(which)과 be동사 생략

which = and + it(institution)

* The most important public purpose of marriage remains uniting men and women in a "formal partnership" **that** will last through "the prolonged period of dependency of a human child."

결혼의 가장 중요한 공적인 목적은 여전히 "공식적인 동반자관계" 속에서 남자와 여자를 결합하는 것인데 그러한 동반자 관계는 "오래 지속되는 한 아이의 의존 기간" 내내 지속될 것이다.

= The most important public purpose of marriage remains uniting men and women in a "formal partnership", **and it(formal partnership)** will last through "the prolonged period of dependency of a human child."

주격 관계대명사 that = and + it(formal partnership)

* To say these arguments for marriage are not religious in nature is not to disparage the important place of faith and morality in public life or the higher law foundation of moral truth.

결혼의 찬성에 대한 이러한 주장들이 사실상 종교적이지 않다고 말한다고 해서 그것이 공공생활에서 신앙과 도덕의 중요한 자리나 도덕적 진리라는 도덕률의 토대를 폄하하는 것이 아니다.

= **To say (that)** these arguments for marriage are not religious in nature **is** not to disparage the important place of faith and morality in public life or the higher law foundation of moral truth.

To say에서 in nature까지가 주어이고 본동사는 nature 다음의 is

higher law 도덕률(인간이 정한 법률보다 한층 높은 것으로 여겨짐으로)

* This nation was founded on truths **said** to be "self-evident."

이 나라는 "자명하다"라고 일컬어졌던 진리에 기초하여 건국되었다.

= This nation was founded on truths **(which was) said** to be "self-evident."

과거분사(said) 앞에서 관계대명사의 주격(which)과 be동사 생략

be founded on = be based on ~ ~에 기초하다

* Concepts like inalienable rights have meaning only in reference to a higher law

that binds even the state.
양도할 수 없는 권리와 같은 개념들은 도덕률과 관련하여야만 의미를 갖는데 도덕률은 국가 마저도 결속시킨다.
= Concepts like inalienable rights have meaning only in reference to a higher law, **and it(higher law)** binds even the state.
주격 관계대명사 that = and + it(higher law)
in reference to ~ ~과 관련하여

* Religion **Harnessed** to Support Same-Sex Marriage
동성 결혼을 지지하기 위해 이용되는 종교
= Religion **(which is) Harnessed** to Support Same-Sex Marriage
과거분사(harnessed) 앞에서 관계대명사의 주격(which)과 be동사 생략

* If religion is viewed as the primary obstacle to making same-sex marriage a reality in law, **it should be no surprise if** some activists wish to exclude certain religious viewpoints from the same-sex marriage debate.
만일 종교가 동성결혼이 법의 현실이 되게 하는데 주요한 장애라 한다면 몇몇 활동가들이 동성 결혼 논란에서 몇 가지 종교적인 관점을 배제하고 싶어한다하더라도 놀랄 일이 아니다.
it should be no surprise if ~ ~라 해도 놀랄 일이 아니다

* **in support of ~** ~을 지지하여

* A wide range of religious institutions supported same-sex marriage legislation **that** was vetoed by Governor Schwarzenegger.
다양한 종교적 단체들이 동성 결혼 법제화를 지지했는데 그 법률은 주지사 슈왈제네거에 의해 거부되었다.
= A wide range of religious institutions supported same-sex marriage legislation, **and it(legislation)** was vetoed by Governor Schwarzenegger.
주격 관계대명사 that = and + it(legislation)

* There was significant religiously based political opposition to Proposition 8, the marriage amendment California voters passed in 2008.
제안 8에 대한 중요한 종교에 기반을 둔 정치적 반대가 있었는데, 그 제안 8은 결혼 수정안으로, 캘리포니아 유권자들이 2008년에 그 수정안을 통과시켰다.

= There was significant religiously based political opposition to Proposition 8, **(and it was)** the marriage amendment **(which)** California voters passed in 2008.

= There was significant religiously based political opposition to Proposition 8, (and it was) the marriage amendment, **and** California voters passed **it(marriage amendment)** in 2008.

,와 the marriage amendment는 동격

Proposition 8, the marriage amendment = Proposition 8, ~~and it was~~(being) the marriage amendment

목적격 관계대명사 which 생략 = and + it(marriage amendment)

* **No on Prop 8** 제안 8에 대한 반대

* **urged** citizens **to oppose** Proposition 8
시민들에게 제안 8을 반대하도록 촉구했다
urge + 목적어 + to + 동사원형 (~하도록) 촉구하다

* **interfaith 'friend of the court' brief**
종교를 초월한 우정의 법정 의견서

* **Far from disclaiming** religious support for same-sex marriage
동성 결혼 찬성에 대한 종교적 지지를 부인하기는커녕
far from + do+ing ~ = instead of + do+ing ~ ~하기는커녕

* **The National Religious Leadership Roundtable**
전국 종교 지도자 원탁회의

* President Washington also had the insight to warn **that** Americans should indulge only with caution **the supposition that** "morality can be maintained without religion.
워싱턴 대통령은 미국인들이 도덕이 종교 없이 유지될 수 있다는 가정을 오직 조심스럽게 받아들여야 한다고 경고할 정도의 통찰력을 또한 가졌다.
the insight to warn = the insight (enough) to warn
warn + that ~ that절은 warn의 목적절
the supposition와 that이하는 동격

* Reason and experience both **forbid** us **to expect** that National morality can prevail in exclusion of religious principle.
이성과 경험 두 가지 모두가 우리로 하여금 국가의 도덕이 종교적 원칙을 배제하고 승리할 수 있다고 기대하지 못하게 한다.
forbid + 목적어 + to + do ~ ~을 금지하다, 방해하다
in exclusion of ~ ~을 배제하고

* Everyone has a world view and everyone inevitably **brings** that world view **to bear on issues** of public policy, including marriage.
모든 사람은 세계관을 가지고 있으며 모든 사람은 불가피하게 그러한 세계관을 결혼을 포함하는 공공정책의 문제에 쏟는다.
bring ~ to bear on something ~을 어떤 것에 쏟다, 집중하다
that은 world view를 수식하는 지시형용사

* Marriage **has** "more **to do with** the morals and civilization of a people than any other institution."
결혼은 어떤 다른 관습보다도 국민의 문명과 도덕률과 더 관련이 있다.
have to do with ~ ~와 관계가 있다

* What is **at stake** is not just technical legal equality, but fundamental social norms and public values in the United States.
문제가 되는 것은 단지 기술적인 법적인 평등이 아니라 미국에서의 근본적인 사회적 규범과 공적인 가치이다.
at stake 위태로운, 문제가 되는

* Commissioner on the U.S. Equal Employment Opportunity Commission
미 연방 고용기회균등 위원회 위원장

* **make the case for ~** ~에 대해 찬성 주장을 하다

* an argument, Professor Feldblum observes, "**that** is hardly ever heard in political circles."
그것은 정계에서는 좀처럼 들리지 않는 주장이라고 펠드블럼 교수는 말하고 있다
= **(and it is)** an argument, **and it(argument)** "is hardly ever heard in political

circles," Professor Feldblum observes
주격 관계대명사 that = and + it(argument)
hardly ever 거의 ~않는

* Current advocates for gay rights are not really engaging their opponents **unless** they are engaged with the moral nature of their opponents' views and arguments.
만일 그들이 그들 반대자들의 견해와 주장들의 도덕적 속성에 관계되지 못한다면 현재의 동성애자 권리 옹호자들은 실제로 그들 반대자들을 사로잡지 못할 것이다.
unless = if ~ not 만일 ~아니라면

* These law professors are not the only advocates **prepared** to advance moral arguments for same-sex marriage.
이러한 법률 교수들이 동성 결혼 찬성의 도덕적 주장을 진전시키기 위해 준비되어있는 유일한 옹호자들은 아니다.
= These law professors are not the only advocates **(who are) prepared** to advance moral arguments for same-sex marriage.
= These law professors are not the only advocates, **and they** are prepared to advance moral arguments for same-sex marriage.
과거분사(prepared) 앞에서 관계대명사의 주격(who)과 be동사 생략
who = and + they

* **allude to ~** ~을 넌지시 언급하다, ~을 내비치다

Unit 16

Ten Important Reasons to Include the Humanities in Your Preparation for a Scientific Career[1)]

WARMING UP

- I wasted a lot of time in college being **forced to** take humanities classes that **had nothing to do with** my area of study
- The need **for** science majors **to** take courses in the humanities has been contentious ever since
- Scientists do not learn enough about the humanities - **to the detriment of** society
- Some applicants to college **regard** a strong core curriculum requirement **as** a negative factor
- Scientists chafe at the stereotype **held** by some **that** they belong to a class of socially awkward "geeks" that are unable to communicate their ideas clearly
- **Put in** Africa, **and** you'd be amazed at how many courses at this university deal with Africa from so many perspectives
- The diploma we receive at graduation defines and symbolizes **who** we are and **what** we are qualified to do

1) This article was written by Dalbert. The source is https://blogs.sciencemag.org/sciencecareers/2011/05/ten-important-r.html

1. manifestation 징후, 표시
2. ongoing 계속 진행 중인
3. rhetoric 수사학
4. moral philosophy 윤리학
5. divinity = theology 신학
6. break with 관계를 끊다
7. form 만들다
8. room 같이 쓰다
9. mingle 섞이다, 어울리다
10. truism 자명한 이치
11. assure 보장하다
12. vis-a-vis ~와 비교하여, ~에 대하여
13. liberal art 교양과목
14. contentious 논쟁을 초래할
15. required 필수의

*It is common to hear undergraduates and recent college graduates preparing for a career in science complain: "I think I wasted a lot of time *in college being forced to take humanities classes that had nothing to do with my area of study." This is one of many *manifestations[1] of the *ongoing[2] centuries-long battle over the relationship between the sciences and the humanities.

From a historical point of view, until the mid-19th century, the humanities (i.e., grammar, *rhetoric[3], history, literature, languages, and *moral philosophy[4]) *held the upper hand. *At Oxford and Cambridge Universities, the gold standard models for American education, the areas of study consisted mainly of classics, mathematics, or *divinity[5].

However, in 1847 Yale College *broke with[6] this tradition and *formed[7] the School of Applied Chemistry. This became the Yale Scientific School and in 1861 it was renamed the Sheffield Scientific School. Sheffield's 3-year undergraduate program focused on chemistry, engineering, and independent research. It offered the best scientific training in America. The "Sheffs" studied and lived apart from other undergraduates *taking the classic curriculum and *roomed[8] together in the "college yard." The two groups did not *mingle[9]. The old *truism[10] that a classical education *assured[11] success was being challenged. Science had begun its separation and was ascending *vis-a-vis[12] the *liberal arts[13] in American universities.

*The need for science majors to take courses in the humanities has been *contentious[14] ever since. The *required[15] core curriculum at most colleges and universities has *atrophied[16] over the years, while at the same time governmental funds for support of any new research in the humanities has *dried up[17]. *Authorities[18] both within and outside of science have expressed concern that scientists do not learn enough about the humanities - *to the detriment of society.

In this environment, it's difficult for the undergraduate to determine the *desirability[19] of taking courses in the humanities - or which and how many to take. In fact, *some applicants to college regard a strong core curriculum requirement as a negative factor, opting instead for programs with a minimum number of required core courses and maximum *flexibility[20].

*All this considered, I would offer the following 10 reasons why students *pursuing[21] science careers should *augment[22] their education with a strong foundation in the humanities.

16. atrophy
위축되다
17. dry up
바싹 마르다, 고갈되다
18. authorities
관계자
19. desirability
바람직함, 타당성
20. flexibility
탄력성
21. pursue
추구하다
22. augment
늘리다
23. land-grant
미국 정부로부터
무상으로 토지
따위가 주어져 설립된
24. cultured
교양 있는
25. forces
영향력을 지닌 사람
26. altruism
이타심

1. The humanities prepare you to fulfill your civic and cultural responsibilities.

The reason that *John Harvard[2)] left his library to the college in Cambridge, Massachusetts, that Jane and *Leland Stanford[3)] founded Stanford University, and that states established *land-grant[23] colleges was to educate *cultured[24] and useful citizens. The humanities provide an insightful understanding into moral, ethical, political, and ideological *forces[25]. A successful society depends upon *altruism[26],

2) John Harvard(1607~1638) 영국태생의 미국 선교사, 자선가.

3) Leland Stanford(1824~1893) 미국의 철도 개발자, 정치가, 자선가, California 주지사, 상원의원을 역임했음. Stanford 대학을 설립했음.

27. charity
자선

28. civility
공손함

29. generosity
너그러움

30. aesthetic
심미적

31. key
가장 중요한, 핵심적인

32. biography
전기

33. introduce
접하게 하다

34. natural selection
자연도태

35. reveal
밝히다

36. link
관련성

*charity[27], *civility[28], compassion, and *generosity[29], and the humanities evaluate and emphasize the importance of these characteristics. The liberal arts introduce *aesthetic[30] values to the student. While it may not be obvious how these characteristics are essential to finding a research position in academia or industry, they are *key[31] to a full and meaningful life.

2. Studying the humanities allows you to become familiar with and use the creative ideas from great minds outside of science.

*Biography[32], literature, and history offer a window into the understanding of human nature and society. They *introduce[33] us to thoughts and ideas from outside our specialist areas and can have relevance to finding new directions and enhance creative thinking.

For example, a classic case that demonstrates the influence of humanities on science can be seen in Charles Darwin's development of the theory of evolution by *natural selection[34]. In his *On the Origin of Species*, his autobiography, and other writings, Darwin *revealed[35] that the principal insight that led to his theory of evolution was his knowledge of *Malthus' population theory[4]. This states that populations increase geometrically while food supplies grow arithmetically. Robert Young, who carefully traced this *link[36] in his 1969 publication, *Malthus and the Evolutionists: the Common*

4) Malthus' population theory (인구론) 영국의 경제학자인 Thomas Robert Malthus(1766~1834)가 제안한 이론으로 그의 저서 '인구론(An Essay on the Principle of Population)'에서 그는 식량 생산은 산술적으로 증가하는 반면에 인구는 기하급수적으로 증가한다고 주장했음.

Context of Biological and Social Theory, points out that assumptions in the humanities about human nature and society contribute fundamentally to *approaches taken in the scientific study of nature.

3. The *state-of-the-art[37] scientific knowledge and techniques you learn in college have a limited *shelf life[38]; mastering the humanities provides tools for extending it.

Just as cars have an approximate 10-year road life and *high-tech[39] *gadgets[40] last 2 or 3 years before they become *obsolete[41], *the preparation for a scientific career one receives in graduate school leaves the individual competitive for a finite period only. *The study of humanities, both in its pursuit and the perspective it provides, rewards the student with the skills needed for self-critical *reflection[42], *adaptability[43], and *self-teaching[44]. *These are the functions needed to be an independent learner, thereby extending one's scientific knowledge and teaching abilities throughout his or her professional career.

4. Humanities study strengthens your ability to communicate and work with others.

*Scientists *chafe at[45] the *stereotype[46] held by some that they belong to a class of socially awkward "*geeks[47]" that are unable to communicate their ideas clearly. The old "classical" liberal arts education was pursued *in large measure because the materials studied and the methods of study enhanced one's ability to work well

37. state-of-the-art 최신의
38. shelf life 유통기한
39. high-tech 첨단기술의
40. gadget 장치, 도구
41. obsolete 더 이상 쓸모가 없는
42. reflection 반영
43. adaptability 적응성
44. self-teaching 자습
45. chafe at ~에 짜증내다
46. stereotype 고정관념
47. geek 괴짜

48. gain advancement 진급하다
49. grant 보조금
50. proficiency 숙달, 능숙
51. clinical practice 임상실습
52. Hispanic (스페인어를 사용하는) 라틴 아메리카계의
53. intelligible 이해할 수 있는
54. pay off 성공하다(성과를 올리다)
55. handsomely 훌륭하게
56. collaboration 공동연구

with others and communicate properly via the spoken and written word. These rewards still apply and remain useful in securing good jobs, *gaining advancement[48] and promotions, and obtaining *grants[49].

5. You will gain knowledge of foreign languages and foreign cultures.

With globalization, this is increasingly seen as a requirement for a successful career in commerce and industry. It is also helpful in science and medicine. When I was in college number of years ago, it was a widely held belief that a *proficiency[50] in German - scientific German, in particular - was of great importance to scientists and physicians. While this has been helpful to me throughout the years, *my lack of proficiency in Spanish has been a handicap in my *clinical practice[51], requiring the use of a translator with *Hispanic[52] patients unable to speak English.

Although we assume English to be the universal language of science and medicine, this isn't the case in every country. Moreover, all non-English speaking countries retain their national pride. Years ago, a colleague of mine was invited to give a "name" lecture in Japan. He spent a great deal of time and effort translating his lecture into Japanese and rehearsing it so it would be *intelligible[53] to his Japanese audience. His efforts *paid off[54] *handsomely[55] *in terms of subsequent *collaborations[56], visiting professorships, and fellowship applications from Japan.

6. The walls that exist among disciplines has been lowered and students can move across disciplines more freely.

The concept of a core curriculum has changed and students have increasing flexibility, largely as a result of information technology. Victor Coelho, *associate provost[57] at Boston University, gives a good illustration:

Recently I worked with the Office of Information Technology on this course selection database that *crawls[58] through all the *course descriptions[59] at BU. You can put in keywords to find all the courses with descriptions having those words, and you would be amazed at how many people are discussing the same thing. For instance, in *typing in[60] theoretical physics, *you would have no idea that there's an art history course discussing theoretical physics.

Or *put in Africa, and you'd be amazed at how many courses at this university deal with Africa from so many perspectives. It showed me how *fluid[61] a university could be. *You could actually see all of the possibilities of a university teaching in a holistic manner, allowing students to stay *tethered[62] to a major, but have that tie be very, very long.

7. *Students can benefit from advice on which courses to take.

Without the benefit of experience or advice, students choosing courses in an abstract manner can *make poor decisions. In many instances, students do not know the value of a particular course until after they've taken it. It is difficult to determine how useful a course

57. associate provost
교무부처장

58. crawl
기어가다, 느리다

59. course description
강좌 설명서

60. type in
입력하다

61. fluid
부드러운

62. tethered
묶여있는

63. advanced calculus 고급 미적분학

64. career track 경력으로 인정받을 수 있는 일

65. knowledgeably 유식하게

66. concerned 우려하고 있는

67. interdisciplinary 학제간의

68. diploma 졸업장

69. complement 보완물

in Russian literature - or *advanced calculus[63] - will be in one's career without information from other people further advanced on the same *career track[64]. To provide that information is the job of one's advisor or mentor, who can *knowledgeably[65] speak to the importance and usefulness of particular courses.

8. Humanities study helps you understand the impact that science, technology, and medicine has had on society and understand the future scientific needs of society.

*The study of literature, history, and philosophy shed light on the influence science has had on the quality of people's lives and on the shaping of society, both positively and negatively. These studies also inform us of society's needs and are important considerations for the *concerned[66] scientist to appreciate and learn from, including the consideration in where he or she chooses to work and what projects they undertake.

9. *Interdisciplinary[67] learning adds value to one's degree.

In a significant measure, *the *diploma[68] we receive at graduation defines and symbolizes who we are and what we are qualified to do. But *its true value is derived from what we have put into our head and our heart. A broad knowledge that includes the essentials of the humanities is an important *complement[69] to our scientific training.

10. Humanities study teaches you that the *supposedly[70] sharp dichotomies[71] that separate science from humanities do not really exist.

It is a general belief among scientists that science deals with facts and the humanities deals with values. But as Robert Young *astutely[72] notes: "Science, technology and medicine - *far from being value-neutral - are the *embodiment[73] of values in theories, things and *therapies[74], in facts and *artifacts[75], in procedures and programs . . . I am suggesting that science is part of culture . . . [and] that research traditions cannot be reasonably claimed to be set above the *prevailing[76] world view of the *epoch[77]."

And that, in summary, I believe the most *compelling[78] reason why the knowledge of values gained through the study of the humanities is important to you as a scientist.

70. supposedly
아마, 추정 상으로

71. dichotomy
이분

72. astutely
통찰력 있게,
날카롭게

73. embodiment
전형

74. therapy
치료

75. artifact
인공물

76. prevailing
우세한, 지배적인

77. epoch
시대

78. compelling
설득력 있는,
강력한

GRAMMAR

형용사(Adjective)와 부사(Adverb)

1. 형용사의 특성

1) 형용사는 명사를 수식한다.

a beautiful song

2) 보어로 사용된다.

She is beautiful.(주격보어)

She make me happy.(목적격보어)

3) 비교형과 최상형을 만든다.

happier, happiest

more beautiful, most beautiful

2. 부사의 특성

1) 부사는 동사를 수식한다. 즉 행위에 대하여 더 많은 정보를 주기 위해 사용된다.

She sang beautifully.(아름답게 노래불렀다)

2) 형용사를 수식하여 형용사의 의미에 영향을 준다.

I'm terribly tired.(아주 피곤하다)

3) 다른 부사들을 수식한다.

He went terribly quickly.

4) 문장 전체를 수식한다.

Actually, I can't come.

5) 전치사구를 수식한다.

You're completely out of your mind.

3. 형용사와 부사의 차이

형용사는 어떤 것이 무엇이고, 어떻게 보이는지를 말한다. 이러한 형용사는 두 가지 방식으로 사용될 수 있다.

1) 한정적(attributive) 위치

a beautiful song

2) 서술적(predicative) 위치

She is beautiful.

부사는 행위에 대하여 더 많은 정보를 주는데 그 행위가 언제, 어디서, 어떻게 행하여졌는지를 말한다.

She sang beautifully.

You always misunderstand me.

PHRASES and STRUCTURES

* **It** is common **to hear** undergraduates and recent college graduates preparing for a career in science **complain**:
흔히 대학생과 과학 분야의 직업을 준비하는 최근의 대학 졸업자들이 다음과 같이 불평하는 것을 듣는 것은 일반적이다:
It ~ to + do 구문 It는 가주어 to이하는 진주어
지각동사(hear) + 목적어 + 동사원형(complain) 구문

* in college being forced to take humanities classes **that had nothing to do with** my area of study
나의 공부분야와 전혀 관계도 없었던 인문학 수업을 이수하도록 강요받은 대학에서
= in college being forced to take humanities classes, **and they(humanities classes)** had nothing to do with my area of study
주격 관계대명사 that = and + they(humanities classes)
have nothing to do with ~ ~와는 전혀 관계가 없다

* **hold the upper hand** 우위를 점하다

* At Oxford and Cambridge Universities, the gold standard models for American education
옥스포드와 캠브리지 대학에서, 그런데 그 대학들은 미국 교육의 표준 모델인데
= At Oxford and Cambridge Universities, **(and they are)** the gold standard models for American education
콤마(,)는 동격으로 사용됨: **~~and they~~**~~(Oxford and Cambridge Universities)~~ **~~are~~(being)**
gold standard 금본위제도(금이 기준이 되는 제도), 즉 표준 혹은 기준을 가리킴

* **taking the classic curriculum** 고전적인 교과과정을 이수하면서

* **The need** for science majors to take courses in the humanities has **been** contentious ever since.

과학전공자들이 인문학 강좌를 이수할 필요성이 그 이후 줄곧 많은 논쟁이 되어왔다.
주어는 the need 본동사는 be
to take의 의미상의 주어는 science majors

* **to the detriment of** ~ 결국 ~을 해치며

* Some applicants to college **regard** a strong core curriculum requirement **as** a negative factor, **opting** instead for programs with a minimum number of required core courses and maximum flexibility.
몇몇 대학 지원자들은 강한 핵심 교과과정 필수과목을 부정적인 요소로 간주하고, 대신 최소로 적은 수의 필수 핵심 강좌와 최대의 탄력성이 있는 프로그램을 선택한다.
= Some applicants to college regard a strong core curriculum requirement as a negative factor, **and they opt** instead for programs with a minimum number of required core courses and maximum flexibility.
opting(분사구문) = ~~and they~~~~(some applicants)~~ **opt**
regard A as B A를 B로 간주하다
opt for ~ ~을 선택하다

* **All this considered,**
이러한 모든 것을 고려해 볼 때
= **When I consider all this** 이 문장을 수동형으로 고치면 다음과 같고
= **~~When~~ all this ~~is~~(being) considered** 이 문장에서 when과 is가 생략되어 본문의 문장이 파생되어 나옴

* approaches **taken** in the scientific study of nature
자연에 대한 과학적 연구에서 받아들여지는 접근들
= approaches **(which are) taken** in the scientific study of nature
과거분사(taken) 앞에서 관계대명사의 주격(which)과 be동사 생략

* **<u>The preparation</u>** for a scientific career one receives in graduate school **<u>leaves</u>** the individual competitive for a finite period only.
개인이 대학원에서 받는 과학계통의 직업에 대한 준비는 개인이 단지 한정된 기간에 대해서만 경쟁력 있게 해 준다.
= **<u>The preparation</u>** for a scientific career **(which)** one receives in graduate school

leaves the individual competitive for a finite period only.

= The preparation for a scientific career, **and** one receives **it(preparation)** in graduate school leaves the individual competitive for a finite period only.

목적격 관계대명사 which 생략 = and + it(preparation)

주어는 the preparation 본동사는 leaves

leave + 목적어 + 보어(형용사) (결과로서) ~상태로 되게 하다

The insult **left** me **speechless**. 그 모욕에 나는 어안이 벙벙해졌다.

* The study of humanities, both in its pursuit and the perspective it provides

인문학에 대한 연구는 그 연구가 제공하는 추구와 관점 모두에 있어서

= The study of humanities, both in its pursuit and the perspective **(which)** it provides

= The study of humanities, both in its pursuit and the perspective, **and** it provides **them(pursuit and perspective)**

목적격 관계대명사 which 생략 = and + them(pursuit and perspective)

* These are the functions **needed** to be an independent learner, thereby **extending** one's scientific knowledge and teaching abilities throughout his or her professional career.

이러한 것들이 독립적인 학습자기 되기 위해 요구되는 기능들인데, 그렇게 함으로써 학습자는 그의 혹은 그녀의 직업경력 내내 자신의 과학적 지식과 교육능력을 확대하게 된다.

= These are the functions **(which are) needed** to be an independent learner, thereby **he extends** one's scientific knowledge and teaching abilities throughout his or her professional career.

과거분사(needed) 앞에서 관계대명사의 주격(which)과 be동사 생략

thereby extending = thereby he extends

* Scientists chafe at the stereotype **held** by some **that** they belong to a class of socially awkward "geeks" that are unable to communicate their ideas clearly.

과학자들은 고정관념에 짜증을 내는데 그 고정관념은 몇몇 과학자들에 의해 그들이 한 무리의 사회적으로 불편한 괴짜들에 속한다고 여겨지는 것으로 그 괴짜들은 그들의 생각을 분명하게 전달할 수 없다.

= Scientists chafe at the stereotype **(which is) held** by some that they belong to a class of socially awkward "geeks", **and they(geeks)** are unable to communicate their ideas clearly.

과거분사(held) 앞에서 관계대명사의 주격(which)과 be동사 생략

hold + that ~라고 생각하다, 주장하다

주격 관계대명사 that = and + they(geeks)

* **in large measure** 꽤 많이, 상당히

* My lack of proficiency in Spanish has been a handicap in my clinical practice, **requiring** the use of a translator with Hispanic patients **unable** to speak English.

스페인어에서의 나의 능숙성이 부족한 것은 나의 임상실습에서 장애가 되었으며 임상실습은 히스패닉계의 부모를 가진 번역자의 사용을 필요로 했는데 그들은 영어를 말할 수 없었다.

= My lack of proficiency in Spanish has been a handicap in my clinical practice, **and it(clinical practice) required** the use of a translator with Hispanic patients, **(and they were) unable** to speak English.

requiring(분사구문) = ~~and it(clinical practice)~~ required

unable 앞에서 접속사(and) + 주어(they) + be동사 생략

* **in terms of ~** ~면에서

* You would have no **idea that** there's an art history course discussing theoretical physics.

당신은 이론 물리학을 논의하는 미술사 강좌가 있다는 것을 모를 것이다.

idea와 that절은 동격

have no idea 모르다

* **Put in Africa, and** you'd be amazed at how many courses at this university deal with Africa from so many perspectives.

아프리카를 입력해 보아라. 그러면 여러분은 아마 이 대학에서 얼마나 많은 강좌들이 너무나 많은 관점에서 아프리카를 다루는지를 보고 놀랄 것이다.

put in = type in 입력하다

명령문, and 구문 ~해라, 그러면 ~다

* You could actually see all of the possibilities of a university teaching in a holistic manner, **allowing** students to stay tethered to a major, but **have** that tie **be** very, very long.
여러분은 실제로 대학이 총체적으로 교육하는 모든 가능성을 볼 수 있는데 그것은(총체적으로 가르치는 것) 학생들이 전공에 여전히 묶여있으나 그 끈이 아주 아주 길게해 주도록 한다.
= You could actually see all of the possibilities of a university teaching in a holistic manner, **and it(teaching in a holistic manner) allows** students **to stay** tethered to a major, but have that tie be very, very long.
allowing(분사구문) = ~~and it(teaching in a holistic manner)~~ allows
allow + 목적어 + to + do ~에게 허락하다, ~하게 하다
have(사역동사) + 목적어 + 동사원형 목적어가 ~하게 하다
in a holistic manner 총체적으로

* Students can benefit from advice on **which** courses to take.
학생들은 어떤 강좌를 수강할 것인지에 관한 충고로부터 혜택을 입을 수 있다.
which는 지시형용사(어떤)

* **make poor decisions** 그릇된 결정을 하다

* The study of literature, history, and philosophy **shed light on** the influence science has had on the quality of people's lives.
문학, 역사, 철학에 대한 연구는 과학이 사람들의 삶의 질에 끼쳐온 영향을 밝혔다.
= The study of literature, history, and philosophy shed light on the influence **(which)** science has had on the quality of people's lives.
= The study of literature, history, and philosophy shed light on the influence, **and** science has had **it(influence)** on the quality of people's lives.
목적격 관계대명사 which 생략 = and + it(influence)
shed light on ~ ~을 밝히다
have an influence on ~ ~에 영향을 미치다

* The diploma we receive at graduation defines and symbolizes who we are and what we are qualified to do.
우리가 졸업 때 받는 졸업장은 우리가 누구이고 무엇을 할 자격이 있는지를 규정하고 상징한다.
= The diploma **(which)** we receive at graduation defines and symbolizes **who** we

are and **what** we are qualified to do.

= The diploma, **and** we receive **it(diploma)** at graduation defines and symbolizes **who** we are and **what** we are qualified to do.

목적격 관계대명사 which 생략 = and + it(diploma)

who(누구)와 what(무엇)은 의문대명사로 사용됨

* Its true value is derived from **what** we have put into our head and our heart.

그것의 진정한 가치는 우리가 우리의 가슴과 머리에 넣는 것에서 생겨난다.

= Its true value is derived from **the thing which** we have put into our head and our heart.

= Its true value is derived from the thing, **and** we have put **it(the thing)** into our head and our heart.

선행사 포함 관계대명사 what = the thing which = and + it(the thing)

* **far from being** value-neutral

그런데 그러한 것들은 조금도 가치중립적이지 않다

= **(and they(science, technology and medicine) are) far from being value-neutral**

far from being = **~~and they(science, technology and medicine) are~~(being) far from being**

be far from be+ing 조금도 ~하지 않다

Unit 17

Nietzsche and Moral Nihilism[1)]

WARMING UP

- Again we have to **remind** ourselves **of** the passage in *the Gay Science*
- Negation **is dependent on** the very thing that it negates
- We have to understand negation, **or** what Nietzsche call negative will to power
- **Having negated** the world, and **seen** nothing positive in it, it has **ended up with** the ultimate negation of destroying itself
- Those who refuse to adapt, conform and fall into line, **have little or no** power
- **Without** active forces, there **would** not be any reactive
- The nihilist is the one **who** reduces life to nothing
- They are left with the negation of the world, but **simply** have **no** belief system to replace religion, morality and philosophy

1) This article was written by Dr W Large. The source is https://www.arasite.org/WL3/nietnihil.html

In popular culture, the philosopher *Nietzsche[2)] is usually associated with moral nihilism. We might define nihilism as the absence of the highest values. Associated with *moral nihilism[3)] is *moral relativism[4)]. Moral relativism is the belief that all values, precisely because there are no higher values, are merely the expression of personal *preference[1]. Ironically, however, *it is exactly this kind of moral viewpoint that Nietzsche is criticising. Rather than being a nihilist he is an anti-nihilist. Nihilism is a *diagnosis[2] of the *decadence[3] of Western culture, *rather than a position that Nietzsche wants, and still less, wants us to aspire to.

What is the cause and origin of nihilism in contemporary society? It is the continued destruction of all meaning and *signification[4]. It is the belief that nothing really *matters[5] any more, because nothing really has any meaning. We have no system of beliefs or values which could *orientate[6] us. The old systems of belief, like religion and morality, still exist, but *at best we only follow them *half-heartedly[7], and *at worst, think that they have no meaning whatsoever. They exist only the edges of our lives and consciousnesses. But *it isn't just the world that doesn't have any meaning anymore. We ourselves don't have any meaning to ourselves. Why should we choice one course of action over the other? *What does it really matter anymore, since no-one's individual

1. preference 선호
2. diagnosis 진단
3. decadence 타락, 퇴폐
4. signification 의의, 가치
5. matter 중요하다
6. orientate 지향하게 하다
7. half-heartedly 냉담하게, 성의 없이

2) Nietzsche(1844~1900) 독일의 철학자, 시인.

3) moral nihilism 도덕적 허무주의는 허무주의의 철학의 한 이론으로 도덕이 존재하지 않으며 어떠한 행위, 생각이나 행동도 도덕적으로 옳거나 틀린 것은 없다는 주의임.

4) moral relativism 도덕적 상대주의는 보편적이며 불변하는 가치는 존재하지 않고, 한 사회 안에서도 개인의 행동을 규제할 어떤 근거도 없기 때문에 도덕문제에 관한 한 누구에게나 획일적으로 적용되는 규범은 없다는 입장을 취하고 있음.

life really has any significance in the *grand scheme[8] of things as Michel Haar describes,

Nothing is worth much anymore, everything *comes down to the same thing, everything is *equalized[9]. Everything is the same and *equivalent[10]: the true and the false, the good and the bad. Everything is *outdated[11], *used up[12], *old dilapidated[13], dying: an *undefined[14] *agony[15] of meaning, an unending *twilight[16]: not a definite *annihilation[17] of significations, but their indefinite collapse.

It would be quite *absurd[18], therefore, to claim that this is what Nietzsche actually desires. On the contrary, he wants to diagnose how we got there. Our culture is like the character God in *Philip Pullman[5)]'s *Dark Materials* *trilogy[19]: old and *worn out[20], barely alive, and certainly nothing to really believe in anymore.

The most dangerous side of this nihilism, however, is that *in the end it becomes happy and satisfied with itself. Once we used to feel horror and *terror[21] at the fact that religion, morality and philosophy don't really have any meaning, but now we're quite happy to live in a world without meaning. One example of this satisfaction is the death of God. *Again we have to remind ourselves of the passage in *the *Gay Science*[6)], where Nietzsche writes of the madman who rushes into the marketplace and declares that God is dead. Many

8. grand scheme 거창한 계획
9. equalize 동등하게 하다
10. equivalent 동등한
11. outdated 구식인
12. used up 써서 낡은
13. old dilapidated 낡고 황폐해진
14. undefined 확실하지 않은
15. agony 고통
16. twilight 황혼
17. annihilation 전멸
18. absurd 터무니없는, 황당한
19. trilogy 3부작
20. worn out 닳아서 못쓰게 된
21. terror 두려움

5) Philip Pullman(1946~) 영국의 소설가.

6) The Gay Science 니체가 1882년에 출간한 책으로 종종 The Joyful Wisdom로 번역됨.

people read this as Nietzsche is simply celebrating *atheism[22], but if we read this passage more carefully we can see that what it really describes is how the ordinary people don't really *care[23] at all whether God is dead or not. This is what is truly *terrifying[24]. Not that God is dead, but that no-one even noticed that he had died:

*Have you not heard of that madman who lit a lantern in the bright morning hours, ran to the market place, and cried *incessantly[25]: 'I seek God! I seek God!' – *As many of those who did not believe in God were standing around just then, the provoked much laughter. Has he got lost? asked one. Did he *lose his way like a child? asked another. Or is he hiding? Is he afraid of us? Has he *gone on a voyage? *Emigrated[26]? – Thus they *yelled[27] and laughed.

How can this famous scene be a declaration of atheism, *when the people that the madman announces the death of god to are in fact already atheists? No, *this is not what Nietzsche thinks is significant for us to understand. The truth of this passage comes a little later, when the madman tells them that it is us who have killed God: 'We have killed him – you and I'. And yet, even though we are the murderers of God *we still have no idea of what a universe without God, without any values really means, because as such we still *cling to[28] the ideal world even though it is absent. It is not enough to *negate[29] values, *because then all you are left with is *negativity[30], and **negation[31] is dependent on the very thing that it negates. I say

22. atheism
무신론

23. care
관심을 가지다

24. terrifying
겁나게 하는

25. incessantly
끊임없이

26. emigrate
이민을 가다

27. yell
고함을 치다

28. cling to
~에 매달리다,
집착하다

29. negate
(존재)부인하다

30. negativity
존재를 부정하는 것

31. negation
존재에 대한 부정

32. paradoxically
역설적으로

33. critique
평론

34. present
보여주다, 나타내다

35. disinterested
사심이 없는

36. valuation
(가치)평가

37. self preservation
자기보호

38. hypocritical
위선적인

39. simplistic
지나치게 단순화한

40. petty
하찮은

that I don't believe in God, but **paradoxically[32] this non-belief is just as much dependent on the idea of God, as the belief in God is, for without the idea of God how would it be possible to be an atheist. We have to *get beyond both the belief and non belief. We have to get, to use a title to one of Nietzsche's books, Beyond Good and Evil.

The real source of nihilism is negation, and therefore to understand nihilism we have to understand negation, or *what Nietzsche call negative will to power. There two sources of values for Nietzsche in the world: *reactive and active. Nihilism in all its forms is reactive, and this is precisely the reason why Nietzsche's philosophy cannot be nihilism, *for it is against reactive will to power that it is written.

Nietzsche's *critique[33] of morality is that in fact it is secondary. Morality *presents[34] itself as a *disinterested[35] objective *valuation[36] of the world, but underneath it is just another form of will to power: the desire for *self preservation[37], even if that means dominating others. All morality is *hypocritical[38], not because it is false or wrong, which would be too *simplistic[39], since all human beings live by values, even if the supreme value in our age might be to value nothing, but because it presents itself *as though it were not of this world, above *petty[40] politics and striving, objective and absolutely true.

Nietzsche is not criticising values in general, but reactive values, and it is these values that have led to the nihilism of the West. *Having negated the world, and seen nothing positive in it, it has ended up with the ultimate negation of destroying itself.

Active and reactive values describe the relations of dominance and *subordination[41]. What is reactive is always a response to what is active. It subordinates itself to more dominating forces. But it is important to realize that this subordination is not an absence of power. *It is just as much an expression of power, Nietzsche believes, to dominate as subordinate oneself. In the second case, one obtains power by *accommodating[42] and *regulating[43] oneself to the *status quo[44]. This is exactly how the power of modern societies operates. It is the power of *adaptation[45] and utility, and those who are better adapted have more power, and *those who refuse to adapt, conform and fall into line, have little or no power. *Be like everyone else, or else! This is the *motto[46] of our societies, and our schools and universities are nothing but machines to produce this *submission[47].

Because our societies, or perhaps society itself, is essentially reactive, it is much harder to describe what active forces are. *One thing that we do know is that they must be first, because without active forces, there would not be any reactive, for what would they be reacting against? This is the first step away from nihilism. For nihilism says that what is first is negation. But this is precisely how reactive forces speak: negate! What is active, on the contrary, is what is creative, what imposes forms and dominates. Its first word is not negate, but create, and what one must first create is oneself beyond the reactive forces of society. *Again simply to negate society, and the values implicit within it, is not enough, for this is to be dependent on the values of the very society one despises, and have negated it all

41. subordination 복종
42. accommodate 수용하다
43. regulate 조절하다
44. status quo 현재의 상황
45. adaptation 적응
46. motto 좌우명
47. submission 항복, 굴복

48. justification 정당한 이유
49. redeem 구원하다
50. affirm 단언하다
51. moralizer 도덕가

that one is left with is *a black hole[7]. The point is to create new values that leap beyond the negative values of society. This is what Nietzsche calls the 'Dionysian power'.

Perhaps the best way to understand this power is through the distinction Nietzsche makes between *Dionysus[8] and Jesus. *The life of Jesus, as those who have seen Gibson's film *The Passion* know, is a life that is the *justification[48] of suffering and which makes of life itself something that causes suffering and which must be justified and legitimated as suffering. This must be distinguished from Dionysus, or at least what this Greek god represents for Nietzsche. Here life does not need to be justified, and even if there is pain, then this is a justified part of life. It does not have to be paid for somewhere else, as in the suffering of Jesus, for example. Life does not need to be *redeemed[49], for this is nothing to be redeemed. Rather life is to be *affirmed[50] *as it is.

Why then is Nietzsche not a nihilist? *Because the nihilist is the one who reduces life to nothing. In this sense *it is the Christian or the moralist who is the nihilist. For without Jesus, or morality, life would be exactly nothing. It is because they experience life as nothing *in itself that they need the extra moral or religious order above life. The modern nihilist is merely the believer without God, the Christian without Jesus, the *moralizer[51] without morals. They are left with the negation of the world, *but simply have no belief

7) black hole 검은(black) 구멍(hole), 즉 강한 중력에 의해 빛조차 빠져 나올 수 없어서 검게 보이는 천체를 뜻함.

8) Dionysus 고대 그리스 신화의 포도주와 풍요, 포도나무, 광기, 다산, 황홀경, 연극의 신이며, 죽음과 재생의 신으로 분류되기도 함. 로마 신화의 바쿠스 (Bacchus)에 해당함.

system to replace religion, morality and philosophy. Without God life is meaningless. But this means that Christianity has to prove that life without God is meaningless. *Now that God is dead, all we are left with in the meaningless of life. All that could happen in the future is that we would get new beliefs (capitalism, *nationalism[52]) that would simply cover over this the death of God. Nihilism is merely the last *symptom[53] of belief, its last stages and final development. It is not the opposite of belief, but merely its final form, as *Deleuze[9)] so *eloquently[54] describes it:

Previously life was *depreciated[55] from the height of higher values. Here on the contrary, only life remains, *but it is still a depreciated life which now continues in a world without values, stripped of meaning and purpose, sliding every further towards its nothingness.

One cannot be a nihilist and affirm life, and Nietzsche's philosophy is nothing but the affirmation of life *as what it is. This is why he is so critical of religion, morality and philosophy. *For they all begin with the same presupposition that life doesn't amount to much, and must be *supplemented[56] by a religious, moral, and essentially *metaphysical[57] 'other world'. Yes the nihilist *gets rid of this 'other world', *but she is still left with the hatred of the world that all these beliefs first began with as their original *impetus[58]. *In one sense, nihilism is worse than morality, religion and philosophy, *for it denies life, but has no recompense at all for the life which has been destroyed.

52. nationalism 민족주의
53. symptom 징후
54. eloquently 유창하게
55. depreciate 가치가 떨어지다, 평가절하하다
56. supplement 보충하다
57. metaphysical 형이상학의, 극히 추상적인
58. impetus 자극(제)

9) Gilles, Deleuze(1925~1995) 프랑스의 철학자로 후기 구조주의 대표학자.

GRAMMAR

혼동하기 쉬운 형용사와 부사

1. -ly로 끝나는 형용사

1) 많은 형용사들은 -ly를 붙여 부사로 사용되지만 -ly로 끝나는 몇몇 단어들은 부사가 아니라 형용사로 사용된다:

He spoke to me in a very friendly way. (형용사: 친절한)
Her singing was lovely. (형용사: 아름다운)

2) 몇몇 단어들은 부사와 형용사로 둘 다 사용된다: daily, weekly, monthly, yearly, early

A daily paper is published daily. (일간(매일의) 신문은 매일 출판된다)
형용사 부사

We got up early to catch an early train. (이른 열차를 타기 위해 일찍 일어났다)
부사 형용사

2. 형태는 같지만 형용사나 부사로 사용된다.

cheap	Do you like this shirt? I bought it really cheap. (cheaply도 가능) (그것을 정말로 싸게 샀다)
dead	부사로 'exactly' 혹은 'completely'를 의미한다. dead right(정확히 똑바로), dead sure(완전히 확실한), dead drunk(완전히 취한), dead tired(완전히 지친) deadly는 형용사로 '치명적인'을 의미 한다: a deadly poison(치명적인 독약)

easy	몇몇 표현에서 easily 대신 사용된다. take it easy, go easy(빠르지 않게), easy come easy go
fair	play fair, fight fair(공정하게)
fast	A fast(quick) car goes fast(quickly) fast가 '완전히'를 의미한다: fast asleep fast가 '꽉', '움직이기 불가능한'을 의미한다: hold fast, stick fast
hard	부사로서 형용사와 유사한 의미를 갖는다. Hit it hard(그것을 세게 쳐라). I'm working too hard this year. (열심히)
high	부사로 높이를 가리킨다. He can jump really high. (높이) highly는 극단적인 정도를 표현한다: It's highly amusing. (아주)
just	일반적인 부사로 '얼마 전'을 의미한다. justly는 '정당하게'를 의미하는 부사이다: He was justly punished for his crimes.
late	부사로서 형용사와 유사한 의미를 갖는다. I hate arriving late. (늦게) lately는 'recently'를 의미한다: I haven't been to the theater much lately. (최근에 극장에 많이 가보지 못했다) late(형용사) = 죽은(故): the late Dr. A(고(故) A박사) late(형용사) = 요전의, 최근의: the late typhoon(요전의 태풍)
loud	부사로서 동사 뒤에 사용된다. Don't talk so loud - You'll wake the whole street.
most	much의 최상급으로 사용된다. 'very'를 의미할 수도 있다. Which part of the concert did you like most? (가장) You're a most unusual person. (매우) mostly는 '주로', '대개'를 의미한다: My friends are mostly teachers. 또한 한정사로 '대부분의'를 의미한다: Most people agree with my attitude. I've eaten most of the salad.

3. **Hardly**

hardly = very little, almost not at all.

Sarah wasn't very friendly to me at the party. She hardly spoke to me.

(= she spoke to me very little, almost not at all)

(사라는 파티에서 나에게 아주 친절하지 않았다. 그녀는 나에게 거의 말을 하지 않았다)

George and June want to get married, but they've only known each other for a few days. I don't think they should get married yet. They hardly know each other.(= they know each other very little)

(조오지와 준은 결혼하기를 원하지만 그들은 서로 안지가 몇일 밖에 되지 않는다. 그들이 벌써 결혼해야 된다고는 생각하지 않는다. 그들은 서로 거의 알지 못한다)

※ hard와 hardly는 완전히 다르다.

He tried hard to find a job, but he had no luck.(=he tried a lot, with a lot of effort)

(그는 일자리를 찾으려 열심히 시도했지만 운이 없었다)

I'm not surprised he didn't find a job. He hardly tried to find one.

(=he tried very little)

(나는 그가 일자리를 찾지 못한 것에 놀라지 않았다. 그는 일자리를 찾으려 거의 시도 하지 않았다)

PHRASES and STRUCTURES

* **It is** exactly this kind of moral viewpoint **that** Nietzsche is criticizing.
니체가 비판하고 있는 것이 바로 정확히 이러한 종류의 도덕적인 관점이다.
It is ~ that 강조 구문

* rather than a position **that** Nietzsche wants, and still less, wants us to aspire to
니체가 원하는 입장 그리고 더더구나 우리로 하여금 열망하기를 원하지 않는 입장이라기보다는
= rather than a position, **and** Nietzsche wants **it(a position)**, and still less, wants us to aspire to **(it = a position)**
목적격 관계대명사 that = and + it(a position)
rather than ~ ~보다는
still less 더더구나 ~아닌
aspire to ~ ~하기를 열망하다

* **at best** 기껏해야

* **at worst** 최악의 경우에

* **It is**n't just the world **that** doesn't have any meaning anymore.
어떤 의미도 더 이상 갖지 않는 것은 단지 세상인 것만은 아니다.
it is ~ that 강조 구문

* What does it really matter anymore?
그게 정말 더 이상 무슨 상관인가?

* **comes down to** ~ 결국 ~이 되다, ~에 이르다

* **in the end** 결국

* Again we have to remind ourselves of the passage in the Gay Science, **where** Nietzsche writes of the madman **who** rushes into the marketplace and declares

that God is dead.

또한 우리는 *Gay Science*에서의 구절을 상기해야 하는데, 그 책에서 니체는 미친 사람에 관해 쓰고 있는데 그 사람은 급하게 시장으로 달려가서 신은 죽었다고 선언한다.

= Again we have to **remind** ourselves **of** the passage in the Gay Science, **and there** Nietzsche writes of the madman, **and he(the madman) rushes into** the marketplace and declares **that** God is dead.

where = and + there

remind A of B A에게 B가 생각나게 하다

who = and + he(the madman)

rush into 급하게 ~하다

that = declares의 목적절을 이끄는 접속사

* Have you not heard of that madman **who** lit a lantern in the bright morning hours, ran to the market place, and cried incessantly?

  그 미친 사람에 관해 들어본 적이 없는가, 그런데 그 사람은 밝은 아침 시간에 손전등에 불을 켜고 시장으로 달려가서 끊임없이 외쳤다.

  = Have you not heard of that madman, **and he(that madman)** lit a lantern in the bright morning hours, ran to the market place, and cried incessantly?

  who = and + he(that madman)

  lit = light의 과거형

* As many of those who did not believe in God were standing around just then, **the provoked** much laughter.

  신을 믿지 않았던 많은 사람들이 바로 그 때 주위에 서 있자 화난사람들은 더 크게 웃었다.

  the provoked 화난사람들

* **lose his way** 길을 잃다

* **gone on a voyage** 항해하다

* when **the people that** the madman announces the death of god to **are** in fact already atheists

  그 미친 사람이 사람들에게 신의 죽음을 선언했을 그 때 그 사람들은 사실 이미 무신론자들이다

  = when the people, **and** the madman announces the death of god to **them(the**

people) are in fact already atheists
목적격 관계대명사 that = and + them(the people)
when절에서 주어는 the people 본동사는 are
announce + 목적어 + to + 사람 사람에게 ~을 선언하다

* This is not **what** Nietzsche thinks is significant for us to understand.
이것은 니체가 생각하는 우리가 이해하기 위해 중요한 것은 아니다.
= This is not what **(Nietzsche thinks)** is significant for us to understand.
what은 선행사를 포함하는 관계대명사
Nietzsche thinks는 삽입절

* We still have no idea of **what** a universe without God, without any values really means, because as such we still cling to the ideal world even though it is absent.
우리는 신이 없는 우주, 즉 어떠한 가치도 없는 우주가 정말로 무엇을 의미하는지 여전히 모른다. 왜냐하면 그렇게 우리는 여전히 이상세계가 존재하지 않는다하더라도 그 이상세계에 집착하기 때문이다.
without God, without any values **콤마(,)는 동격**(신이 없는, 즉 어떠한 가치도 없는)
what은 means의 목적어 역할을 하는 의문대명사(무엇)

* because then all you are left with is negativity
당신이 그 때 함께 남겨지는 것 모두가 존재를 부정하는 것이기 때문이다
= because then all **(that)** you are left with is negativity
= because then all, **and** you are left with **it(all)** is negativity
목적격 관계대명사 that = and + it(all)

* Negation is dependent on the very thing **that** it negates.
존재를 부정하는 것은 그 부정이 부정하는 바로 그것에 의존한다.
= Negation is dependent on the very thing, **and** it(negation) negates **it(the very thing)**.
목적격 관계대명사 that = and + it(the very thing)
be dependent on ~ ~에 의존한다

* Paradoxically this non-belief is **just as** much dependent on the idea of God, **as** the belief in God is, for without the idea of God how would it be possible to be an

진 그 모든 것이 블랙홀이라는 것을 부정하는 것이기 때문이다.

= Again simply to negate society, and the values implicit within it, is not enough, for this is to be dependent on the values of the very society **(which)** one despises, and have negated **(that)** it all **that** one is left with is a black hole.

= Again simply to negate society, and the values implicit within it, is not enough, for this is to be dependent on the values of the very society, **and** one despises **it(the very society)**, and have negated **(that)** it all, **and** one is left with **it(it all)** is a black hole.

목적격 관계대명사 which 생략 = and + it(the very society)

첫 번째 생략된 that은 negate동사의 목적절을 이끄는 접속사

it all 다음의 that은 목적격 관계대명사 = and + it(it all)

it all은 동격(그것 모두)

* The life of Jesus, as those who have seen Gibson's film *The Passion* know, is a life **that** is the justification of suffering and **which** makes of life itself something **that** causes suffering and **which** must be justified and legitimated as suffering.

예수의 삶은 깁슨의 영화 *The Passion*을 보았던 사람들은 알다시피 고통의 정당한 이유이고 고통을 인생 자체의 어떤 것으로 생각하는 삶인데, 인생 자체의 어떤 것은 고통을 야기하고 고통으로 정당화되고 합법으로 인정되어야 하는 것이다.

= The life of Jesus, as those who have seen Gibson's film The Passion know, is a life, **and it(life)** is the justification of suffering and, **and it(life) makes** (suffering) **of** life itself something, **and it(life itself something)** causes suffering and, **and it(life itself something)** must be justified and legitimated as suffering.

주격 관계대명사 that = and + it(life)

which = and + it(life)

주격 관계대명사 that = and + it(life itself something)

which = and + it(life itself something)

make A of B A를 ~라고 이해(생각)하다

* **as it is** 있는 그대로

* Because the nihilist is the one **who** reduces life to nothing

왜냐하면 허무주의자는 삶을 무로 바꾸는 사람이기 때문이다

= Because the nihilist is the one, **and he(the one)** reduces life to nothing

who = and + he(the one)

reduce + 목적어 + to 목적어를 ~로 바꾸다, ~로 옮기다

* **It is** the Christian or the moralist **who** is the nihilist.

허무주의자는 바로 기독교인이거나 도덕주의자이다.

it is ~ who 강조 구문

* **in itself** 그 것 자체가, 본질적으로

* but **simply** have **no** belief system to replace religion, morality and philosophy

그러나 종교, 도덕, 철학을 대체할 어떠한 신앙체계도 전혀 가지고 있지 않다

simply ~ no 전혀 ~아니다

* **Now that** God is dead

신이 죽었기 때문에

now that ~ ~이므로, ~이기 때문에

* but **it is** still a depreciated life **which** now continues in a world without values, **stripped** of meaning and purpose, sliding every further towards its nothingness

그러나 가치가 없는 세계에서, 의미와 목적이 박탈된 채 삶의 무(존재하지 않음)를 향해 더 미끄러져 가면서 지금도 계속되는 것은 바로 여전히 가치가 떨어진 삶이다

= but **it is** still a depreciated life **which** now continues in a world without values, **(and it(life) is) stripped** of meaning and purpose, and it slides every further towards its nothingness

it is ~ which 강조 구문

stripped(분사구문) = ~~and it(life) is~~(being) stripped

* **as what it is** 있는 그대로

* For they all begin with the same **presupposition that** life doesn't **amount to** much.

왜냐하면 그들(종교, 도덕, 철학) 모두는 삶이 상당한 것이 된다는 같은 추정으로 시작하기 때문이다.

presupposition과 **that**절은 동격
amount to ~ ~에 이르다
amount to much 상당한 것이 되다
amount to little 무가치하다

* **get rid of** 제거하다, 없애다

* but she is still left with the hatred of the world **that** all these beliefs first began with as their original impetus
그러나 그녀(다른 세계)는 여전히 세상의 증오와 함께 남겨지는데, 모든 이러한 믿음들은 그들의 원래 자극으로 처음에 그러한 증오와 함께 시작을 했다
= but she is still left with the hatred of the world, **and** all these beliefs first began with **it(hatred)** as their original impetus
목적격 관계대명사 that = and + it(hatred)

* **In one sense** 어떤 의미에서

* for it denies life, but has no recompense at all for the life **which** has been destroyed
왜냐하면 그것(허무주의)은 삶을 부정하지만 파괴되어진 삶에 대해 전혀 어떠한 보상도 하지 않기 때문이다
= for it denies life, but has no recompense at all for the life, **and it(life)** has been destroyed
which = and + it(life)
no(not) ~ at all 전혀 ~아니다

Unit 18

Science and Religion[1)]

WARMING UP

- A person who is religiously enlightened appears to me to be one who has, **to the best of his ability**, liberated himself from the fetters of his selfish desires
- For science can only ascertain what is, but not what should be, and outside of its domain value judgments of all kinds **remain necessary**
- **To** this there also **belongs** the faith in the possibility that the regulations valid for the world of existence are rational, that is, comprehensible to reason
- This qualification **has to do with** the concept of God
- The **main source** of the present-day conflicts between the spheres of religion and of science **lies in** this concept of a personal God
- **Hardly** anyone could be found who would deny these partial successes and **ascribe** them **to** human self-deception
- **The more** a man is imbued with the ordered regularity of all events **the firmer** becomes his conviction that there is no room left by the side of this ordered regularity for causes of a different nature

1) This article was written by Albert Einstein, is taken from: Science, Philosophy and Religion, A Symposium, published by the Conference on Science, Philosophy and Religion in Their Relation to the Democratic Way of Life, Inc., New York, 1941. The source is https://www.update.uu.se/~fbendz/library/ ae_scire.htm

1. perceptible 인지할 수 있는
2. thoroughgoing 아주 철저한, 완전한
3. reconstruction 복원
4. conceptualization 개념적인 해석
5. aspiration 열망
6. fetter 속박, 구속
7. superpersonal 초인적인
8. overpowering 아주 강한
9. divine Being 신, 하느님
10. devout 독실한, 신앙심이 두터운

*It would not be difficult to come to an agreement *as to what we understand by science. Science is the century-old endeavor *to bring together by means of systematic thought the *perceptible[1] phenomena of this world into as *thoroughgoing[2] an association as possible. *To put it boldly, it is the attempt at the posterior *reconstruction[3] of existence by the process of *conceptualization[4]. But *when asking myself what religion is I cannot think of the answer so easily. And *even after finding an answer which may satisfy me at this particular moment, *I still remain convinced that *I can never under any circumstances bring together, even to a slight extent, the thoughts of all those who have given this question serious consideration.

At first, then, instead of asking what religion is I should prefer to ask what characterizes the *aspirations[5] of a person who gives me the impression of being religious: *a person who is religiously enlightened appears to me to be one who has, to the best of his ability, liberated himself from the *fetters[6] of his selfish desires and *is preoccupied with thoughts, feelings, and aspirations to which he clings because of their *superpersonal[7] value. It seems to me that what is important is the force of this superpersonal content and the depth of the conviction concerning its *overpowering[8] meaningfulness, *regardless of whether any attempt is made to unite this content with a *divine Being[9], *for otherwise it would not be possible to count Buddha and Spinoza as religious personalities. Accordingly, a religious person is *devout[10] in the sense that he has no doubt of the significance and *loftiness[11] of *those superpersonal *objects[12] and goals which neither require nor are capable of rational foundation. They exist with the same necessity and *matter-of-factness[13] as he himself. In this sense religion is the age-old endeavor of mankind to become clearly and completely conscious of these values and goals and constantly to strengthen and extend their effect. If one conceives of religion and science according to these definitions then a conflict between them appears impossible. *For science can only *ascertain[14] what *is[15], but not what should be, and outside of its domain value judgments of all kinds remain necessary. Religion, on the other hand, deals only with *evaluations[16] of human thought and action: it cannot *justifiably[17] speak of facts and relationships between facts. According to this interpretation *the well-known conflicts between religion and science in the past must all be *ascribed to[18] a *misapprehension[19] of the situation which has been described.

For example, a conflict arises *when a *religious community[20] insists on the absolute truthfulness of all statements recorded in the Bible. This means an *intervention[21] on the part of religion into the *sphere[22] of science; this is where the struggle of the Church against the *doctrines[23] of Galileo and Darwin *belongs[24]. On the other hand, *representatives[25] of science have often made an attempt to arrive at fundamental judgments *with respect to values and ends on the basis of scientific method, and in this way have set themselves in opposition to religion. These conflicts have all *sprung from[26] fatal

11. loftiness 고상함
12. object 대상
13. matter-of-factness 사실성
14. ascertain 확인하다
15. is 존재하다
16. evaluations 평가
17. justifiably 정당하게
18. ascribed to ~의 탓으로 돌리다
19. misapprehension 오해
20. religious community 종교계
21. intervention 간섭
22. sphere 영역
23. doctrine 학설, 교리
24. belong 제자리에 있다
25. representative 대표
26. spring from ~로부터 일어나다

27. reciprocal
상호간의

28. attainment
달성

29. imbued with
젖어있는, 가득 찬

30. genuine
진짜의

31. profound
심오한

32. lame
절뚝거리는

33. legitimate
정당한, 적당한

34. qualify
자격을 주다,
뒷받침하다

35. evolution
진화

36. fantasy
공상, 환상

37. phenomenal world
현상계

38. disposition
기질, 성향

errors.

Now, even though the realms of religion and science *in themselves *are clearly marked off from each other, nevertheless there exist between the two strong *reciprocal[27] relationships and dependencies. Though religion may be that which determines the goal, *it has, nevertheless, learned from science, in the broadest sense, what means will contribute to the *attainment[28] of the goals it has set up. But science can only be created by those who are thoroughly *imbued with[29] the aspiration toward truth and understanding. This source of feeling, however, springs from the sphere of religion. *To this there also belongs the faith in the possibility that the regulations valid for the world of existence are rational, that is, comprehensible to reason. I cannot conceive of a *genuine[30] scientist without that *profound[31] faith. The situation may be expressed by an image: science without religion is *lame[32], religion without science is blind.

Though I have asserted above that in truth a *legitimate[33] conflict between religion and science cannot exist, I must nevertheless *qualify[34] this assertion once again on an essential point, with reference to the actual content of historical religions. This qualification *has to do with the concept of God. During the youthful period of mankind's spiritual *evolution[35] *human *fantasy[36] created gods in man's own image, who, by the operations of their will were supposed to determine, or at any rate to influence, the *phenomenal world[37]. Man sought to alter the *disposition[38] of these gods *in his own favor by means of magic and prayer. *The idea of God in the religions taught at present is a *sublimation[39] of that old concept of the gods. Its *anthropomorphic[40] character is shown, for instance, by the fact that men *appeal to[41] the Divine Being in prayers and *plead for[42] the *fulfillment[43] of their wishes.

Nobody, certainly, will deny that the idea of the existence of an *omnipotent[44],

*just[45], and *omnibeneficent[46] *personal God[47] is able to *accord[48] man *solace[49], help, and *guidance[50]; also, by virtue of its simplicity it is accessible to the most undeveloped mind. But, on the other hand, *there are decisive weaknesses attached to this idea in itself, which have been painfully felt since the beginning of history. That is, if this *being[51] is omnipotent, then every *occurrence[52], including every human action, every human thought, and every human feeling and aspiration is also His work; how is it possible to think of holding men responsible for their *deeds[53] and thoughts before such an *almighty[54] Being? *In giving out punishment and rewards He would to a certain extent be passing judgment on Himself. *How can this be combined with the goodness and righteousness ascribed to Him?

*The main source of the present-day conflicts between the spheres of religion and of science *lies in[55] this concept of a personal God. *It is the aim of science to establish general rules which determine the reciprocal connection of objects and events in time and space. For these rules, or laws of nature, absolutely general *validity[56] is

39. sublimation
승화, 구현

40. anthropomorphic
인간화 된, 신·동물·사물을 의인화해서 보는

41. appeal to
~에 호소하다

42. plead for
~을 호소하다(바라다)

43. fulfillment
성취, 달성

44. omnipotent
전능한

45. just
공정한

46. omnibeneficent
모든 곳에서 선을 베푸는

47. personal God
인격신

48. accord
부여하다

49. solace
위안

50. guidance
가르침

51. being
존재

52. occurrence
발현

53. deed
행동

54. almighty
전능한

55. lies in
~에 있다

56. validity
타당성

57. found
(…에 입각해서) 만들다,
(…에) 근거를 두다
58. self-deception
자기기만
59. temporal
속세의
60. planetary
행성의
61. apparatus
기구, 장치
62. development
개발품
63. henomenological
현상학적
64. fail
도움을 못주다
65. causal connection
인과관계
66. penetrate
침투하다
67. regularity
규칙적인 패턴

required - not proven. It is mainly a program, and faith in the possibility of its accomplishment in principle is only *founded[57] on partial successes. But *hardly anyone could be found who would deny these partial successes and ascribe them to human *self-deception[58]. *The fact that on the basis of such laws we are able to predict the *temporal[59] behavior of phenomena in certain domains with great precision and certainty is deeply embedded in the consciousness of the modern man, *even though he may have grasped very little of the contents of those laws. He need only consider that *planetary[60] courses within the solar system may be calculated *in advance *with great exactitude on the basis of a limited number of simple laws. In a similar way, though not *with the same precision, it is possible to calculate in advance the mode of operation of an electric motor, a transmission system, or of a wireless *apparatus[61], even when dealing with a novel *development[62].

To be sure, when the number of factors *coming into play in a *phenomenological[63] complex is too large, scientific method in most cases *fails[64] us. One need only think of the weather, in which case prediction even for a few days ahead is impossible. *Nevertheless no one doubts that we are confronted with a *causal connection[65] whose causal components are in the main known to us. Occurrences in this domain are beyond the reach of exact prediction because of the variety of factors in operation, not because of any lack of order in nature.

We have *penetrated[66] far less deeply into the *regularities[67] obtaining within the realm of living things, but deeply enough nevertheless to *sense[68] at least the rule of fixed necessity. One need only think of the systematic order in *heredity[69], and in the effect of poisons, as for instance alcohol, on the behavior of organic beings. What is still lacking here is a *grasp[70] of connections of profound generality, but not a knowledge of order in itself.

*The more a man is imbued with the ordered regularity of all events the firmer becomes his conviction that there is no room left by the side of this ordered regularity for causes of a different nature. For him neither the rule of human nor the rule of divine will exists as an independent cause of natural events. To be sure, the doctrine of a personal God *interfering[71] with natural events could never be refuted, in the real sense, by science, for this doctrine can always *take refuge in those domains in which scientific knowledge has not yet been able to *set foot.

But I am persuaded that such behavior on the part of the representatives of religion would not only be unworthy but also fatal. For a doctrine which is able to maintain itself not in clear light but only in the dark, will *of necessity lose its effect on mankind, with *incalculable[72] harm to human progress. In their struggle for the ethical good, teachers of religion must have the *stature[73] to give up the doctrine of a personal God, that is, give up that source of fear and hope which in the past placed such vast power in the hands of priests. *In their labors they will have to avail themselves of those forces which are capable of cultivating the Good, the True, and the

68. sense
감지하다

69. heredity
유전

70. grasp
이해

71. interfering
개입하는

72. incalculable
헤아릴 수 없이 많은, 막대한

73. stature
지명도, 위상

Beautiful in humanity itself. This is, to be sure, a more difficult but an incomparably more worthy task. (This thought is convincingly presented in Herbert Samuel's book, Belief and Action.) After religious teachers accomplish the *refining process[74] indicated they will surely recognize with joy that true religion has been *ennobled[75] and made more *profound[76] by scientific knowledge.

If it is one of the goals of religion to liberate mankind as far as possible from the *bondage[77] of *egocentric[78] *cravings[79], desires, and fears, scientific reasoning can aid religion in yet another sense. Although it is true that it is the goal of science to discover rules which permit the association and *foretelling[80] of facts, this is not its only aim. It also seeks to reduce the connections discovered to the smallest possible number of mutually independent conceptual elements. It is in this striving after the rational unification of the *manifold[81] that it encounters its greatest successes, even though it is precisely this attempt which causes it to *run the greatest risk of falling a prey to illusions. But whoever has undergone the intense experience of successful advances made in this domain is moved by profound *reverence[82] for the rationality made *manifest[83] in existence. By way of the understanding he achieves a

*far-reaching[84] *emancipation[85] from the *shackles[86] of personal hopes and desires, and thereby attains that humble attitude of mind toward the *grandeur[87] of reason *incarnate[88] in existence, and which, *in its profoundest depths, is inaccessible to man. This attitude, however, appears to me to be religious, in the highest sense

74. refining process
정제과정

75. ennobled
품격이 높아진

76. profound
심오한

77. bondage
속박

78. egocentric
자기중심적인

79. craving
갈망

80. foretell
예언하다

81. manifold
여러 가지의

82. reverence
숭배, 경의

83. manifest
분명한

84. far-reaching
지대한 영향을 가져올

85. emancipation
해방

86. shackle
족쇄, 구속

87. grandeur
장엄함

88. incarnate
인간의 모습을 한

of the word. And so it seems to me that science not only *purifies[89] the religious impulse of the *dross[90] of its *anthropomorphism[91] but also contributes to a religious

*spiritualization[92] of our understanding of life.

The further the spiritual evolution of mankind advances, the more certain it seems to me that the path to genuine *religiosity[93] does not lie through the fear of life, and the fear of death, and blind faith, but through striving after rational knowledge. In this sense I believe that the priest must become a teacher if he wishes to *do justice to his *lofty[94] educational mission.

89. purify
정화하다

90. dross
찌꺼기

91. anthropomorphism
신인동형설

92. spiritualization
정화

93. religiosity
독실함

94. lofty
고귀한

GRAMMAR

접속사와 전치사

1. 접속사(Conjunction)

접속사는 단어(word)와 단어, 구(phrase)와 구, 절(clause)과 절을 연결하는 역할을 하는 단어이다. 특히 종속접속사는 주절과 종속절을 연결해 주는 접속사로서 접속사 뒤에는 항상 주어와 동사가 온다.

등위(coordinate)접속사	단어와 단어, 구와 구, 절과 절을 대등하게 연결하는 접속사로 and, but, or... 등
종속(subordinate)접속사	주절(main clause)과 종속절(subordinate clause)을 연결하는 접속사로 when, while, since, because, if, that ... 등

2. 전치사

명사(구) 앞에 위치하여 그 명사(구)와 전치사 앞의 다른 어구와의 관계를 밝혀주는 단어를 말한다. 따라서 전치사 다음에는 항상 명사나 명사 상당어구가 와야 한다.

1) 명사

What time do we arrive at Cardiff?

2) 명사구

I am glad of your success.

3) 대명사

I entirely agree with you.

4) 동명사

He went away without saying good-bye.

5) 부정사

Nothing remains but to die.

6) 절

Your success will depend on what you do.

7) 형용사

I regard it as important.

전치사와 함께 사용된 명사는 전치사의 목적어로서 전치사구를 형성하며, 그 전치사를 포함하는 전체 문장 내에서의 역할은 주로 형용사구나 부사구이다.

He doesn't want to marry a woman without money.

(그는 돈이 없는 여자와 결혼하기를 원치 않는다)

without money는 앞의 woman을 수식하는 형용사구의 역할을 한다.

He died at the age of eighty.(그는 80의 나이에 죽었다)

at the age of eighty는 때를 나타내는 부사구의 역할을 한다.

3. 전치사와 다른 품사와의 관계

1) 전치사와 부사

전치사의 목적어가 탈락하면 부사가 된다.

They ran across the road.(전치사)

They ran across.(부사)

2) 전치사와 형용사

Bring your chair near the fire.(전치사)

I'll come and see you in the near future.(형용사로서 명사 수식)

Winter is near.(형용사로서 주격보어로 사용됨)

3) 전치사와 접속사

전치사 다음에는 명사가 오지만 접속사 다음에는 주어와 동사가 온다.

I met him the day before yesterday.(전치사)

It may be many years before we meet again.(접속사)

다음의 since를 보자.

He has been ill since leaving college.(전치사)

He has worked since he left school.(접속사)

I have not seen him since.(부사)

즉 전치사는 뒤에 목적어로서 명사를 취하며, 접속사는 주어와 동사를 취하고, 부사는 단독으로 사용된다.

PHRASES and STRUCTURES

* **It** would not be difficult **to** come to an agreement.
합의에 도달하는 것은 어려울 것이다.
It은 가주어 to 이하는 진주어
come to an agreement 합의에 도달하다

* as to **what** we understand by science
우리가 과학으로 이해하는 것에 관하여
as to ~ ~에 관하여
what은 선행사를 포함하는 관계대명사

* to bring together (by means of systematic thought) the perceptible phenomena of this world into **as** thoroughgoing an association **as possible**
체계적인 생각에 의하여 이 세상의 인지할 수 있는 현상들을 가능한 완전하게 연관시켜 묶으려는 것
by means of ~ ~에 의하여
bring together 묶다
as + 형용사 + as possible 가능한 한 ~한

* **To put it boldly** 노골적으로 말하면

* when asking myself **what** religion is
종교가 무엇인지 나 자신에게 물어볼 때
what은 의문대명사(무엇)

* even after finding an answer **which** may satisfy me
나를 만족시킬 답을 발견한 이후에 조차도
= even after finding an answer, **and it(the answer)** may satisfy me
which = and + it(the answer)

* I still **remain convinced**. 나는 여전히 확신한다.
remain + 형용사 여전히 ~하다

* I can never (under any circumstances) bring together, even to a slight extent, the thoughts of all those **who** have given this question serious consideration.
어떤 환경 하에서도 나는 이러한 문제에 진지한 고려를 했던 모든 사람들의 생각들을 아주 조금까지도 결코 묶을 수 없다.
I can never (under any circumstances) bring together, even to a slight extent, the thoughts of all those, **and they(those)** have given this question serious consideration.
who = and + they(those)

* **A person** **who** is religiously enlightened **appears** to me to be one **who** has, to the best of his ability, liberated himself from the fetters of his selfish desires.
종교적으로 깨달음을 얻은 사람은 나에게는 최대한 능력을 발휘해 그의 이기적인 욕망의 속박으로부터 자신을 자유롭게 한 사람인 것처럼 보인다.
= A person, **and he(person)** is religiously enlightened appears to me to be one, **and he(person)** has, to the best of his ability, liberated himself from the fetters of his selfish desires.
who = and + he(person)
주어는 a person이고 본동사는 appear
one = a person
to the best of his ability 능력을 최대한 발휘해

* is preoccupied with thoughts, feelings, and aspirations **to which** he clings because of their superpersonal value
초인적인 가치 때문에 그가 집착하고 있는 생각, 느낌, 열망들에 사로잡혀 있다
= is preoccupied with thoughts, feelings, and aspirations, **and** he clings **to them(thoughts, feelings, and aspirations)** because of their superpersonal value
to which = and + to them(thoughts, feelings, and aspirations)
is preoccupied with ~ ~에 사로잡혀있다
cling to ~ ~에 집착하다, 매달리다

* regardless of whether any attempt is made **to unite** this content with a divine Being
이러한 내용을 하느님과 합치기 위해 행하여지는 어떤 시도와도 상관없이
regardless of ~ ~에 상관없이
make an attempt 시도를 하다

to unite에서 to부정사는 부사적 용법으로 '~하기 위해'
unite A with B A와 B를 합치다

* for otherwise **it** would not be possible **to count** Buddha and Spinoza **as** religious personalities
왜냐하면 그렇지 않다면 부처와 스피노자를 종교적인 인물로 간주하는 것이 가능하지 않을 것이기 때문이다
otherwise 그렇지 않다면
it ~ to 구문
count A as B A를 B로 간주하다

* those superpersonal objects and goals **which** neither require nor are capable of rational foundation
합리적인 기초가 가능하지도 않고 필요로 하지도 않는 그러한 초인적인 대상과 목표
= those superpersonal objects and goals, **and they(objects and goals)** neither require nor are capable of rational foundation
which = and + they(objects and goals)
neither A nor B A도 아니고 B도 아닌

* For science can only ascertain **what is**, but not **what** should be, and outside of its domain value judgments of all kinds remain necessary.
왜냐하면 과학은 무엇이 존재하는지, 무엇이 존재해야하는지가 아닌지를, 오로지 확인만 할 수 있고, 그 존재 영역 밖에는 모든 종류의 가치 판단들이 여전히 필요하기 때문이다.
what은 의문대명사(무엇)
is 존재하다

* The well-known conflicts between religion and science in the past must all be ascribed to a misapprehension of the situation **which** has been described.
과거의 잘 알려진 종교와 과학 사이의 갈등은 모두 기술되어져 왔던 상황의 오해 탓으로 분명히 돌려져야 할 것이다.
= The well-known conflicts between religion and science in the past must all be ascribed to a misapprehension of the situation, **and it(the situation)** has been described
which = and + it(the situation).

must be ~ ~임에 틀림없다

* when a religious community insists on the absolute truthfulness of all statements **recorded** in the Bible
종교계가 성경에 기록된 모든 진술들의 절대적인 진실성을 고집할 때
when a religious community insists on the absolute truthfulness of all statements **(which are) recorded** in the Bible
과거분사(recorded) 앞에서 관계대명사의 주격(which)과 be동사 생략

* **with respect to** ~ ~에 관하여

* **in themselves** 본래

* **are** clearly **marked off from** each other
서로 분명히 다르다
This type is clearly marked off from the rest.
이 형은 다른 것과는 뚜렷이 다르다.

* It has, nevertheless, learned (from science), in the broadest sense, what means will contribute to the attainment of the goals it(religion) has set up.
그럼에도 불구하고 종교(it)는 (과학으로부터), (넓은 의미에서), 어떤 수단들이 종교(it)가 설정한 목표를 달성하는데 기여할 것인지를 배워왔다.
= It has, nevertheless, learned (from science), in the broadest sense, **what** means will contribute to the attainment of the goals **(which)** it(religion) has set up.
= It has, nevertheless, learned (from science), in the broadest sense, what means will contribute to the attainment of the goals, **and** it(religion) has set up **them(the goals)**.
what은 의문형용사(어떤)
목적격 관계대명사 which 생략 = and + them(the goals)

* To this there also belongs the faith in **the possibility that** the regulations valid for the world of existence are rational, that is, comprehensible to reason.
존재 세계에 타당한 법규들이 합리적이라는, 즉 이치에 맞다는 가능성을 믿는 것도 또한 여기(종교)에 속한다.

= **The faith** in **the possibility that** the regulations valid for the world of existence are rational, that is, comprehensible to reason also **belongs to** this there.
the possibility와 that은 동격 that ~라는 가능성
the faith 이하는 주어, 동사는 belongs
belong to ~ ~에 속하다

* **has to do with ~** ~와 관계가 있다, 관련되다

* Human fantasy created gods in man's own image, **who**, by the operations of their will were supposed to determine, or at any rate to influence, the phenomenal world.
인간의 공상이 인간의 이미지 속에 신을 창조했는데 그 신은, 그들의 의지로, 현상계를 결정하기로 되어있는데, 다시 말해 어쨌든 현상계에 영향을 미친다.
= Human fantasy created gods in man's own image, **and they(gods)**, by the operations of their will, **were supposed to** determine, or at any rate to influence, the phenomenal world.
who = and + they(gods)
were supposed to ~ ~하기로 되어있었다

* **in his own favor** 자신에게 유리하게

* **The idea** of God in the religions **taught** at present **is** a sublimation of that old concept of the gods.
현재 가르치는 종교에서의 신이라는 개념은 그러한 신이라는 낡은 개념의 구현이다.
= The idea of God in the religions **(which is) taught** at present is a sublimation of that old concept of the gods.
주어는 the idea, 본동사는 is
과거분사(taught) 앞에서 관계대명사의 주격(which)과 be동사 생략

* There are decisive weaknesses **attached** to this idea in itself, **which** have been painfully felt since the beginning of history.
이러한 생각에 본질적으로 붙게 되는 결정적인 약점들이 있는데 그 약점들은 역사의 시작 이래로 고통스럽게 느껴져 왔다.
= There are decisive weaknesses **(which are) attached** to this idea in itself, **and they(weaknesses)** have been painfully felt since the beginning of history.

과거분사(attached) 앞에서 관계대명사의 주격(which)과 be동사 생략

attached = which are attached = ~~and they are~~ attached

which = and + they(weaknesses)

* In giving out punishment and rewards He would **to a certain extent** be passing judgment on Himself.

벌과 보상을 나누어주는데 있어서 하느님은 어느 정도까지 그 자신에 대한 판단을 내릴 것이다.

to a certain extent 어느 정도까지

pass judgement 판단을 내리다

* How can this be combined with the goodness and righteousness **ascribed** to Him?

이것이 신에게 부여된 선량함과 올바름과 어떻게 결합될 수 있는가?

= How can this be combined with the goodness and righteousness **(which are) ascribed** to Him?

과거분사(ascribed) 앞에서 관계대명사의 주격(which)과 be동사 생략

ascribe A to B B에 A를 부여하다, A를 B탓으로 돌리다

* The <u>**main source**</u> of the present-day conflicts between the spheres of religion and of science <u>**lies**</u> in this concept of a personal God.

오늘날 종교와 과학의 영역 사이의 갈등의 주요한 근원은 이러한 인격화된 신이라는 개념에 있다.

주어는 main source이고 본동사는 lies

* **It** is the aim of science **to** establish general rules **which** determine the reciprocal connection of objects and events in time and space.

일반적인 규칙을 정하는 것이 과학의 목적인데 그 규칙들은 시간과 공간 속에서 사물과 사건들의 상호 연관성을 결정한다.

= It is the aim of science to establish general rules, **and they(rules)** determine the reciprocal connection of objects and events in time and space.

which = and + they(rules)

It은 가주어, to이하는 진주어

* Hardly anyone could be found **who** would deny these partial successes and ascribe them to human self-deception.

우리는 이러한 부분적인 성공을 부정하고 그 성공들을 인간의 자기기만 탓으로 돌릴 사람들을 거의 찾을 수 없을 것이다.

= We could **hardly** find **anyone, and he(anyone)** would deny these partial successes and ascribe them to human self-deception.

who = and + he(anyone)

* **The fact that** on the basis of such laws we are able to predict the temporal behavior of phenomena in certain domains with great precision and certainty **is** deeply embedded in the consciousness of the modern man.

그러한 법의 토대위에서 우리가 몇몇 영역에서의 현상들의 일시적인 행동을 아주 정확하게 그리고 확실하게 예측할 수 있다는 사실은 현대인의 의식 속에 깊이 내장되어 있다.

주어는 the fact, 본동사는 is

that은 the fact과 동격

with great precision and certainty 아주 정확하게 그리고 확실하게

with + 추상명사 = 부사

is deeply embedded in 깊이 내장되어 있다

* even though he may have grasped very **little** of the contents of those laws

비록 그가 그런 규칙들의 내용을 거의 파악하지 못했을 지라도

little은 부정적인 의미로 사용됨

* **in advance** 미리

* **with great exactitude** 아주 정밀하게

* **with the same precision** 같은 정밀도로

* **coming into play** 작동하기 시작하는

* Nevertheless no one doubts that we are confronted with a causal connection **whose** causal components are in the main known to us.

그럼에도 불구하고 우리가 인과관계에 직면하고 있다고 아무도 의심하지는 않는데, 그 인과관계의 요소들은 대체로 우리에게 알려져 있다.

= Nevertheless no one doubts that we are confronted with a causal connection, **and**

its(connection's) causal components are in the main known to us.
whose = and + its(connection's)
are confronted with ~ ~에 직면하다
in the main 대체로

* **The more** a man is imbued with the ordered regularity of all events **the firmer** becomes **his conviction that** there is no room left by the side of this ordered regularity for causes of a different nature.
인간이 모든 사건들의 질서화 된 규칙성으로 가득 차 있으면 있을수록 다른 자연의 이유들 때문에 이러한 질서화 된 규칙성 면에 의해서 남겨지는 여지가 없다는 그의 확신은 더 확고해 진다.
the + 비교급 ~, the + 비교급 = ~하면 할수록 점점 더 ~하다
his conviction과 that 절은 동격
is imbued with 가득 차 있다

* **take refuge in ~** ~에서 위안을 구하다

* **set foot** 발을 들여놓다

* **of necessity** 필연적으로

* In their labors they will have to avail themselves of those forces **which** are capable of cultivating the Good, the True, and the Beautiful in humanity itself.
그들의 노력으로 그들은 그러한 힘들을 이용해야할 것인데 그러한 힘들은 인류 자체에서 진, 선, 미를 기를 수 있다.
= In their labors, they will have to avail themselves of those forces, **and they(forces)** are capable of cultivating the Good, the True, and the Beautiful in humanity itself.
which = and + they(forces)
In their labors 그들의 노력으로
avail themselves of ~ ~을 이용하다

* **run the greatest risk of** 최대의 위험을 무릅쓰다

* **falling a prey to ~** ~의 희생양이 되다, ~의 먹이가 되다

* **in its profoundest depths** 가장 깊은 곳에서

* **do justice to somebody/something** ~을 공정하게 대하다, ~을 제대로 다루다

구문 분석과 해설

중급영문독해

2020년 8월 24일 초판 1쇄 발행

지은이	석종환
펴낸이	권순기
부장	박현곤
행정팀장	김성균
디자인	이희은
편집보조	이희성

펴낸곳	경상대학교출판부 | 출판등록 1989년 1월 7일 제16호
주소	경남 진주시 진주대로 501
전화번호	055) 772-0801(편집), 0802(디자인), 0803(도서 주문)
팩스	055) 772-0809
전자우편	gspress@gnu.ac.kr
홈페이지	http://gspress.gnu.ac.kr
페이스북	https://www.facebook.com/gnupub

책값은 뒤표지에 있습니다.

이 도서의 국립중앙도서관 출판시도서목록(CIP)은 서지정보유통지원시스템 홈페이지(http://seoji.nl.go.kr)와 국가자료공동목록시스템(http://www.nl.go.kr/kolisnet)에서 이용하실 수 있습니다.
(CIP제어번호: CIP2020034214)